The Wind Doesn't Need a Passport

The publisher gratefully acknowledges the generous support of the General Endowment Fund of the University of California Press Foundation.

The Wind Doesn't Need a Passport

STORIES FROM THE U.S.-MEXICO BORDERLANDS

Tyche Hendricks

UNIVERSITY OF CALIFORNIA PRESS

BERKELEY   LOS ANGELES   LONDON

University of California Press, one of the most
distinguished university presses in the United States,
enriches lives around the world by advancing scholarship
in the humanities, social sciences, and natural sciences. Its
activities are supported by the UC Press Foundation and
by philanthropic contributions from individuals and
institutions. For more information, visit www.ucpress.edu.

University of California Press
Berkeley and Los Angeles, California

University of California Press, Ltd.
London, England

Library of Congress Cataloging-in-Publication Data

Hendricks, Tyche.
    The wind doesn't need a passport : stories from the
U.S.-Mexico borderlands / Tyche Hendricks.
        p.   cm.
    "Portions of this work originally appeared, in different
form, in the San Francisco Chronicle series "On The
Border."
    Includes bibliographical references and index.
    ISBN 978-0-520-25250-9 (cloth : alk. paper)
    1. Mexican-American Border Region—Social
conditions.   I. Title.
HN79.A165H46   2010
303.48'209721—dc22   2009046593

Manufactured in the United States of America
19 18 17 16 15 14 13 12 11 10
10 9 8 7 6 5 4 3 2 1

This book is printed on Cascades Enviro 100, a 100% post
consumer waste, recycled, de-inked fiber. FSC recycled
certified and processed chlorine free. It is acid free,
Ecologo certified, and manufactured by BioGas energy.

For Paul,
my partner on the journey

CONTENTS

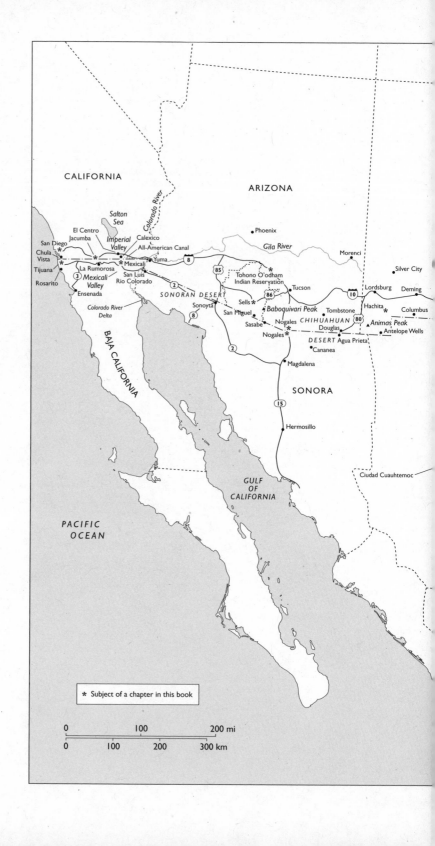

CALIFORNIA

ARIZONA

Salton
Sea

Colorado River

El Centro
Jacumba
Calexico
Imperial
Valley
All-American Canal

San Diego
Chula
Vista
Tijuana
La Rumorosa
Mexicali
3 Mexicali
Valley
San Luis
Rio Colorado
Yuma
Rosarito
Ensenada

Phoenix

Gila River

Morenci

Silver City

8

85
Tohono O'odham
Indian Reservation

Tucson

Lordsburg
10
Deming

SONORAN DESERT

2

Colorado River
Delta

8
Sonoyta
San Miguel
Sasabe

86
Sells
Baboquivari Peak

CHIHUAHUAN
Nogales
DESERT
Nogales
Tombstone
Douglas
Agua Prieta
Cananea

80
Hachita
Columbus
Animas Peak
Antelope Wells

BAJA CALIFORNIA

2

Magdalena

SONORA

15

Hermosillo

Ciudad Cuauhtemoc

PACIFIC
OCEAN

GULF
OF
CALIFORNIA

* Subject of a chapter in this book

0		100		200 mi

0	100	200	300 km

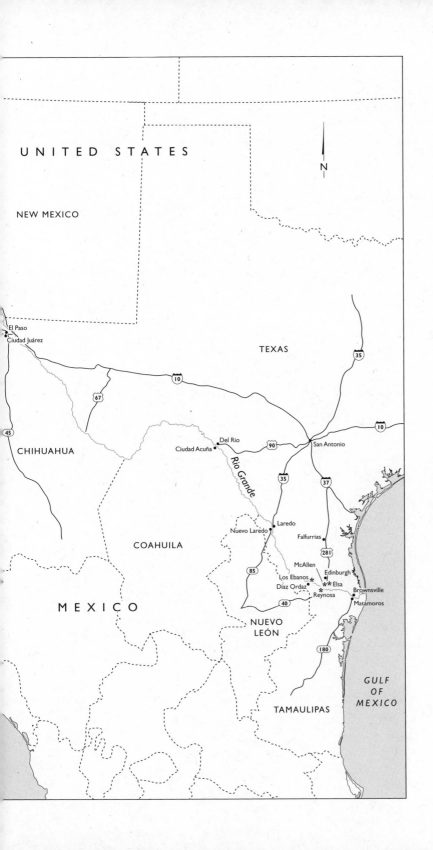

Introduction

THE GREEN-BROWN WATER OF THE Rio Grande swirls and eddies as it flows eastward past the overhanging trees on the shore at Los Ebanos, Texas, site of the last hand-pulled ferry crossing on the U.S.-Mexico border. The steel barge, tethered to a system of cables and pulleys, plies the river from 8:00 a.m. to 4:00 p.m. each day. The ferry's deck can accommodate three cars, a dozen pedestrians, and a few stocky men in feed store caps and dusty blue jeans who grasp a rope spanning the river and pull rhythmically, leaning their bodies into the work. On the thirty-ninth pull, the ferry floats across the midline of the river, leaving the United States and entering Mexico.

Elsewhere along its length, the international line is marked by a steel wall flooded with stadium lights or a few strands of barbed wire tacked to wooden fence posts. At the San Ysidro port of entry, a painted yellow stripe across twenty-four lanes of traffic indicates the place where one country ends and the other begins. At Reynosa, a plaque in the center of a bridge over the Rio Grande marks the dividing line. Here at Los Ebanos, the river's midpoint exists somewhere on the muddy bottom, but no sign points it out. It must be imagined.

When most Americans think of the border, they think of a line on a map or a fence erected in the desert sand. Politicians talk about "sealing the border" and debate how much hardware and manpower are needed to accomplish the task. The 1,952-mile border is indeed a boundary—a dividing line between two countries with distinct histories, traditions, and languages. It is the world's longest frontier between a developed and a developing country. But the border is also a very permeable membrane where commerce and culture, air and water, workers and students, pollution and disease flow back and forth daily. The rapid transmission of swine flu and the alarming proximity of cutthroat drug battles are only the most headline-grabbing examples of how the United States and Mexico are linked.

Here on the ferry on the river's surface, people, cars, bicycles, groceries, and small loads of goods travel back and forth. There are some tourists, drawn by the quaintness of this international gateway between two country villages, but most passengers here are local. They live in Los Ebanos, named for the grand ebony trees growing there, or the Mexican town of Díaz Ordaz, a couple of miles down the road. They take the ferry (50 cents for pedestrians, $2.50 for vehicles) to work, to the supermarket, or to visit relatives. They know each other and the ferrymen and the customs inspectors on each bank. For them, the border is not so much a boundary line as it is a meeting point, a place where different parts of their lives converge.

More than that, the border is the axis of a region. There are obvious differences between life on the Mexican side and the American side. And each section of the border—from the Lower Rio Grande Valley to the Paso del Norte to the high Sonoran Desert to the Tijuana/San Diego metropolis—has its own particular character. Some scholars have described these subregions as transborder corridors, each with a distinctive culture defined by its geography, economy, and population.[1] But in every part of the borderlands and on both sides of the line, the region is defined by its proximity to the border and to the country on the other side. The land is one continuous place. The histories are interconnected. And the people who inhabit the borderlands interact frequently across the international divide.

It's not as if there is no border line. Homeland Security inspections are a fact of life, even at the rustic ferry crossing at Los Ebanos. And binational tensions play out frequently, whether over pollution, truck traffic, or the causes and consequences of drug-related violence. But equally real are the relationships that link the two sides, as the little hand-pulled barge does each day. The border's influence, like the muddy water, laps at both countries.

At this juncture where the United States and Mexico meet, a border culture has evolved that sets the region apart from other parts of either country. Michael Dear, a geographer at the University of California, Berkeley, calls

Figure 1. Motorist waits to be inspected by a U.S. Customs and Border Protection agent before crossing the border from Mexico into the United States at San Ysidro, California. Photo by Sandy Huffaker Jr.

the U.S.-Mexico borderlands a "third nation," a hybrid place where many residents have adopted a transnational mind-set, conducting their lives in both countries even as the border wall is being constructed between them.[2] For University of Arizona historian Oscar J. Martínez, who has examined the varying levels of transborder interaction in the lives of Mexican and American residents, the borderlands is a binational region.

"Nowhere else do so many millions of people from two so dissimilar nations live in such close proximity and interact with each other so intensely," Martínez wrote.[3] "What distinguishes borderlanders from the rest of the citizenry is the effect of the boundary on their daily lives. On the one hand, the border is a barrier that limits activity and hinders movement, but, on the other, it offers tremendous opportunities to benefit from proximity to another nation."[4]

I first went to the border as a reporter for the *San Francisco Chronicle* to cover undocumented immigration—an issue most Americans now associate with the border. In my reporting in Mexico, I met migrants in Sonoran border towns waiting for the right moment to try their luck at jumping the fence: a brother and sister from Oaxaca carrying a Fresno phone number and a supply of leathery, homemade corn tortillas; a couple from Chiapas hoping to make it over with their two small children; a pregnant woman from Mexico City who had become separated from her husband on their first attempt to cross. On the Arizona side of the line, I spent time with Border Patrol agents tracking migrants, or "cutting for sign," in the desert; with armed vigilantes who boasted of nighttime immigrant patrols; and with a county medical examiner working to identify the hundreds of bodies of those who had died trying to make it to America. In reporting their stories, I felt as if the two sides of the line were parallel worlds cut off from one another.[5]

But in the course of multiple reporting trips over several years, other stories came into focus, and with them a fuller sense of the borderlands as a dynamic region that straddles the boundary and extends into two countries. It's a place that's alive with the energy of cultural exchange and international commerce, freighted with the burdens of too-rapid growth and binational conflicts, and underlain by a deep sense of history. My reporting took me to communities large and small along the length of the U.S.-Mexico line. I explored the borderlands by car and by foot, on horseback, in a propeller plane, and in the back of a pickup truck, often traveling with a newspaper photographer. I shared meals with border residents and listened to their stories. I was invited into their homes and visited their churches, factories, hospitals, farms, and jails. My editor at the *Chronicle* asked me to answer for our readers the question, "What is the border?" The answer I found is that the border is much more complicated, indeed much richer, than most people who live hundreds of miles from it usually imagine. Both nations have made a symbol of the border, often with overheated rhetoric, but for twelve million people, it is simply home.[6] It is more a borderlands than a border line.

Social scientists have studied the border region, quantifying its economic activity and categorizing its people. And political commentators have expounded on the problems they feel the border signifies. But life at the border can't be encapsulated in statistics or rhetoric. The best way to understand the border, I believe, is to listen to the people who live there. This book is a collection of stories about the lives of Mexicans and Americans for whom the border region is home. The problems with which they wrestle, the values they hold, and the ways they navigate this binational region reveal the border's pressing concerns—from immigration to the environment, and from drug smuggling to manufacturing. Those concerns in turn have a broad impact in both countries. The daily lives of border residents also reveal the paradox here: that what appears to be a place of separation is also common ground.

In the chapters that follow, through the stories of people who inhabit the borderlands, I will explore the powerful cultural, economic, familial, even psychological ties that weave the two sides of the border together into a binational region. I'll look at the manifold ways people and goods traverse this region, with increasing difficulty but in patterns that have important historical roots and contemporary relevance. And I'll probe the often-neglected idea that solutions to borderlands problems such as toxic pollution and violent crime can be resolved only through cross-border collaborations involving the people and governments of both countries.

What happens at the U.S.-Mexico border touches both countries in more ways than we might imagine. And the scale of cross-border exchange is vast. The value of goods traded between the two countries is almost $350 billion annually,[7] and 90 percent of that travels across the international boundary over land.[8] Workers, shoppers, and students flock daily in both directions, adding up to more than two hundred million entries into the United States and a like number of crossings into Mexico. Border agents seized 2.78 million pounds of narcotics in 2008,[9] and that's estimated to be just a small fraction of the drugs that make it across. Most of the cash the drugs sold for is returned to Mexico, along with firearms smuggled by drug cartels. Hundreds of thousands of people also cross the border without authorization; for years the U.S. Border Patrol made roughly a million arrests of people who attempted the crossing, though that number has fallen in recent years as the U.S. economy has declined and immigration enforcement has increased.[10] Every year hundreds of migrants don't make it. Bent on reaching the United States, many trust profit-seeking smugglers to lead them across unfamiliar territory. They die of heat or cold or thirst. Or they drown or suffocate or perish in car crashes.

From afar the border looks like a barrier, albeit an imperfect one. It has become an emblem in the U.S. debate over immigration—a locus for economic anxiety, cultural change, national muscle-flexing, and political grandstanding. In recent years, the border region has been depicted as a rugged terrain populated by hordes of illegal immigrants hiking north through the desert hills and by Border Patrol agents, and sometimes vigilante militias, equipped with pistols and binoculars, intent on stopping them.[11] The border's symbolism as a dividing line was most vividly expressed in a 2006 law mandating the construction of almost seven hundred miles of steel fence along the international line at a cost of several billion dollars. It's unlikely that a border wall, particularly a partial one, could actually halt illegal immigration, but construction was swift, though not free from legal challenges. Many Americans embraced the idea of a fence as a tangible way to assert a physical boundary—and with it a sense of control over this country's economic and cultural destiny. As Minuteman volunteer Britt Craig put it one night as he pitched camp in the rural hills of eastern San Diego County: "A border is like your skin. There's got to be a place where you stop and something else begins."[12]

Even President George W. Bush, who worked unsuccessfully for an immigration overhaul that would have given low-skilled workers a legal way to enter the United States, finally embraced border fencing as a means to show Americans, especially more restrictionist members of his own Republican party, that he was serious about border enforcement. Posing before a new stretch of double steel fence, complete with razor wire, in the Yuma, Arizona, desert, he told reporters: "Manpower can't do it alone. There has to be some infrastructure along the border to be able to let these agents do their job. . . . The American people have no earthly idea what's going on down here."[13]

Whether the fence was responsible for the decrease that began in 2007 in the number of illegal immigrants arrested at the border or whether the decline had more to do with the slowing U.S. economy, as many scholars believe, Bush's emphasis on enforcement was not enough to push through a "comprehensive" immigration reform bill that year. But it wasn't the first time an American politician has used the border as a symbolic stage, or the last. President Barack Obama has deemphasized fencing as a solution for the border. Although the fence was largely built by the time he took office in early 2009, he allowed construction to continue to complete the 670 miles planned by the Bush administration. During his first year, however, Obama and his Homeland Security secretary, Janet Napolitano, calibrated the U.S. message on border enforcement, emphasizing collaboration with Mexico while still maintaining a tough stance on security.[14]

"It looks like you're doing something. That's the mentality we've seen from every administration in the United States since the 1980s, at the national and state level, whether Democrat or Republican. Looking tough, posturing at the border, is a winning strategy," said David Shirk, a University of San Diego political science professor who directs the university's Trans-Border Institute. "Whether it's building a fence to control immigration or trying to interdict drugs at the border, it doesn't really work. But it costs us tremendously at the border."[15]

That's what happens when the border is used as a symbol. Up close, though, the border is much more than a hurdle for undocumented immigrants and a stage for Minutemen. It is mountain, desert, ranchland, river, sprawling cities, and remote villages. At its western end, where a series of twenty-foot lengths of steel rail have been pounded vertically into the Pacific sand, the surf washes flotsam indiscriminately onto the beaches of San Diego and Tijuana. In the east, the border is an estuary, where the Río Bravo del Norte (as Mexicans know the Rio Grande) meanders between Brownsville and Matamoros and through a humid salt marsh, where egrets and roseate spoonbills forage, before emptying into the Gulf of Mexico. It is a place that people have inhabited and explored for centuries.

The border region is a complex, interconnected world where factory managers from Texas commute across the Rio Grande to work in the maquiladora industrial parks and transsexual prostitutes in Tijuana cater to American sexual appetites. It's an interwoven place where farmers in the irrigated desert of the Mexicali Valley produce green vegetables in winter for the U.S. market, and 10 percent of the student body at the University of Texas at El Paso—1,800 college students—crosses over a bridge from Ciudad Juárez each day. It's a mutual aid agreement between the fire departments of Calexico and Mexicali. A Mexican family goes north seeking an orthopedic surgeon to care for an injured child. An American without dental insurance crosses south looking to get an affordable filling. A smuggler humps a bale of dope across the desert on a moonless night. The border is a visit to a Mexican grandfather on the ancestral *rancho*. It's a new DVD player purchased at a Texas Wal-Mart. It's a series of watersheds where creeks flow both north and south, and a flyway where birds migrate more readily than people. The borderlands in both countries are home to cowboys, whose grandparents homesteaded on the grassland frontier a century ago, and Indians, whose ancestors eked out an existence in the Sonoran Desert for millennia.

I was especially struck by the intimate nature of relationships across the border when I was reporting on the binational AIDS epidemic. The human immunodeficiency virus has spread across the border from north to south and back again, reflecting the continuous movement and interaction of people between San Diego and Tijuana. "Just because someone says they're a resident in one place doesn't mean they don't have a life, including a sexual life, on the other side too," remarked Dr. María Luisa Zúñiga, an epidemiologist at the University of California at San Diego. And just as the virus traveled across the borderlands, so Zúñiga and other scientists and health care professionals were also crossing the border line, collaborating on binational solutions to stop the deadly spread of the disease and to care for those infected.[16]

I am certainly not the first writer to examine the U.S.-Mexico border. Scholars have written about border history, commerce, and culture and the mechanics and politics of immigration and national security. Much of this scholarship has informed my work, although it often deals with very specialized themes and is geared toward an academic audience. Historian Oscar J. Martínez has contributed finely textured accounts of the region and its people in all their variety. Historians Paul Ganster and David E. Lorey have traced the economic and social origins of contemporary issues in the borderlands. David Spener, a sociologist, and Kathleen Staudt, a political scientist, have provided a theoretical framework for thinking about borders both abstractly and concretely. Geographer Lawrence A. Herzog has charted the development of twin border cities, their contrasts, and their shared use of space. Sociologist Pablo Vila has investigated the ways that border residents construct their sense of identity, often by distinguishing themselves from others they consider different either nationally or ethnically. Economists Joan B. Anderson and James Gerber have analyzed labor, trade, manufacturing, environmental impacts, binational institutions, and human development at the border. Geographer Joseph Nevins has described the evolution of the border from a territorial "frontier" to an international "boundary" with a legal and physical infrastructure to enforce it, while political scientist Peter Andreas has argued that the escalation of policing that boundary is closely connected to the opening of the border to greater economic flows in a symbolic reassertion of U.S. territorial authority. Sociologists Douglas S. Massey, Jorge Durand, and Nolan J. Malone have developed a perceptive analysis of the forces of global development that underlie labor migrations, and historian Mae M. Ngai has traced the causes, consequences, and dynamics of undocumented Mexican migration to the United States. These authors constitute a selection—by no means a complete list—of the range of scholarly thinkers in the area of border studies.

Nonfiction writers, meanwhile, including Luis Alberto Urrea and Ted Conover, have given us vivid tales of border dwellers and border crossers in recent decades. Journalists, too, have documented the world of the border. A few notable recent examples come to mind. Rubén Martínez, in his book *Crossing Over,* and Sonia Nazario, in *Enrique's Journey,* recounted gripping narratives of migration. Sam Quinones gathered stories of migrants that are at once flamboyant and earthy in *Antonio's Gun and Delfino's Dream.* In her 2000 book *Lives on the Line,* former *Arizona Republic* reporter Miriam Davidson gracefully described the changing reality of Ambos Nogales in a time of rapid industrialization and heightened border enforcement. Two *Los Angeles Times* reporters have also ably chronicled the border. Sebastian Rotella, in his 1998 book *Twilight on the Line,* captured·the rough world of drug lords and politicians in Tijuana. And in his 2004 book *Hard Line,* Ken Ellingwood traced the conflictive saga of illegal immigration across California and Arizona. Reuters reporter Tim Gaynor focused on the cat-and-mouse drama of border agents and smugglers in his 2009 *Midnight on the Line.*

What distinguishes this book, I hope, is a view of the border not just as a line (as emphasized in the titles of the preceding books) but as a region. Though I have drawn on the academic literature about the borderlands to give my readers a greater sense of context, I have not aimed to produce a scholarly treatment of the place. Rather, this volume is fundamentally a work of journalism that tells human stories about people and communities along the entire length of the border. Each story individually seeks to illuminate something about a particular area and a particular issue. Together they add up to a multifaceted view of the borderlands, a region that is more complex than policy makers tend to understand. The border is not something to be "sealed," though we can surely find better ways to regulate the flow of goods and people across this permeable boundary. Here in this two-thousand-mile-long region, which reaches both north and south, Americans and Mexicans have a long track record of coexistence. Their lives are shaped by the presence of the boundary line but also by the country next door. Right now they bear the brunt of the border's problems, but they might help point us toward the solutions.

So I invite the reader to take a look at the borderlands, meet some of its inhabitants, and listen to their perspectives. The story unfolds from east to west, starting in the Lower Rio Grande Valley, where a binational culture is most deeply rooted, and heading westward, chapter by chapter, to the Pacific, where I examine perhaps the thorniest problem the United States and Mexico must tackle.

In chapter 1, at the border's eastern end, near the mouth of the Rio Grande, a teenager in South Texas wrestles with the tension between her parents' Mexican traditions and her very American aspirations. For Maribel

Saenz, growing up on the border encompasses a quintessential Tejano blend that mixes volleyball practice and Fourth of July fireworks with Norteño dancing and fittings in Mexico for a *quinceañera* dress. Maribel's borderland is a hybrid world, and for her the true frontier is the one she crosses in leaving her Mexican American community for college further north.

In chapter 2, in a Reynosa shantytown on the Mexican side of the line, María de la Luz Modesto butchers a chicken for her children's soup while her husband toils in a maquiladora assembly plant. Beside a glittering swimming pool in a McAllen subdivision across the river, Char Taylor encourages her friends, a group of maquiladora managers' wives, to contribute to a fund drive for Mexican orphans. Though the two women are strangers, their lives are intertwined through the binational economy of export manufacturing. But their experiences are like mirror images of each other, reflecting the opportunities of the border economy but also its stark inequities.

In chapter 3, in the southwest corner of New Mexico, cows outnumber people and Lawrence Hurt and his brothers raise beef cattle on land their grandparents homesteaded a century ago. Sitting right on the border, the Hurts are tied to Mexico by work, marriage, and geography. Their ranch in the Boot Heel has been relatively untouched by illegal immigration, but because it is one stretch of border not slated for fencing, it could become the "cattle chute" into which northbound migrants are funneled by fences to the east and west. The interdependence of the borderlands is clear here, but so are its tensions.

In Nogales, Sonora, in chapter 4, Dr. Enrique Contreras, a Mexican physician at a public hospital, often finds himself caring for Mexicans from further south who are trying to make it across the border to the United States. His resources are strained, as are those of American doctors on the other side of the fence, but Contreras is getting help from Arizona hospitals whose view of health care—and of the community they serve—doesn't stop at the border. With the help of donated equipment, Contreras can now treat even complex cases in Mexico, rather than transferring them to the U.S. side. The pragmatic approach to cross-border problem solving here is based on personal relationships between Mexican and American medical providers.

Perhaps nowhere is the artificial nature of the border between the United States and Mexico so glaring as it is on the Tohono O'odham Indian Reservation in southern Arizona, the focus of chapter 5, where the original inhabitants of the Sonoran Desert have made their home for eons. O'odham tribal leader Harriet Toro frequently drives through a gap in the fence to tend to the needs of Mexican members of the tribe. But with the international boundary cutting through their ancestral land, Toro and her tribe are now on the front line in a grim struggle to cope with drug runners and with migrants who perish in the heat. The brutal impact of failed border policies is felt most keenly here, by people who predate the border line.

In chapter 6, at the point where the Colorado River crosses the border, its waters are drained from the riverbed to coax vegetables from the desert in California and Baja California, leaving nothing for wildlife habitat but leakage and waste. The region is also criss-crossed by power lines and natural gas pipes in a growing energy network that connects Mexico to the United States but compromises the environment in both countries. San Diego engineer Bill Powers is part of another kind of network, a binational environmental movement fighting for clean air and water on both sides of the border. It's a grassroots effort that aims to convince policy makers in both countries to see that their interests span the international divide.

Alone on a hill outside the California town of Jacumba, Minuteman Britt Craig stands sentry to protect his country. His story unfolds in chapter 7. Decades earlier, Craig was wounded in Vietnam and came home to an ungrateful America, but guarding the border has renewed Craig's patriotism. Though the Minuteman movement fizzled, the group's name became a household word, striking a chord with Americans frustrated by illegal immigration and anxious over the changes of a globalizing world. For Craig, finding the Minutemen helped him find a sense of mission and a place on the border under the bright stars. He and his compatriots have come to the border not to reach across it but to assert its power of separation.

In chapter 8, Agustín Bravo counsels addicts at a drug rehabilitation center on a cliff above the Pacific Ocean after years of running marijuana across the border for Tijuana's drug lords. Bravo, who is recovering from a methamphetamine addiction, is one of countless Tijuanans whose lives have been shattered as the border drug trade has escalated, narcotics have been bottled up in Mexico, and violence has exploded between competing cartels and the police. Another unlikely counselor to those in the grip of drugs and violence is Mother Antonia, an eighty-year-old American nun who lives inside Tijuana's state prison and doggedly navigates the halls of power in the United States and Mexico to salvage lives from the drug trade. They dwell in a teeming binational metropolis where cross-border commerce, both legal and illicit, is constantly flowing.

Figure 2. As dusk settles, a man leaps off the hand-pulled barge that ferries across the Rio Grande between Los Ebanos, Texas, and Díaz Ordaz, Tamaulipas. Photo by Chris Stewart/San Francisco Chronicle.

The border was created as the outcome of a war. And it often seems like a battleground today. It is at the core of debates about immigration, trade, labor, drugs, culture, the environment, and national security. The openness or restrictiveness of the border changes with the political tides. And discussion of the border is high drama. But in a place like Los Ebanos, Texas, the little village with the hand-pulled ferry, people are accustomed to living with an international boundary running through their world. They have learned to accommodate themselves to the politically wrought changes in the same way they might cope with flood or drought. For them, the border is nothing more dramatic than a hand-pulled ferry connecting two small towns.

At dusk in Los Ebanos, when the border stations are locked, the barge is chained to an ebony tree, and the boatmen and customs agents have gone home, stillness settles on the river. The small stucco chapel is empty. So is the baseball diamond beside the elementary school. An old woman waters the flowers struggling in her dooryard. A donkey brays, its voice rending the twilight curtain of insect chirrs and bird calls. Somewhere in the dusty village of four hundred people a dog barks. Another answers. For centuries, people forded the river at this shallow spot. In 1950 the crossing became an official U.S. port of entry and a sign was mounted over the customs inspection station. The printing on the sign has faded with the years, but it's still legible. *"Bienvenidos a Los Estados Unidos,"* it reads in welcoming Spanish.

ONE

Elsa

"We want to hold our kids close forever"

THE THUNK AND SLAP OF a volleyball game echoed through the junior high school gymnasium in Elsa, Texas. Sweat streaming from her forehead and a long dark ponytail flopping on her shoulders, Maribel Saenz connected with the ball, setting it up for a teammate who spiked it over the net. With a whoop of glee, the seventeen-year-old led her fellows in a brief victory dance. But the game eventually went to the other team, led by Mari's sister, Carolina, a lanky fifteen-year-old and the strongest player on the court.

The relative cool of the gym was a welcome respite from July's steamy heat in this little South Texas farm town twenty minutes from the Mexican border. And the morning pickup game provided a bit of diversion for a handful of Mexican American teenagers on summer break. Coach Mary Cruz, who grew up a "gym rat" herself an hour north in Falfurrias, had known Maribel and her sister since she began coaching them as sixth graders. "They're very well-mannered kids," said Cruz, as she stretched her hamstrings on the bleachers, half watching the game. "Their parents are very old-fashioned. Her mom has said to me, 'If she does anything wrong, you let me know about it.'"

Elsa, with a population of 5,500, is the kind of town where it's not too hard to keep an eye on a teenager. It's a town where just about everyone turns out for high school football games, and scores of fans drive hours to support the Edcouch-Elsa Yellowjackets at away games.

The town is in the heart of South Texas—a region with some of the strongest and most enduring cross-border ties anywhere. Maribel's life was deeply embedded in that world, and the conflicts she faced in coming of age were uniquely those of a border girl. In Elsa, as in most of the Lower Rio Grande Valley, store clerks address their customers in Spanish as often as English. Nine out of ten residents of the region are Hispanic.[1] Some, like Maribel's parents, are immigrants from Mexico. But many families in the area trace their roots to the land grants of the eighteenth century, when both sides of the Rio Grande were settled by ranchers from Spain. Still other families have migrated back and forth across the river over time. The long relationship with Mexico has helped shape a distinctive Tejano culture, blending Mexican and American traditions.

Maribel and Carolina were in their element browsing the mall in McAllen or gossiping with friends at the local Whataburger, but they also drew freely on their Mexican roots. "At Caro's *quince* we put on CDs," said Maribel after the game was over. "My sister likes to dance to hip-hop. I like Norteño and Colombiano."

In her final year of high school, Maribel didn't challenge her immigrant parents openly, but her plans extended well beyond their dream that she stay close to home and join the family plumbing business, where they hoped she would put her fluent English to use in the front office. When it came to dating, though, her parents prevailed. In her wallet she carried a photo of Luis, a football player she'd been seeing for seven months. At her parents' insistence, however, the couple always took along Carolina and the girls' thirteen-year-old brother Juan Carlos when they went on a date. "At first I was so embarrassed, but then I got used to it," said Maribel. "Now we don't go out, though, because Luis got sick of going with my little brother. I see him at school or at the football workout and we talk on the phone. That's it."

Like countless Tejano teenagers in this border region, she felt torn between staying true to her parents' traditional Mexican values, which emphasize family connectedness above all, and striking out on an individual American path to success. Maribel mused about applying to colleges as far away as California and Washington, D.C. "My parents won't be thrilled," she acknowledged. "I told them I want to leave the Valley, and they were like, '¿Porqué? ¡Tan lejos!' I'm going to tell them it's best for me."

The Rio Grande meanders to the Gulf of Mexico through a vast alluvial plain where Mexico and the United States have rubbed off on each other for generations. In the Mexican state of Tamaulipas, the flat river valley—known there as La Cuenca, the basin—is part irrigated farmland, part thorn scrub, and part urban sprawl. The cities of Reynosa and Matamoros have burgeoned in recent decades with the proliferation of foreign-owned manufacturing plants or *maquiladoras*. On the Texas side, the Valley—as locals call this three-thousand-square-mile region, is a checkerboard of cotton, sorghum, citrus, tomato, and sugarcane fields—punctuated by an occasional water tower. Strip malls of Wal-Marts and Home Depots flank U.S. Route 83 as it hugs the river. The small cities of McAllen and Brownsville are hubs of border commerce. But the back roads are dotted with modest farmhouses and struggling *colonias,* or shantytowns.

Some Texans draw an imaginary demarcation they call the Mexican-Dixon line from El Paso east to Houston, which essentially consigns heavily Latino South Texas to Mexico. The sense of living in a world apart is common among Valley residents. "We're pretty cut off from the rest of Texas through distance, geography, culture, and custom," said Juan Ochoa, a Mexican-born lawyer who teaches junior high school in the Valley town of La Joya. "You drive sixty miles out of here and there's a federal checkpoint that says, 'Protecting America's Frontier.' It's as if the United States starts sixty miles north of here."

The border region today is shaped by its history. The entire borderlands, including all of the U.S. Southwest, once belonged to Mexico (and before it, the colony of New Spain). In Spanish, the word for border is *la frontera,* the frontier. For the Spanish colonizers, and later Mexican leaders, these northern territories were a frontier to be conquered by missionaries, soldiers, and settlers, in much the same way as the United States approached its own western frontier. In the chaotic years after gaining independence from Spain in 1821, Mexico had trouble establishing control over its outlying northern provinces and permitted Americans to colonize Texas. By 1835, more than twenty thousand English-speaking Americans—with little loyalty to Mexico—had settled there. When Mexican president Antonio López de Santa Anna acted to centralize power, reduce the authority of Mexico's states, and enforce the country's law against slavery, the Texas settlers rebelled, declaring independence from Mexico in 1836. But when the United States, bent on westward expansion and motivated by a sense of manifest destiny, moved to annex Texas in 1845, Mexico resisted, still considering the state part of its national territory. War erupted in 1846, and a U.S. invasion of Mexico culminated in the taking of Mexico City nearly two years later.[2]

Under the Treaty of Guadalupe Hidalgo, which ended the fighting in 1848, Mexico ceded one-third of its territory (one-half, counting Texas), and the United States paid $15 million in compensation. University of Southern California geographer Michael Dear has called it "the most important belligerent land grab in history."[3] With the stroke of a pen an estimated seventy-five thousand to one hundred thousand Mexicans, many of them Native Americans (whose own claims to the land predated the existence of either nation), became U.S. citizens. Though nominally guaranteed the full protections of the U.S. Constitution, these first Mexican Americans were soon relegated to second-class status.[4] The physical boundary between the two countries was adjusted in 1853 by the Gadsden Purchase, by which the United States bought an additional strip of land in southern Arizona and New Mexico to obtain a more favorable route for the transcontinental Southern Pacific Railroad. With the boundary thus established, the frontier was converted into a border, an edge, where the two countries began marking off their territorial limits.[5]

Cities and towns along the border exist as pairs: one Mexican, one American. Some, like Laredo, began as single communities that were divided in two when the international boundary was established. In other cases, a second town grew up after the Mexican-American War, as a counterpart to the original city across the border: Brownsville began as a U.S. fort across the river from the colonial city of Matamoros; El Paso grew as a railroad town opposite old El Paso del Norte, later renamed Ciudad Juárez; and the little cow town of Tijuana—south of the eighteenth-century Spanish mission and garrison at San Diego—gained importance only after the war placed the border there. More recent settlements—Ambos Nogales (the pair of towns of the same name, one in Sonora, one in Arizona), Douglas/Agua Prieta, and Calexico/Mexicali—emerged side by side later in the nineteenth century as gateways between the two countries. Nowadays, the Mexican cities tend to be much larger than their U.S. counterparts, a consequence of industrialization, tourism, and U.S.-bound migrants who haven't made it over the border.[6]

The inhabitants of this fast-growing, in-between place at times feel like outsiders, misunderstood even within their own countries. "The border is really a bundle of paradoxes," says Jorge Bustamante, a Mexican sociologist on the faculty of the University of Notre Dame and founder of Tijuana's Colegio de la Frontera Norte, a research institute on border issues. "It's sort of a sandwich between the prejudices from the North and from the South."[7]

In Mexico, the border region, distant as it is from Mexico City, has nevertheless developed rapidly over the past two generations, its economy and population growing on the foundation of a manufacturing base and proximity to U.S. resources. Mexican border residents benefit from the relative prosperity of their region. But because the border has long been an outpost, remote from the center of the country's political power and culture, its inhabitants are sometimes viewed with suspicion as not being Mexican enough. In the 1960s, the Mexican government went so far as to launch a campaign in border cities to strengthen national identity through educational and cultural programs and insistence on the use of proper Spanish, unadulterated by Anglicisms.[8] Mexicans who live near the border may be derided by their countrymen as being too *agringados,* says Bustamante, yet they are, if anything, more adamantly Mexican because when they cross into the United States, "we know for sure that we are not gringos."

On the American side of the line, the border region varies from affluent, conservative, predominantly white San Diego County on California's Pacific Coast to the low-income, politically liberal, overwhelmingly Mexican American counties of Cameron and Hidalgo in South Texas. In the Lower Rio Grande Valley, where 85 percent of the population is Hispanic, residents complain of neglect by officials in Austin and Washington, D.C., feeling that because they live so far south in Texas—or rather, so close to Mexico—their needs and aspirations are little appreciated. Yet Valley natives point to the musical, culinary, and literary offerings their region has generated; while Tejano writer and anthropologist Américo Paredes and Tex-Mex *conjunto* accordionist Narciso Martínez may not be household names, they have contributed to the roots of American culture.

After the volleyball game, the players exchanged high fives and clustered, chattering, around the water fountain, then drifted out into the parking lot. "See you at home," called Carolina. She and Maribel each climbed into her own beat-up sedan and departed. Neither girl had a driver's license. But in the way of many country kids, both were competent drivers. Maribel drove home to change out of her sweat-soaked gym clothes. She steered her little Kia over the back streets of town, crossed herself as she passed the Sacred Heart Catholic Church, and pulled into her driveway. "We have *gallinas,*" she said, switching seamlessly between English and Spanish, her first language and the tongue she shared with her parents. She showed off the chicken coop and the young orchard. "And my mom has her papayas and banana trees . . . *apenas están creciendo.*"

The Saenzes' modern brick ranch house was set back from the road behind a low cyclone fence. For Juan and Raquel Saenz, purchasing the house two years earlier was the culmination of decades of hard work and savings. They had each immigrated to Texas as teenagers, he from the border state of Nuevo Leon, she from a little *terreno* in Zacatecas. The couple had met and married in Houston, eloping after Raquel's family refused to bless the union. They had settled in Elsa when Maribel was ten, Carolina eight, and Juan Carlos six. Together with his four brothers, Juan Saenz had built a flourishing plumbing company, installing water and sewer lines for new construction projects throughout the Valley.

The town had its own bank, the Elsa State Bank and Trust Co., and an H.E.B. supermarket. But the main drag, State Route 107, was struggling, flanked by a used muffler shop, a trailer park, a convenience store announcing, "WIC accepted here," and an evangelical church housed in a corrugated metal warehouse, the Iglesia Betesda de la Palabra Viviente. A farmer sold tomatoes from the back of a pickup truck. A scrawny horse grazed a stubbly field beside an irrigation canal. A tire swing dangled from a tree in the corner of a dirt yard.

The Saenz's new, four-bedroom suburban home—one of a handful in town that display prosperous aspirations—was a welcome change from the family's previous abode, a cramped little house close to the school. But just like its humbler neighbors, the Saenz home sat in the path of a yellow crop duster that targeted the cotton fields surrounding it. "In the morning you can see the planes overhead spraying pesticides," said Maribel. "Sometimes they don't aim right and it lands on the house. My mom yells 'Get indoors!' I think sometimes people get sick."

Inside, the house was as neat as a pin, with a cheerful sunflower motif in the kitchen. The key rack held rosaries and a green flyswatter. A small bowl of chili peppers sat on the dining table. Carolina was already home, standing by the fridge eating crackers topped with chicken salad she dipped from a plastic container. Her cell phone rang. "Hi Mom . . ." she answered. "*En la casa. ¿Y tu?*" The girls arranged to meet their mother for lunch, and Mari headed for the shower. In the living room hung enormous studio portraits of Maribel and Carolina dressed in formal gowns at their *quinceañeras,* the coming-of-age celebrations that marked each girl's fifteenth birthday. The framed photographs dominated even the overstuffed furniture.

More than three hundred friends and relatives had attended Maribel's *quince.* Her pale pink satin dress had been handmade across the border in

Mexico, and she had been escorted down the aisle of the church by fourteen attendants, representing the fourteen years of her childhood. Following the mass, her parents had hosted a catered *fiesta* under a tent in their back yard. "We danced the whole night away. It was crazy," remembered Mari, transported. "Even when the band took a break we put on the radio and kept dancing. It went on until three in the morning."

For Maribel's mother, the most important moment had come at the beginning of the evening when her daughter knelt on the dance floor and all four grandparents prayed over her. "One by one, her *abuelitos* went to her and gave her their blessing," recalled Raquel Saenz. "We were so proud, because she had always been so well-behaved—she didn't drink or go with boys—and she was growing into a beautiful young woman. I didn't have a *quinceañera* because my parents were so poor. I wanted it to be possible for my daughters."

For several decades after the Mexican-American War put this once-Mexican territory firmly in the control of the United States, Texans of Mexican descent, or Tejanos, continued to exert leadership in the Rio Grande Valley—as landowners and merchants, local politicians and law enforcement. The English-speaking white Americans (known in the region as Anglos) who first settled here intermarried with Tejano families, converted to Catholicism, and adapted themselves to Mexican American traditions. But over time, and with the backing of occupying U.S. troops and the Texas Rangers, the state's mounted frontier police force, the balance of power tipped toward the Anglos. With the arrival of the first railroad line in Brownsville in 1904, the shift accelerated drastically.[9]

The Valley's economy had been dominated by Tejano cattle ranches that produced beef for the local market. But some Anglo ranchers began clearing the chaparral and experimenting with irrigation systems to water row crops. Once the railroad opened an easy route to a national market for agricultural products, a land boom ensued. In the first decades of the twentieth century, cash-poor *rancheros* found themselves unable to pay their skyrocketing tax bills and were forced to surrender their lands. In some cases they were expelled by intimidation and threats. In a few short years, a wholesale transfer of land ownership from Tejanos to Anglos took place.[10]

Real estate developers advertised aggressively to midwestern farmers, touting the Valley's rich alluvial soil, eleven-month growing season—and docile Mexican labor. The region's once-proud *vaqueros* were reduced to working as field hands, stooped over endless rows of cotton, cabbages, and onions, under the watchful eye of a crew boss. And the new wave of Anglos, who arrived by the thousands, were not inclined to adapt themselves to Tejano ways. Instead, many cultivated disdain for ethnic Mexicans and often outright racism.[11]

In 1915 and 1916, fueled by a bitter sense of injustice and inspired by the Mexican Revolution just over the border, some Tejanos launched an uprising, seeking to force the Anglo settlers out of South Texas. A couple of hundred loosely organized rebels sabotaged railroad lines and launched sometimes brutal raids on Anglo farms, then melted back into the countryside or retreated south across the Rio Grande. But the rebellion, known as the Plan de San Diego, was unsuccessful in its aims. And it unleashed a furious backlash of anti-Mexican vigilantism, including hundreds, possibly thousands, of lynchings and summary executions, according to historian Benjamin Heber Johnson, whose book *Revolution in Texas* gives a thorough account of the period.[12] The violence unleashed on Mexicanos by local Anglo landowners and sheriffs, and above all the Texas Rangers, echoed the campaign of terror endured by African Americans in the post-Reconstruction South. In the years that followed, Anglos cemented their control of the region through poll taxes and whites-only primaries, which disenfranchised Tejanos, and through the racial segregation of schools, neighborhoods, and public facilities.[13]

Juanita Garza, sixty-two, traced her family roots in the Valley back to 1760—before the American Revolution. But her parents had sent her and her siblings to school in San Antonio, 250 miles north, rather than put them through the segregated public schools in Weslaco, six miles south of Elsa. "Where I grew up, there were three schools: one was for Anglo Americans, another was for Mexican Americans, and then African Americans had their own little shack of a school," said Garza, now a professor teaching border history at the University of Texas–Pan American (UTPA) nearby. "My parents sent some of us off to boarding school for high school. It was either we went to a school where we were segregated or we went to a school where there was integration but it was away. My parents weighed what was worse." Their commitment to education and equity eventually led Garza's mother and father to establish a religious school in Weslaco, open to students of all backgrounds. Her mother went on to serve on the local school board in the 1970s and finally helped oversee the integration of the public schools.

Elsa, like many Valley farm towns, was segregated from its inception. Fifteen miles north of the border, the settlement, along with its smaller neighbor Edcouch, was established in 1927 when the Southern Pacific

Railroad laid track across the broad delta. Scottish speculator William George had bought the land in 1916 and persuaded the railroad to build its new line across his property. He named the new community after his wife and held a land sale, advertising Elsa as "The Planned Valley Town" and offering residential lots for $75 to $600 and business lots for $150 to $850 apiece. Parcels to the south of the tracks were reserved for Anglo residents and businesses and were served by paved roads and a sewer system. Those to the north included the "Mexican colony," which had no such amenities. The city fathers enacted a Hispanic curfew during those early decades, allowing Tejanos to cross the tracks to shop during the daytime but subjecting to arrest any Hispanic caught on the south side after sunset. Mexican Americans found work in the area's cotton gins and vegetable packing sheds, but few made it to high school.[14]

Frank Guajardo, a graduate of Edcouch-Elsa High School, had been born just over the border in Mexico. His grandparents, Texans who had owned a small *rancho* on the north bank of the river, fled to Tamaulipas in the 1920s when the Texas Rangers were persecuting Tejanos. His wife's ancestors, also Mexican American, had lived in Texas for more than two hundred years. The emphasis on family was a source of strength for Guajardo, age forty, founder of a college-prep program in which Maribel participated called the Llano Grande Center, named for the broad plain here that constituted one of the first Spanish land grants north of the Rio Grande, made to Capt. Juan José Hinojosa in 1778.

"When our first child was born, my wife and I were still in grad school," Guajardo said. "We decided that we wanted him to be raised not just by his parents but by his grandparents, his *tíos* and *tías*. So for us, living many miles away from home in San Antonio didn't make sense. What made sense was to go home." Guajardo earned his PhD at the University of Texas at Austin, then settled back in Edinburg, the seat of Hidalgo County, where he joined the faculty of the College of Education at UTPA. Since moving back home he had taken his three kids to dinner at grandma's house every Sunday.

On the Fourth of July, Guajardo accompanied his fifteen-year-old son Danny and a teenage friend to a minor league baseball game between the Edinburg Roadrunners and the El Paso Diablos. Many in the overwhelmingly Hispanic crowd were decked out in American flag T-shirts, and a number of women had thrust little plastic flags into their buns or ponytails in celebration of the holiday. As the balmy evening descended, families chatted in Spanish and English over the booming voice of the announcer calling the lineup. "Now at bat, Al-e-jaaan-dro Fer-naaan-dez, No. 19 for El Paso." Vendors hawked watermelon—by the slice or the whole melon—and roasted ears of corn, slathered with butter and salt, American style, or chili pepper and lime juice, *a la Mexicana,* depending on the customer's preference.

Meandering through the crowd and greeting friends, Guajardo suddenly spotted an old hero: Pedro Borbón, a former major league pitcher who had played ten seasons for the Cincinnati Reds, was lounging at the back of the open-air stands, taking in the game. The aging Dominican player had made an unlikely move to the Rio Grande Valley two decades earlier, after having fallen in love with a local girl who had cut his hair at a barbershop there. Family ties in the Valley being what they are, the girl was not prepared to move away just because she had married a baseball star, so Borbón settled down and pursued a second career in the Mexican leagues. "When I was a kid I used to listen to your games on the radio when my family drove north to Michigan to pick crops," Guajardo told Borbón, his all-time favorite ball player. "That's how I learned English."

Guajardo also ran into one of his former students, a graduate of the Llano Grande program who was home from Occidental College for the summer. Celebrating Independence Day in the United States was bittersweet, said the young woman, who had crossed the river from Mexico without papers a decade before, because she sometimes felt she didn't quite belong in either her adopted country or the country of her birth. Then after a pause, the young woman observed: "I love living at the border because it's not a crash of cultures, it's a flow of cultures. Coming here tonight, I can enjoy baseball but still be Mexican."

After the game, the fans rose to their feet to sing the national anthem and watch the indigo sky erupt with fireworks. Little boys ran around waving glow sticks, while young men smooched in the dark with their girlfriends. Guajardo and the boys ambled out of the stadium. In the Valley the most American of holidays had taken on a quintessential Tejano twist.

As Guajardo's family did a generation ago, many Mexican Americans from the Valley even today spend half the year as migrant workers, following the harvest to California or Michigan with their children in tow. The border region struggles economically. The median household income in Hidalgo County, which includes Elsa, is $30,000 (well below the national average of almost $51,000), and almost 40 percent of all families with children in the county live in poverty.[15] Just 58 percent of Hidalgo County's adults have a high school diploma, compared to 79 percent of Texans and

84 percent of Americans overall. And in the seven counties along the river that make up the greater Rio Grande Valley, four in ten students are classified as "English learners," seven times as many as in the United States overall.[16]

But Guajardo bristled at the notion that such statistics mean that the Valley's youth are incapable of success. "We've been conditioned by signals in the mainstream that suggest that along the border, schools, economies, and people are expected to do according to one level of achievement," said Guajardo. "Those assumptions . . . suggest a lower level of expectations for people from here. But when we think that way, we're not able to cultivate genius; we cultivate mediocrity. We say, 'You're not going to find the cure for AIDS.' 'You're not going to be the next governor of Texas.'"

Through the Llano Grande Center, Guajardo and his colleagues take youngsters like Maribel on annual tours of elite East and West Coast universities to show them the educational possibilities beyond the Valley. The center has helped dozens of students garner scholarships to schools like Yale and Stanford. But the program also teaches the kids to value their own culture and community. Llano Grande kids have interviewed their grandparents for oral history projects and produced a video documentary that persuaded the city council to clean up a derelict park. Perhaps most remarkable is how many of the center's alumni return to the region after college. But Guajardo said family ties still keep many Hispanic kids from going away to college in the first place, just as they did when he was a youth.

How much young people feel the pressure to break away depends on how close they are to their family and how traditional their parents are, said Juanita Garza. "For the most part, the break does come. It's very American. But it's a major difference between Anglo society and Hispanic. We want to hold our kids close forever. It's okay if they're married and come back to live with us. But that's not part of the American way of doing things. It's totally different in the Valley."

At thirty-nine, Raquel Saenz was a pillar of maternal wisdom and warmth, though her eyes still twinkled with some of the same spunk that enlivened her daughters' faces. She met the girls, and Maribel's best friend Marylu Rodríguez, at Elsa's new Subway sandwich shop and chatted and joked easily with them over lunch. Carolina, the athlete of the family, wolfed down two subs, then prepared to head back to school to run bleachers and lift weights at a football team practice that was open to all students. "Caro can eat a whole pizza by herself," teased Raquel fondly. "She's always working out."

For Raquel, maintaining a close relationship with her children—and keeping them physically close—was of paramount importance. She knew the pain of separation firsthand and told her oldest daughter: "It's better for the family to stay close. It's better for you to study in the same town and marry in the same town."

By the time she was nine, Raquel had been in charge of looking after her younger siblings and feeding and watering the livestock on her family's small plot of land in rural Zacatecas. When she was fifteen, instead of preparing for a coming-of-age party, Raquel left home with her eighteen-year-old brother and made her way north. "There were eleven children in my family and not enough food," she recalled. "We were the oldest. There wasn't any work, so we came here."

Swimming across the Rio Grande was "the hardest thing I had done in my life. I was so afraid. It seemed like an impossible mission." But the pair made it across and found their way to Houston, where Raquel got work in a factory, making dining room chairs. Other siblings joined them over time. Her education, which had been interrupted after ninth grade, was resumed only many years later, when she was already a mother of three trying to help her kids with their homework.

In Houston Raquel met Juan Saenz, three years her senior, and the two began courting. But with their parents back home in Mexico, Raquel's brothers assumed the job of protecting her honor. "My *tíos* were very strict," said Maribel. "She would only get to see him outside the house for ten minutes." Raquel reflected later that she had missed out on her own mother's influence during those teenage years—someone to whom she could confide her romantic yearnings and get a sympathetic hearing. Even when her father migrated to Texas and Juan asked him for her hand, the young couple was denied. And so one night, after Raquel turned eighteen, they eloped.

Though she and her husband had since become citizens of the United States as well as Mexico, and could travel freely across the border, Raquel was still seized with pity when she heard stories of migrants drowning in the river or dying in the desert as they attempted the same crossing she had once made. "She'll say, '*O, pobre gente,*' because she went through it too," said Maribel. With Mexico so close, Raquel easily maintained a connection to the country of her birth. She took her daughters on grocery errands across the border a couple of times a month, purchasing her husband's favorite tortillas and *aguacates,* or shuttling the children to doctor or dentist appointments in Mexico.

Maribel and Marylu finished their lunch of turkey subs and Sun Chips and bade Raquel goodbye, then drove the fifteen minutes into Edinburg, the county seat, to enroll in college-level summer classes at UTPA. The girls knew that if they took four college-level courses and kept up a B average they'd qualify for a four-year scholarship at UTPA, through a program designed for students from South Texas counties underserved by the state's public universities. It was their ticket to the future.

Sitting in a counselor's office, Maribel trained the same fierce concentration on the registration process as she had on the volleyball earlier in the day. "I think the principal is out of town. Do we really need his signature on this form, or is a counselor's enough?" she asked. Then: "I've already taken pre-calc in high school. Do I need to take it again?"

Jaime Garza, the counselor in charge of the federally funded GEAR UP program, was brisk but encouraging. "We try to make sure their first experience is going to be positive," said Garza, who spent his days helping students who were the first in their families to make it to college.

Over the years, the obstacles for students like Maribel and Marylu to getting a quality education and a shot at college have been formidable. In 1977 the U.S. Commission on Civil Rights found that 19 percent of Mexican American adults in Texas were illiterate. Seven years later the National Commission on Secondary Schooling reported that the majority of Mexican American students in Texas attended "inferior and highly segregated schools."[17]

In 1987 two Latino civil rights groups, the Mexican American Legal Defense and Education Fund and the League of United Latin American Citizens, joined forces to bring a lawsuit against the state of Texas. They charged the government with short-changing the border region's largely Latino population out of full access to higher education. The Texas Supreme Court did not find the state guilty of discrimination but noted that the state legislature had failed to establish a "first-class" university system for border residents—who accounted for one in four of the state's residents. The legislature got the message and in 1993 launched the South Texas Initiative, which pumped $600 million into five public colleges in the region and brought them into the state university system.[18]

Those resources—combined with the federal program for first-time students, the guidance of the Llano Grande Center, and more than a little personal gumption—put college within the girls' reach in a way it would not have been a generation earlier. "Since I was little I knew I wanted to go to college. I instilled it in myself," said Marylu, sixteen, on the drive back to Elsa. "But if GEAR UP wasn't paying, I wouldn't have the money to go to college classes."

The youngest of seven children of Mexican immigrant farmworkers, Marylu had watched one sister get pregnant and drop out of high school. Two others had gotten their diplomas only to end up working at the local supermarket. A fourth sister, though, had gone on to earn her bachelor's degree at UTPA and become a social worker. "She said she chose social work because of our family, because we were poor," said Marylu, her dark eyes pensive. "Well, we still are. But she wants to help other poor kids have a chance." Marylu's oldest sisters had helped her cover the cost of clothes and other expenses, filling in what their parents couldn't, because they didn't want her to take a job and lose the focus on her studies. "They know that school will get us out," she said.

The rich yellow walls of Maribel's tidy bedroom were decorated with family photos, school sports memorabilia, and a beribboned corsage from the previous year's homecoming dance. Dozens of stuffed animals lined the headboard of her double bed, and a stack of folded laundry sat on the bedspread. The girls plopped down, and Maribel idly ran a brush through her glossy hair, which showed delicate streaks of crimson from a recent coloring experiment. As they talked, Marylu settled herself comfortably on the bed behind Maribel, took the brush, and began weaving her friend's hair into braids. The talk turned to boys.

Maribel and Luis had known each other since eighth grade. But it hadn't been until the previous Christmas that he had started getting sweet on her. When she had gone to Houston for the holidays, they had gotten to talking on the phone—long, lingering conversations where little was said but much was expressed. She chafed at her parents' protectiveness and the sibling chaperones they required, yet accepted them at the same time.

"They won't let me go out without my sister or let her go out without me. I guess they figure we'll look out for each other," Maribel reflected. "To my parents, it's like 'We're being free with her.' I think they're so strict because my mom was brought up really strict. My mom supports me, even about Luis. But she says, 'Don't get too serious.' She ran away with my dad and she regrets it. She said it's more supportive to have a church wedding." It was a common refrain, reiterated by Coach Cruz and Maribel's aunts and uncles: "Don't get too serious." If you get pregnant,

Figure 3. As her friend Marylu Rodríguez styles her hair, teenager Maribel Saenz chats about school, while Maribel's sister, Carolina Saenz, braids her own hair at their home in Elsa, Texas, in the Lower Rio Grande Valley. Photo by Chris Stewart/San Francisco Chronicle.

was the unspoken message, you'll ruin your prospects for an education and a career.

Her parents were eager to see their daughter attend college, but they were also anxious to keep her close. Around the dinner table, over a meal of *pollo en mole* that night, Raquel Saenz said she didn't think her daughter was ready to go away. "Mari wants to travel and travel," she said. "Some people go so far to college. They go from California to Miami and from Miami to California. It doesn't make sense to me."

Juan Saenz arrived from work during the meal and was greeted by his wife and daughters, who each stood up in turn and kissed him on the cheek. *"Todavía está un bebe,"* he put in, joining the conversation. "She's still just a baby." Her parents hoped Maribel would live at home and attend UTPA, then put her education to work for the Saenz family's company. "My husband knows how to do the work, but he doesn't speak much English," said Raquel. "Maribel could take charge of the business side of things."

When autumn came, Maribel took her SATs and started filling out college applications. She visited colleges in California on a trip funded by the Llano Grande Center. In spring she was turned down by Stanford and wait-listed by Occidental, but she got offers from Kalamazoo College, Dakota Wesleyan, UT Austin, Texas A&M, and, of course, UTPA.

Dakota Wesleyan was tempting: the school extended Maribel a soccer scholarship and Marylu had accepted an offer to play softball there. But Maribel had decided to study civil engineering—she had glimpsed the field because her father worked with civil engineers, and it seemed a practical, versatile, and portable profession—and the South Dakota school did not offer an engineering major. Texas A&M came through with a four-year scholarship that almost matched the full ride at UTPA, and the huge College Station campus offered engineering. But A&M was eight hours from home. It had an entering class of seven thousand freshmen, more than the entire population of Elsa, and the vast majority of students were Anglos.

"My mom was like, 'No. You have to stay here,'" recounted Maribel. "She got all these people, teachers and counselors and stuff, to tell me I had to stay at UT Pan American because I had four years paid for. But I had already been there. I didn't want to go there any more."

"Our plan was for her to go to the university here in Edinburg," said Raquel. "I did everything in my power to keep her home."

And so the battle began.

"We never really yelled," said Maribel. "But we made each other cry. When I told them I wanted to go because there were better opportunities, I was crying because I knew I was going to miss them."

"She fought me," put in Raquel. "She thought I was keeping her close to home because she was a girl. She said, 'Why do you want me to stay? You taught me to do things for myself. I'm not afraid. I need to grow more.' We cried a lot. She said she was ready. I didn't see it."

A month after her parents delivered Maribel to her dormitory at College Station, they were adjusting to her absence. Raquel missed her daughter acutely. "I'm getting used to it, but it's very, very hard," she said. "She was so animated. When we would cook out and grill *carne asada* she used to put on Mexican music and dance. It's not the same with Maribel gone." But mother and daughter spoke by phone every day. Raquel had already made one visit to the campus, delivering forgotten items from home, and Maribel had plans to return for her father's birthday a few weeks later.

Maribel was embracing A&M traditions full bore, yelling her heart out with her fellow freshmen when the class of 2010 was announced at an all-school gathering. Though the campus was huge, the people were friendly, she said, and more than once strangers helped her find her way when she got lost. She liked her roommate. And her room—its walls a familiar yellow—felt homey.

She had adopted an Aggie greeting: "Howdy." But she did have to make a few adjustments. "I can't talk Tex-Mex any more, with Spanish words that just slip in," she said. "If I speak Spanish here, no one will understand me." For the first time in her life, Maribel felt like a minority. But so far it hadn't shaken her. "Since I grew up with Mexicanos in the majority, nobody can put me down," she said. "In the Valley, the mayors are Mexican, the judges are Mexican. We have the opportunity of meeting Hispanics who are doctors, who have their PhDs."

And surprisingly—but compellingly—Maribel felt something else in College Station that fit with her Tejano upbringing: "There are so many traditions here, you feel like you're part of something bigger than school. You're part of the big Aggie family." She grinned to think she could replicate the familial bonds of the borderlands in this new setting. "You can actually feel the love of family. It's exciting."

TWO

McAllen / Reynosa

"Most people here work in the maquiladoras"

A FAMILY OF GIRAFFES STRUTTED across the fifty-two-inch television screen in Char Taylor's living room. Outside the air was hot and sultry—the bank thermometer in downtown McAllen, Texas, read 103 degrees at 10:00 a.m. In Taylor's subdivision, a few miles west, the turquoise swimming pool sparkled invitingly. Her five-year-old niece Chloe, visiting from Taylor's hometown in Kansas, begged to swim. But the sun was too strong. Better to wait for evening, Taylor said. So the pair stayed indoors, where air conditioning kept the five-bedroom house pleasant. Chloe arranged her Beanie Babies on the couch while Taylor folded laundry and Animal Planet played in the background.

With its cul-de-sacs, verdant lawns, and manmade lagoons, Sharyland Plantation could be a development in any fast-growing region of the United States. But the master-planned enclave is a half mile from the Mexican border, strategically situated near a future bridge to Mexico and a Texas business park under construction.

Char and her husband Tim Taylor, both forty-two, moved here with their two kids in 2003 when Tim was put in charge of the first assembly plant opened in Mexico by his employer, Dayton Superior, an American maker of concrete sealants, rebar, and other construction materials. Dayton's maquiladora is one of hundreds of factories owned by U.S., Asian, and other multinational companies on the Mexican side of the border that manufacture everything from speedboats and circuit breakers to satin brassieres.

The maquiladoras have drawn people from the interiors of both countries toward the border in pursuit of economic opportunity. The Mexicans fill mainly low-wage assembly-line jobs and the Americans a range of positions in design, engineering, distribution, and management. Moving to the border, these Americans and Mexicans have become part of a single, complex, transnational economy. Though some residents of the borderlands, including Char Taylor and her counterparts across the river in the Mexican city of Reynosa, may have few close personal ties to people in the neighboring country, they are nevertheless woven together in the regional fabric of border manufacturing and commerce, with all its possibilities and contradictions.

Suntanned and trim, with voluptuous dark curls, Char popped open a Diet Pepsi, settled back on the sofa and gazed up at her cathedral ceiling to contemplate the life her family had built since moving from Birmingham, Alabama, a year and a half earlier. "When we moved here, we stepped up," said Char, a plumber's daughter, originally from Parsons, Kansas. "It was a step up." She was pleased with the comfortable lifestyle afforded by her husband's new position in Mexico but also uneasy with the glaring contrasts the border forced upon her.

Dayton's factory is in an industrial park just across the Rio Grande in Reynosa, where more than ninety-six thousand workers are employed in about 135 maquiladoras that produce for the U.S. market.[1] It is a nine-mile drive—just three miles away as the crow flies. But the return commute across the international bridge, where street vendors hawk snacks and trinkets, often took Tim upwards of ninety minutes because of the backup getting through U.S. immigration. For Mexican factory workers in plants like Dayton's, the distance can seem a lot further.

María de la Luz Modesto never crossed the bridge to McAllen. Most of her days were spent in her small dusty yard on the eastern edge of Reynosa, washing laundry at an outdoor sink or cooking over a wood fire on the ground. A trash-strewn and deeply rutted dirt road connected her sprawling shantytown to the city's paved streets where buses took her husband to work, her son to school, and herself to the grocery store.

Like the Taylors, Modesto, twenty-eight, and her husband, Sabino Juárez, thirty-three, had relocated to the border for the promise of prosperity. Both had grown up in villages in the southern state of Veracruz. They had been working in Reynosa's maquiladoras when they met and married eight years back. The couple bought a parcel of government land and began building a two-room home for themselves, using dismantled wooden pallets and other salvaged materials. Over time, they replaced the original walls with cinderblock. But the corrugated steel roof was held in place with rocks and lengths of old wire. The house and its environs—a haphazard jumble of impoverished dwellings—reflected the stresses in Mexican border cities where infrastructure and public services have not kept pace with the burgeoning population. "Most people here work in the maquiladoras," said Modesto.

Her children—Angel, six, and Isabel, three—were growing listless as the relentless sun pounded the metal roof. So Modesto draped a sheet across a pair of outdoor clotheslines to improvise a shady place for them to play. She placed a plastic shipping pallet on the ground and covered it with a folded blanket and a couple of pillows. The kids flopped down eagerly, but after a bit wandered back indoors in search of their small stash of crayons. "Life is a little better than in Veracruz," Modesto reflected. "Here we have a little money when the weekend comes. And the school here is closer and better than the one I went to." Still, the harsh conditions of urban life contrasted with the lush tropical landscape in the village of her birth, and Modesto knew firsthand that the work that put cash in her husband's pocket came at a cost.

For a while, Modesto had held down various factory jobs—assembling motors for electronic automobile braking systems, stitching ironing-board covers, and soldering plumbing valves. But she had quit her last position five years earlier when Angel was a baby. Not only was it hard for her to find child care, but she worried about how the job was affecting her health. The incessant din of the machinery at the Nibco plumbing parts factory penetrated her earplugs, and caustic smells seeped in around her face mask. "I didn't like it," she said. "I haven't worked since."

Juárez, her husband, worked for a computer parts maker called Jabil Global Services, where, after a promotion, he earned nine hundred pesos a week, almost $85. But like many Mexican maquiladora workers, the couple and their children lived with no indoor plumbing or electrical service. They paid a neighbor for the use of one tenuous wire, pirated from the house next door, which afforded them a lightbulb and a tiny refrigerator. For the first four years, Juárez and Modesto had carried water in cans to their home from a water pipe down the road. "Finally the government put in pipes for every house," said Modesto, gesturing to a knee-high faucet protruding from the hard ground. "But the water's not fit to drink.

We have to buy drinking water from a truck that comes around." Behind the house stood the privy and an outdoor bathing stall Juárez had built out of scrap wood with an old plastic tablecloth for a curtain. There was no showerhead inside, however, just a plastic bucket, sitting on the ground beside a soap dish and a bottle of shampoo.

Like Char Taylor, María de la Luz Modesto felt her family was better off economically living at the border. But both women wrestled with a sense that they had traded away a connection to the families and values they had grown up with for this new place in the global economy. And the contrast between the material conditions of the two women's lives, just miles apart, could hardly be starker.

The foreign-owned assembly plants—there were 2,800 of them in 2006—were first established in 1965 under Mexico's Border Industrialization Program. The government aimed to create employment in northern Mexican cities to absorb workers returning from the United States after the termination of the Bracero Program, a two-decade-long agricultural guest worker arrangement that ended in 1964. In the process, however, the factories drew new residents from other states further south in Mexico, making them more mobile, no longer rooted by a connection to the land and to family, history, and community. And rather than hiring the men returning from American farms, employers wound up favoring very young women with little worldly experience because they found them especially dexterous, patient with tedious, repetitive tasks, and docile in the workplace.

The maquiladora program took advantage of U.S. tariff rules allowing components of American products to be assembled in other countries and then shipped back to the United States, where they were taxed only on the value added by Mexican workers. To facilitate the process, Mexico permitted foreign companies to import materials and machinery duty-free into the border zone reserved for export-oriented plants.

The arrangement offered American enterprises access to low-wage Mexican labor without the social costs of admitting immigrants to the United States or the difficulty of negotiating with U.S. unions. The lower production costs in maquiladoras have enabled American companies to produce goods more cheaply in Mexico than in the United States, a strategic means by which U.S. companies have endeavored to stay competitive in the global marketplace.

For Mexico, maquiladoras served as the engine of regional development for the northern states and what Canadian sociologist Kathryn

Kopinak has called "the most successful export-industry model, not only throughout Mexico but also in the larger region that reaches to the Caribbean and Central America."[2] Over time, the maquiladora industry became the linchpin of a new Mexican economic policy. After decades of pursuing development by protecting the country's domestic industries with high tariffs on imported goods, Mexico shifted course in the 1980s to pursue an increasingly privatized economy focused on export-oriented development.[3]

As the economic liberalization got underway in earnest, policy makers in the administration of President Carlos Salinas de Gortari called the maquiladora "the most agile vehicle for the integration of Mexican industry with foreign markets."[4] It was the advent of what economist James M. Cypher has dubbed the "maquilization" of the entire Mexican economy, a shift away from the higher wages and greater labor protections prevalent in traditional manufacturing industries and toward the more flexible work rules and lower pay prevalent in the foreign-owned border assembly plants.[5]

In 1989 the Mexican laws governing the assembly plants were relaxed to allow some maquiladora production to be geared toward domestic consumption. And since 2001 all maquiladora output can be sold directly into the domestic Mexican economy. The government allowed Mexican-owned factories producing for export to operate under looser maquiladora rules. It also allowed foreign-owned companies producing in Mexico for the domestic market—notably in the automotive industry—to shift part of their production to export. The combined effect was to blur the distinctions between the maquiladora and nonmaquiladora manufacturing sectors. The North American Free Trade Agreement (NAFTA), which took effect in 1994, extended to all Mexican industry the ability, formerly reserved for maquiladoras, to import materials from the United States (and Canada) and export them as goods, duty free.

Employment at the plants grew rapidly after NAFTA, doubling to a million jobs in the first five years of the trade pact and peaking in late 2000 with 1.3 million workers. "Some observers believe the correlation in maquiladora growth after 1993 is directly due to NAFTA, but in reality it is unclear whether maquiladora growth is more related to trade liberalization, or to economic conditions in the United States," according to a report by the Congressional Research Service.[6] Wages in the maquiladoras have been stagnant or declining for more than a decade, however, in part because Mexico has an oversupply of workers, in part because labor organizing has been suppressed, and in part because Mexican workers are now competing for assembly-line jobs against workers in low-wage countries in Asia, where firms are increasingly shifting their manufacturing operations.

The Mexican industry's reliance on sales to the U.S. market pushed it into decline when the American economy went into recession in late 2000. At the same time, even lower-wage countries were also getting into the export-industry market, including India, Vietnam, and, most of all, China. It wasn't until mid-2003 that the maquiladora sector began to recover. By mid-2007 it employed 1.2 million Mexicans, still below the peak level of jobs. But the sharp downturn in the U.S. economy in 2008 precipitated another contraction in the Mexican export sector.

Mexico's shift to a liberalized, export-focused economy, which culminated with the country's inclusion in NAFTA, has led to more trade and foreign investment and, according to World Bank economists, is beginning to help Mexico get closer to the levels of development of its NAFTA partners.[7] But as long as the success of Mexico's maquiladora sector depends on cheap labor, some economists say, it will continue to face the threat of being undercut by countries where workers are willing to accept even lower wages. In some cases the Mexican factories are merely a way station in a process of offshoring American manufacturing still further. "The effect of foreign competition is often couched in terms of a product cycle, in which product development and testing occur in the United States, initial long production runs take place in Mexico and ultimately product commoditization happens in China or another low-wage competitor. The more quickly and easily a product is commoditized, the quicker it will move to China," according to economists with the Federal Reserve Bank of Dallas.[8]

Mexico retains some advantages, though. Most importantly, it is close to the United States, which has a seemingly insatiable appetite for consumer goods. Bulky items, such as large-screen televisions or refrigerators, that are not cost-effective to ship across the ocean are likely to continue to be made in Mexico. Proximity is also valuable if orders need to be turned around quickly or if there are frequent design changes or retooling of products.[9]

In search of lower wages, some companies have opened maquiladoras in Mexican cities further south, but more than 75 percent of maquila production still takes place in border cities, which offer better access to roads, power, water, and telephone service and are close enough for managers to live in the United States. Mexico's northern border has become a magnet for workers like Modesto and Juárez from elsewhere in Mexico, particularly rural areas, where government support for subsistence agriculture has evaporated in the liberalized economy.

Passage of NAFTA capped a four-year lobbying effort waged by the Mexican government and business world and endorsed by U.S. business interests.[10] In the 1980s, Mexico began shifting away from a protectionist economic strategy, based on import-substitution industrialization and a large public sector, and toward a privatized, liberalized, export-oriented economy. In 1991 President Salinas secured a commitment from the United States and Canada to extend their bilateral free-trade agreement to include all of North America, ensuring Mexico a place at the table with the world's richest nation. In the words of historian William K. Meyers, "NAFTA would be Mexico's ticket out of the third world."[11]

In the United States, NAFTA was marketed as a plan that would stimulate jobs and incomes and reduce Mexican migration to the United States. Much of the debate in the United States centered on what the trade deal's effect would be on U.S. employment. But even at the time, it was understood by some opinion leaders as more of a political gesture to help the Salinas government than a measure that would have much impact on the U.S. economy. "Mexico's government needs NAFTA, and the United States has a strong interest in helping that government," wrote economist Paul Krugman in 1993.[12]

The least developed of the three countries, Mexico has felt NAFTA's impact most intensely. Its gain in jobs in the export manufacturing sector was outweighed by a decline in domestic manufacturing employment and a sharp drop in agricultural jobs. Two million Mexican farmers were displaced, as peasant producers had to compete against heavily subsidized and mechanized midwestern corn growers.[13] Though productivity has increased in both the United States and Mexico, workers are not seeing the returns as higher wages. And real wages for many Mexicans were lower in 2006 than when NAFTA took effect twelve years earlier.[14]

The trade agreement has been neither a disaster nor a success for Mexico overall, but for peasant farmers its effect has been overwhelmingly negative, according to John J. Audley, former director of the Trade, Equity and Development Project at the Carnegie Endowment for International Peace in New York. "For Mexico's rural households the picture is clear— and bleak," Audley wrote in the introduction to "NAFTA's Promise and Reality: Lessons from Mexico for the Hemisphere," a critical assessment of NAFTA ten years out. "NAFTA has accelerated Mexico's transition to a liberalized economy without creating the necessary conditions for the public and private sectors to respond to the economic, social, and environmental shocks of trading with two of the biggest economies in the world. Mexico's most vulnerable citizens have faced a maelstrom of change beyond their capacity, or that of their government, to control."[15]

"Trade agreements do not need to result in this kind of hardship for the world's rural poor," continued Audley. "Negotiated properly, they can open doors to new markets while providing adequate protections from the stress associated with exposure to global competition and the increased pressure on natural resources. Trade should not be seen as an end in itself; instead, it should be used as a tool to strengthen economies through the operation of comparative advantage. At the same time, governments must respond to economic opening with effective policies, such as the deployment of social safety nets and trade adjustment assistance, and develop and implement programs that protect labor rights and the environment."[16]

Forty-six percent of all Mexican jobs are in "informal sector" occupations such as domestic work, street vending, and repairs: low-paid employment that does not provide benefits such as health care and pensions.[17] And Mexico's workforce has grown substantially, with a baby boom reaching employment age during the 1990s and more women working outside the home. Consequently, Mexico has needed almost a million new jobs annually in recent years, far more than the economy has created, to accommodate the growing labor supply.[18] Those factors have created a situation ripe for Mexican workers to migrate, in increasing numbers, to the border, or across it.

Sometimes Mexicans who came to the border for maquiladora jobs have decided to jump the fence to try to earn a better living in the United States. Other times, Mexicans from the interior have come to cities like Tijuana or Juárez intending to migrate to *el norte* but have ended up staying on the Mexican side. Many have joined the ranks of the maquila workers or, lacking family resources or community ties in their new border world, have gotten involved in petty crime, drug use, prostitution, or the cross-border smuggling of people or drugs. New arrivals in Mexican border cities often end up living in shantytowns. The urban infrastructure to meet the needs of these factory workers—for schools, housing, clean water, and electricity—has not kept pace with the population growth.

In the United States in the months leading up to the approval of NAFTA, there was great concern, especially in the labor movement, that the agreement would lead to a massive loss of U.S. manufacturing jobs as companies relocated south of the border where workers could be paid a fraction of U.S. wages—a move that 1992 presidential candidate Ross Perot colorfully asserted would take place with a "giant sucking sound." In fact, by the end of the trade agreement's first decade, more than half a million U.S. workers—concentrated in manufacturing, especially in the apparel industry—had applied for government "trade adjustment assistance" because they could demonstrate that their jobs had been eliminated as a direct result of NAFTA.[19] Labor advocates believe the number of workers who came forward and applied for such assistance was a fraction of the number actually displaced because they faced the onerous requirement of proving that NAFTA was to blame for the disappearance of their jobs.[20]

To this day, the United States continues to lose manufacturing jobs as businesses go abroad in search of lower production costs, but most analysts don't consider NAFTA to be the primary culprit.[21] Rather, the off-shoring of the manufacture of goods for American consumption is a much larger phenomenon that predates NAFTA. At the same time, the maquiladoras helped create almost six hundred thousand American jobs along the border between 1990 and 2002, many of them in retail and the service sector, but many also in shipping and warehousing, product design, remanufacturing, and management, according to the U.S. Government Accountability Office.[22]

In McAllen, business leaders have promoted Reynosa as a manufacturing center, knowing that their own economy grows as a result. And while every other Mexican border city suffered crippling job losses during the maquiladora contraction after 2000, Reynosa merely leveled off briefly and then kept growing. "Our economy has not been affected because we've gone toward higher-end products, things that don't make sense to go to China, that need to be turned around fast," said Nancy Boultinghouse, marketing director for the McAllen Economic Development Corporation. "If you want cell phones in aqua and pink, customized products, and you don't want to wait eight weeks, you want it in two days . . . , if you order your computer as you want it and they program it and send it to you, they can't do that in China, Vietnam, India. It takes too long to ship it over."

Many American border cities also depend heavily on retail sales, as Mexican shoppers with U.S. government-issued border-crossing cards known as "laser visas" throng to American big box stores. "Maquiladora workers spend money in the United States," said Boultinghouse. "The growth of the maquila sector in Reynosa is responsible for the growth of other industries in the United States, and those who come over to shop in the U.S." From the Mexican perspective, however, the Mexican earnings spent north of the border represent money that's no longer circulating in—and stimulating—the local economy on the Mexican side.

John Castany, the general manager of a factory that produces after-market auto parts, believes Reynosa's sector has done so well because the industries that have set up shop there are more diverse than in cities like Tijuana or Ciudad Juárez—making appliances, electronics, and medical, mechanical, and automotive products. Castany, who is also the public relations chair for the local maquiladora trade association, says export-oriented manufacturing has "turned out to be something great for Mexico."

Like Tim Taylor, Castany is raising his family on the U.S. side of the border and commuting from his home in McAllen each day. But unlike Taylor, Castany is Mexican. He grew up in nearby Monterrey, the child of American parents, but got his education at the University of Texas. Fully bilingual and bicultural, he seamlessly navigates the border's binational economy.

Though Castany is a booster for the maquiladora industry, he acknowledges that Reynosa is not keeping pace with the need for housing and public services for the thousands of families that, like Modesto's, have relocated from further south in Mexico. "The population growth on the border creates all kinds of pressures," he said. "You have a need for road infrastructure, school infrastructure. Housing has been a tremendous struggle, though more has been built in the past couple of years. We're definitely lagging, but we're picking up speed."

University of California-Berkeley professor Harley Shaiken, an expert on labor and trade with Mexico, paints a starker picture. "It is inadequate sliding toward desperate," says Shaiken. "The maquilas are paying minimal if any taxes, and the result is an infrastructure that is inadequate to the growth taking place."

Outside the gates of Castany's industrial park, a *colonia* of marginal dwellings speaks for itself. Most of the shacks are hammered together of corrugated metal and thin pine boards scrounged from wooden pallets. Some have walls made of plywood disks, two feet across, taken from dismantled spools of cable—the detritus of the industrial workplace. Railroad tracks traverse the dirt streets. Wastewater flows down open gullies.

In a survey of housing conditions for maquiladora workers in Nogales, Sonora, in 1991, Kopinak, the Canadian sociologist, found that one in three workers lived in homes built of cardboard, mud, sheet metal, or other "nondurable" materials, 13 percent had dirt floors, 19 percent had no running water, 23 percent lacked electricity, and 41 percent lacked sewerage.[23] For maquiladora workers raising their families in Reynosa's shacktowns, conditions are little changed.

The fault, insists Castany, doesn't lie with the factory owners, who pay the taxes they are assessed. The problem, he and others say, is that Mexico's overall tax base is too narrow. The government collects less than 10 percent of the country's gross domestic product in taxes, half the rate in industrialized countries. Shaiken and others agree that the tax base needs enlarging, but they say that one part of the reason is that Mexico, anxious for job-creating investment, has offered excessive tax breaks to the foreign-owned assembly plants.

The maquiladoras ostensibly pay 10 percent of their payroll in taxes, Kopinak says, but the lion's share of that money goes to the federal government in Mexico City, leaving border cities unequipped to respond to the need for electricity, roads, and sewage-treatment plants.[24] In 2002 the Mexican newspaper *El Financiero* quoted a Mexican treasury official as saying that the maquiladora sector pays almost no taxes. The total net take, after tax credits and other subsidies, the official said, was $300 million in 1999, less than 0.5 percent of the nation's tax revenues.[25]

The health and well-being of local residents are what suffers, notes Cypher, an economics professor at California State University at Fresno. "The lack of adequate schools, medical facilities, parks and recreation sites, and sewage and waste disposal, as well as water treatment facilities and publicly supported housing, is all a direct but external result of the maquilization model that imposes virtually no effective taxes on the export firms."[26]

Such matters are undoubtedly influenced by U.S. corporations, but they are beyond the scope of American managers who operate the plants day to day. When Tim Taylor took the Dayton Superior job in Reynosa, he bought a Ford pickup to navigate the Mexican potholes and see past the rickety donkey carts he encountered on the streets. Bit by bit, he accustomed himself to Mexico's reality. "I know I'm in a foreign country, so I make sure I obey the laws," he said. "The way they drive is a little more erratic than the way we drive, but once I learned how, it didn't bother me."

Taylor, an electrical engineer by training, said the language barrier was his biggest challenge. The Taylors' weekly Spanish class was helping, but he still felt at a disadvantage in a culture that he had found put a premium on personal relationships. "I'm not bilingual," he said. "I was told that's not a problem, but ideally, in retrospect, it would be a big plus. Americans tend to be more direct to the point, and in Mexico the relationship portion is maybe more important than getting it done."

South Texas, though it wasn't Kansas, felt a little more comfortable for Taylor. "I'm a minority in McAllen, being that I'm white, but that doesn't really bother me. Everybody is very nice and polite," he said. "There's a difference in what people eat, though. There are fewer of your steakhouses and a lot of taco joints."

Char (who pronounced her name like the first half of Charlotte, though it was actually short for Charlee) embraced her new community with gusto. Many of her neighbors and her son Coltynn's high school class-mates were wealthy Mexicans who had settled north of the border. "They speak mostly Spanish in the lunchroom," she said. "He's picking it up fast." For her part, she looked forward to trying out her new language skills at the supermarket. And she looked to her teacher, who was from central Mexico, for moral support and a better understanding of Mexican culture. "I tell my Spanish teacher, 'What your nationality has brought to us is the value of the family. That's something we've forgotten.'"

Char's daughter Alaina was off at college, and Coltynn would soon leave the nest as well. The rest of her family was nine hundred miles away in Kansas, so it was particularly sweet when her sister consented to send Chloe for a weeklong visit. Char showered hugs on the girl and relished the role of favorite auntie. And she reflected on how her life had changed since she left her hometown.

"Kansas people are farm kids. You're expected to hold a job, go to school, do chores," she said. Char had started junior college in Parsons but had dropped out when she fell in love with her first husband and had her two kids. She worked her way up to a manager's job at the Ace Hardware store and later worked as a supervisor at a cabinetmaking factory. After the marriage ended, her mother helped her with child care. And then she ran into Tim, the "nerd" she remembered from high school math class, who had come back to Parsons after he got his engineering degree at Kansas State. The romance bloomed, he accepted her children as his own, and his career at Dayton took off.

When the company promoted him and transferred the family to Bir-mingham, Char was content to quit working and settle into what she called "the southern way of life." But she never quite shed her small-town midwestern upbringing. "We lived in a very wealthy school district in Alabama, where kids' parents were buying them Lexuses. My way is: if you want a car, you earn the money to buy it." In Texas she was unsettled by the prevalence of nannies and maids, and insisted on cleaning her own house and mowing her own lawn.

But she also had time to enroll in art classes, work out in her home fitness center, serve as president of the Booster Club that supported the athletic teams at Coltynn's school, sit on the philanthropic committee for Dayton Superior, and help lead a social club for wives of U.S. maquiladora executives in the area. The Maquila Women's Association was "a lifesaver," she said, providing new friends, referrals to doctors and hairstylists, and support in making sense of border culture and news reports of drug-related violence in northern Mexico, where the women's husbands worked every day.

At one coffee klatsch, Taylor passed around homemade muffins and encouraged the women to join a fledgling book club. She announced upcoming events, including a bus trip to see the Pope in San Antonio and a tour of a local butterfly garden. Then the conversation turned to the poverty across the river in Reynosa and what the group might do to help. "You realize when you walk over there, you are very, very blessed," said Taylor. "It's very hard when you see a woman with six kids begging. But they recommend we not buy papers from the street kids because their parents keep them out of school to work."

The husbands of the Maquila Women's Association members worked in plants making computer components, auto parts, and construction materials. But those were not the only things produced in the maquiladoras. Some plants made products as simple as Christmas candy. In the kitchen of the Dulces Famosos candy factory in Reynosa, Jesús García extracted a one-hundred-pound batch of sugar, flavored with peppermint oil, from the candy-pulling machine and hoisted it onto a wheeled dolly, where he rolled it into a squat cylinder. "I'm used to the weight," said García, nineteen, flaunting his muscles in the sauna-like kitchen. "And the heat doesn't bother me." He had come north from Veracruz when he was sixteen and had been working in maquiladoras ever since and living with his older sister and her family.

Another man kneaded red food coloring into a small wad cut from the larger batch. He divided it into four lumps, stretched each one into a long, flat band, and laid the red stripes onto García's white mass of taffylike sugar. The men heaved the striped barrel into a machine and set it spinning. Soon it emerged as a long, spiraling, peppermint-striped candy rope, less than an inch in diameter. It passed through machinery out of the

Figure 4. At the U.S.-owned Dulces Famosos candy factory, a maquiladora in Reynosa, Mexico, a worker scoops up peppermint candies for packing. Photo by Chris Stewart/San Francisco Chronicle.

kitchen and into the larger factory, where it was sliced into balls that cooled and hardened. The red-and-white candies were scooped into bins, shaken and sorted by size, inspected, individually wrapped in cellophane, and packaged in twenty-eight-ounce plastic tubs. Some would be sold at See's Candy shops as premium "Pure Cane Sugar Twists"; the rest would be distributed to chain drugstores across the United States under the house label, Bob's "Sweet Stripes."

In the United States, Dulces Famosos is known as Bob's Candies. The family-owned company was bought in 2005 by another label, Farley's and Sathers, maker of Jujyfruits, Now-and-Laters, and the bags of generic lemon drops, candy corn, and chocolate-covered raisins displayed on peg boards in American gas stations. The company is the world's largest producer of candy canes, according to Randy Main, general manager of the Reynosa plant. "This is not robot automation, high-tech city here. We honestly believe the production of this candy is an art. It's semi-handmade and that makes it labor-intensive," said Main, who had overseen the Georgia-based company's first foray into foreign manufacturing. Bob's opened the

Mexican plant in 2000 because the cost of sugar in the United States was so high, he said. "Here in Mexico, with a maquiladora permit, we can buy it at something closer to world price," said Main. "It was more about sugar than labor. But is the labor cost better here as well? Yes it is. I'd be lying if I said otherwise."

The factory floor was sticky with sugar, and nowhere as much as in the kitchen, where García and his coworkers put in four twelve-hour days a week without overtime pay. The company gave them new shoes twice a year, on top of their wages, which ranged from $7 to $16 a day. A bigger hazard than sticky floors, though, was the risk of burns from the boiling sugar syrup, which was poured from great vats onto cold tables to chill before it went into the pulling machines.

As maquiladoras go, though, this may have been among the least toxic. Elsewhere in Reynosa and along the border, workers routinely handled resins, acids, solvents, thinners, and other chemicals. Stories of toxic exposure—for workers and surrounding neighborhoods—abounded.

Workers who glued leather covers onto automobile steering wheels at Auto Trim de México in Matamoros, a factory owned by Florida-based automotive parts supplier Breed Technologies, testified in 2000 in a case against their employer brought under the North American Agreement on Labor Cooperation, NAFTA's labor "side agreement." The glues and solvents that they used daily, bare-handed and with little ventilation and no safety training, were making them sick, the workers said.

"I also frequently get throat infections and sometimes cough up blood," testified one eight-year employee. "I sometimes feel as though I can't breathe properly—that I can't get enough air and that I'm gasping. . . . If I get a lot of glue or solvent on my hands, it causes skin burns. My eyes get very irritated, and I get terrible headaches. I am now often dizzy and have almost constant nausea and stomach pain. I have trouble sleeping at night sometimes because of the pain."[27]

Another worker, Ezequiel Tinajero, who had worked at Auto Trim from 1988 to 1996, told the painful story of losing his newborn child, probably as a result of workplace poisons. "After seven years of being exposed to these toxic substances, in 1995, my wife and I had a daughter that died two hours later; she had anencephaly. After this, we started asking about the cause of death of my daughter, and I started getting information from other co-workers that had had miscarriages that had happened at the plant and from other co-workers that had children with physical defects. Eighteen days after my daughter died, another worker had a daughter that died due to hydrocephaly and the wife of another co-worker had another daughter like my daughter. My friend Bruno had a son with spina bifida."[28]

Several cases of anencephaly, a rare and fatal birth defect in which a baby is born with an incomplete or missing brain, were found at the plant. During the early 1990s, thirty children in Matamoros and Brownsville, Texas, just across the Rio Grande, were born with anencephaly and another twenty-five had spina bifida, a neural tube defect. The Texas families sued local maquiladoras and the Brownsville Public Utility Board, charging that pollution from the plants was responsible. The defendants settled for $17 million in 1995. Clusters of anencephaly also turned up in Del Rio, Texas, across from the maquiladoras in Ciudad Acuña, and in a Tijuana *colonia* just downhill from a shuttered battery factory.[29]

In the 1990s, health and safety surveys by the U.S. General Accounting Office and other researchers found that maquiladora workers faced frequent chemical exposure, ergonomic hazards, poor ventilation, high noise levels, and machines that lacked required safety guards. One study found that maquiladora workers in Nogales, Sonora, were three times as likely as other women to deliver low-birth-weight babies.[30]

Though maquiladora plants have been required by law to return hazardous waste products to the country of origin (usually the United States) for disposal after the manufacturing process, many observers say Mexico's underfunded and politically weak environmental regulatory program has not kept pace with rapid industrialization and that monitoring has been lax.[31] A 2003 statement in Mexico's official digest for government activity said that only 26 percent of the country's hazardous waste was properly handled: "The remaining 74 percent is disposed of in secret dumps or in inappropriate sites, which represents a significant source of contamination not only for the water, air and ground, but also for humans and animals through direct contact."[32] In 1995, the World Bank's Northern Border Environmental Project Loan analyzed compliance with the reshipment requirement and found that just 20 percent of the total quantity of hazardous waste believed to be produced by maquiladoras in Ciudad Juárez was shipped back to the United States.[33]

The U.S. Environmental Protection Agency had developed a computerized database called Haztraks for monitoring toxic substances coming across the border. But the agency pulled the plug on the program in 2003, in part, officials said, because of a two-year backlog in data entry. Since then the agency has relied on a nonprofit organization, the Border Compliance Assistance Center, to compile data from paper shipping manifests.

The center found that imports of hazardous waste from Mexico had reached about forty-three million pounds in 2006, double the amount a decade earlier. An EPA plan to adopt electronic manifests and use radio transmitters to track shipments is years away, critics say. Border officials inspect a very small percentage of toxic waste shipments, and current controls are ineffective and inconsistent, according to the Commission for Environmental Cooperation, a NAFTA body.[34]

In Tijuana, two notorious cases of toxic pollution involved battery recycling operations. One company, Alco Pacific, accumulated more than thirty-one million pounds of lead and other heavy metals at its smelter, then abandoned them when the American owners went out of business and filed for bankruptcy in 1991.[35] Another U.S.-owned company, Metales y Derivados, stockpiled six thousand metric tons of lead, arsenic, antimony, and other toxic substances, abandoning its waste heaps to the elements when Mexican authorities shut the operation down in 1994. Years of community organizing and legal wrangling before the NAFTA environmental commission ensued before any cleanup took place.[36] In the mid-1990s, illicit industrial dump sites were discovered outside Ciudad Juárez, containing hundreds of barrels of hazardous waste, much of it traced back to maquiladoras.[37]

Castany asserts that the maquiladora sector is "an industry that's looked at with a magnifying glass from both sides of the border." Mexico has full-scale environmental laws, just as the United States does, he added. But while Mexican laws governing the environment, workplace health, and safety and labor rights are strong on paper, they are inadequately enforced. When it comes to labor rights in the maquiladora workplace, observers have found that forced overtime, constantly increasing production quotas, and wage and hour violations are commonplace. Workers who complain about conditions or organize resistance are routinely let go.[38]

In decades past, especially in state-run companies, Mexican unions that were affiliated with the ruling Institutional Revolutionary Party achieved decent wages and social benefits for workers, as well as a measure of political power, in exchange for ceding substantial control over labor to the government and ruling party, according to Cirila Quintero Ramírez, a researcher with the Colegio de la Frontera Norte in Matamoros. But as industries and the government restructured to pursue global competitiveness, unions were weakened and wages and benefits fell, especially in the maquiladora sector. Mexico's minimum wage, which is set annually by the official unions, employers, and the government, lost half of its purchasing power between 1990 and 2000.[39]

The peso devaluation of late 1995 played a significant role in the decline in real wages in Mexico, but the fact remains that manufacturing wages in 2001 were lower than in 1980, adjusted for inflation.[40] Still, World Bank economists don't attribute the stagnation to Mexico's economic policies. "An important reason why growth and wages did not perform more favorably after [the enactment of NAFTA in] 1994 was the macroeconomic and financial crisis triggered by the devaluation of December 1994. . . . Trade and [foreign direct investment] cannot be blamed for the lackluster performance of wages," according to Daniel Lederman of the World Bank.[41]

Along much of the border, including the employment centers of Tijuana and Ciudad Juárez, most maquiladora workers have no union representation. Employers frequently sign "protection contracts" with sham unions that are paid by the company and never consult with the workers they nominally represent. Such contracts exist primarily as a defense against worker attempts to organize independent unions. In the state of Tamaulipas, which includes Reynosa, unions have a history of greater strength and almost all workers are unionized. But even there, most locals are affiliated with the official union federations, notably the Confederation of Mexican Workers, or Confederación de Trabajadores Mexicanos, known as the CTM, which is an arm of the long-ruling Institutional Revolutionary Party and has served more to quell labor unrest than to empower workers. Such traditional unions have done slightly better for workers in terms of wages and job security, Quintero found.[42] But these *charro* unions have repeatedly failed workers struggling against unsafe conditions and exploitation and have undercut efforts by workers to form independent unions.[43] A profile of Reynosa's business environment posted on the Internet by the McAllen Economic Development Association had this to say about the city's unions: "The labor union climate in Reynosa is very favorable to industry. Relations between unions and management are peaceful and harmonious. New companies have a choice of selecting one of two union leaders under the CTM or establishing their own in-house union."

In the absence of meaningful collective bargaining power, many workers have sought support from grassroots organizations, often with ties to U.S. church, labor, and human rights groups. Two of these are the Coalition for Justice in the Maquiladoras and the Border Workers' Committee.

At the center of Reynosa's leafy *zócalo,* or town square, a handful of kids fooled around on the empty bandstand. Over a hedge, Teresa Chávez sat on a park bench with a trio of workers who had just been fired by Jabil, the same company where Sabino Juárez worked. Small and sturdy, with short, curly brown hair, Chávez, forty-five, took rapid notes, gave advice, and punched in calls on her cell phone. The workers—two women and a man—said that they had been let go for falsifying a supervisor's signature on a form—a charge that they denied. They were convinced they had actually been targeted for insisting that the company pay workers an annual profit-sharing dividend, as required by Mexican law. Their union, they said, had offered no help, so they had come to Chávez, an organizer with the nonprofit Coalition for Justice in the Maquiladoras.

"In 1998 I had the same fight they're having," said Chávez, who lost her job of nine years at Delphi after showing her fellow workers a copy of the profit-sharing law at a union meeting and rallying them to demand that the auto parts maker pay up. "The company shows a chart of gains and losses, and they make it look like they've had a loss or a tiny gain. In my case they gave us seventy pesos (less than $7). They kept saying they were losing money."

"The company fired me and had guards take me out of the factory," she said. "If workers fight for their rights, they risk losing their jobs. But our objective is to teach all the workers about their labor rights."

Almost daily, Chávez got word of maquiladora workers fired for organizing. This day, she arranged to get the workers an interview on a television news program and planned to bring a complaint before a governmental labor commission. But the workers worried that their employer would blacklist them by sending word around through the maquiladora association not to hire them.

To Chávez, the CTM-affiliated union was anemic. After leaving the *zócalo,* she paid a visit to María de la Luz Modesto, whose husband, Juárez, was on the governing board of Chávez's workers' group. As the women sat chatting under a shade tree in the front yard, Chávez's cell phone rang. When she hung up she was seething.

"Jabil just fired another worker," she reported. "The managers forced her to sign a form saying she was voluntarily resigning, and a union representative just stood by looking on. And then the union rep told her, 'See? This is what happens when you stand up for your rights.' Ay! What powerlessness!"

Chávez had come to activism the hard way. One of her two daughters, herself a maquiladora worker and the mother of a little girl, had experienced premature menopause at the age of twenty-one and had died at twenty-three. Chávez believed her daughter had been poisoned by lead and other toxins in her workplace. She was now raising her granddaughter, six-year-old Alma Valeria, and she was joined in her organizing work by her son and her other daughter, both veteran factory workers as well. "We're not against the source of jobs, but we're opposed to the injustice inside the maquiladoras," said Chávez.

Juárez had hooked up with the Coalition for Justice in the Maquiladoras several years back, when he worked at Erika, known in the United States as Fresenius Medical Care, a dialysis equipment manufacturer, the women said. Female workers at Erika were experiencing a rash of miscarriages—they tracked ninety-eight of them—and suspected that the chemicals they used in the plant were responsible. Juárez was among a group of workers who had organized a work stoppage and succeeded in getting the chemical changed, said Chávez. "But after a while the company changed the chemical back again," she said. "And in 2000 they fired the workers, including Sabino, for causing the company losses."

At Jabil, Juárez was keeping a lower profile. "Sabino's doing fine," said Modesto, his wife. "But he's not organizing. He can't afford to lose his job."

Though maquiladora jobs have rebounded in Mexico in recent years, Chinese competition poses a long-term problem by dampening workers' ability to organize for better wages and working conditions, said Shaiken, the University of California professor. "You don't have to move many plants at all to have a lot of frightened workers," he said. "The hope of an expanding domestic market in Mexico based on higher wages is, in effect, throttled."

A longitudinal study of maquiladora wages published in 2001 found that while the jobs in the industry were much needed, they had not provided for the growth of a middle class, something industrialization has achieved in more developed countries. Instead, inflation and government policies to hold down the minimum wage were responsible for a decline in real wages.[44]

Trade publications say that in the wake of the downturn from 2001 to 2003, maquiladoras increasingly "reinvented themselves as high-tech, lean manufacturing enterprises that emphasize quality instead of low wages." With the lifting of U.S. trade barriers to Chinese goods, Mexico lost its comparative advantage based on low wages, the analysts say, and factories at last began retooling themselves. "Successful maquiladoras will resemble high-tech operations in the U.S. or Western Europe that emphasize efficient production and high quality."[45]

Some scholars have long watched for such a trend. They agree that the plants are much more sophisticated than in the early years of simple assembly processes. But the few high-tech factories continue to be the exception, not the rule. More importantly for the health of the Mexican economy, Mexico has failed to build commercial links between the border factories and Mexican companies that could supply them with materials and components. It has also failed to extend the technological know-how of the foreign companies to increase the skills of Mexican workers.[46]

In some Asian countries, notably South Korea, Singapore, Taiwan, Malaysia, and Thailand, export-oriented development has led to industrial linkages to the domestic economy through technology sharing. That has allowed those countries to develop more complex systems of production that raise local wages and create jobs by increasing the share of production based on local content, according to economist James Cypher. The process of technology transfer in those countries, he argues, has been driven by a strong national political commitment to foster linkages and by state policies that emphasize the internal market as much as the external one.[47]

But Cypher has found that in Mexico the experience has been the reverse. While Mexico's share of the world's manufactured exports rose tenfold between 1980 and 1997, its share of world income fell by 13 percent and its share of world manufacturing "value added" fell by one-third, according to a 2002 report issued by the United Nations Conference on Trade and Development. Mexico's domestic inputs into maquiladora products constituted 2 percent of the product value in 1980 and just shy of 3 percent in 2002. By contrast, Taiwan increased its share of local content in export products from 5 percent in 1967 to 27 percent in 1978.[48]

As foreign investors have bought domestic companies and imports have surged, Mexico's domestic economy is being deindustrialized, asserts Cypher. And as domestic industry's higher wages are being supplanted by the maquiladoras' substandard wages, Mexican purchasing power—and thus the economic stimulus of domestic consumer spending—has dwindled. In addition, with most maquila jobs situated along the U.S. border, Mexican factory workers are more apt to do their shopping in American stores, further weakening the Mexican economy. While 36 percent of Mexicans lived in poverty in 1982, the share was up to 43 percent twenty years later.[49]

In her makeshift outdoor kitchen, María de la Luz Modesto took a hammer to a wooden crate and deftly smashed it into fuel for her cooking fire. Though she had an indoor stove, she said propane was so expensive that she cooked over scrap-wood fires whenever possible. She was preparing to

Figure 5. María de la Luz Modesto takes a moment from plucking a chicken to help her son with his schoolwork outside their home in the border city of Reynosa, Tamaulipas. Photo by Chris Stewart/San Francisco Chronicle.

butcher one of her chickens and balanced a pail of water over the fire to boil so she could scald the bird before plucking it. "The money my husband makes isn't much, but we make it stretch," she said, grabbing the rooster, hanging it up by the ankles and sawing its throat with a kitchen knife. "We can eat chicken once a week, and we don't have to buy it at the store."

But as she pulled handfuls of feathers off the now-damp bird, Modesto frowned. "*Es flaco,*" she said. "He looked like a big fellow, but I guess he was more feathers than meat." Modesto singed the pinfeathers over the fire and began to scrub the chicken skin clean in her sink, which drained into a muddy path between neighboring houses. She would stew the bird all day, season it with tomato, onion, and *hierba buena,* then serve it with tortillas when her husband came home from his twelve-hour factory shift.

As Modesto worked, Angel came out of the house with a school workbook left over from kindergarten. He showed his mother how he had traced the letter R on the page for *reloj,* then asked, "What color am I supposed to make the clock?" "Color it green," she said, reading the directions for him.

To enroll Angel in first grade, his parents were saving up the money to cover registration, books, shoes, and a uniform. Modesto planned to return to work when Isabel was ready for school to ensure that she had enough money to educate both her children. She would take a graveyard shift so she could be home during the day.

"When I was a kid we lived on a ranch and we went to school on horseback or bicycle," she said. "It was pretty remote and sometimes the teacher didn't show up. I finished primary school, but after that, with nine kids in the house and me a girl, my father couldn't afford to keep sending me."

"I want my kids to study, to learn," said Modesto. "I want them to be able to do what they choose."

With the limited resources at her disposal, Modesto was determined to make the economy of the borderlands work for her family, just as Chávez was struggling to do on a broader scale. North of the river, Char Taylor in her own small way also acknowledged the connections between her family's economic interests and those of families like Modesto's across the borderline.

As the meeting of the Maquila Women's Association wound to a close in the community room at Sharyland Plantation, Char Taylor had a suggestion: look through your kids' closets, pull out last year's school backpacks (the ones they don't use anymore), and donate them to a drive for needy Mexican schoolchildren Char was organizing through Dayton Superior. "We wanted to do an orphanage, but we wanted to do more than a check, so we thought, 'Let's do school supplies *and* a check,'" she said.

The Taylors were confident that maquiladora jobs were a boon to Mexico. At the same time, they were acutely aware of the economic chasm that separated them from the workers at Dayton and other Mexican plants. "We live in this great house and sometimes we come back from Mexico and I think it's a sin," said Char later, cuddling Chloe on her lap. "Dayton's moving down here in a gradual way, but the potential to grow is big. The poverty is a big issue for Tim and me, though. We have to go gentler on them, I think."

THREE

Hachita

"A fence is only as good as its weakest point"

LAWRENCE HURT SHIFTED FROM FOOT TO FOOT, dancing like a boxer. He advanced on a group of calves and mother cows and set them trotting into the corral's sorting alley. Then he pulled back—patient, intent, his arms loose at his sides. Inside his dusty leather work boots, he bounced lightly on the balls of his feet.

Beyond him, the khaki-colored grassland of southwestern New Mexico stretched toward the Mexican border. The wiry forty-six-year-old Hurt was part of the third generation of a ranching family, and he knew the terrain intimately. Though the wide landscape appeared almost untouched, Hurt knew, as he scanned the horizon, just where his fences had been cut by smugglers transporting people and dope, where the *coyotes* had busted a water line, where the migrants had strewn trash. He understood why Mexican migrants had begun trekking across his pastures and he sympathized with their plight, but their presence was a source of mounting frustration.

Over the years the Hurt family had had to contend with death and drought and a new generation of neighbors who didn't understand cattle ranching. But the ridges and valleys in their corner of New Mexico had started to suffer the effects of illegal immigration and drug smuggling—problems that had already battered other stretches of the borderlands. The southern and eastern boundaries of the Hurt ranch ran along the U.S.-Mexico border for twenty-eight miles, and Lawrence Hurt and his family

Figure 6. Rancher Lawrence Hurt sorts calves and cows during the fall roundup on his land near the New Mexico-Chihuahua border. Photo by Sandy Huffaker Jr.

had found themselves wrestling with a complicated view of the border. The land that included their property—and the region's cattle ranching tradition—stretched uninterrupted into Chihuahua. And the family had close ties, through work and marriage, to Mexico. But the aggravation and expense of the nation's illegal immigration quandary was becoming their problem, even with a decline in unauthorized immigration. Compared to the Arizona desert to the west, which had been traversed by hundreds of thousands of migrants annually, or the migrant corridor around Columbus, New Mexico, just to the east, the Boot Heel remained pristine, but the threat was an unwelcome distraction from the work of sorting cattle.

With five cow-calf pairs funneled into the alley, Hurt swung the corral gate shut on the remaining herd. The brim of his battered felt cowboy hat shielded his eyes from the mid-morning sun as, prod outstretched, he moved in, clucking softly, and peeled off a couple of cows. "Hup, hup," he encouraged. "Ch-ch-ch-ch-ch." The muscled black animals lumbered forward, and Martín Salazar, a cowboy on Hurt's ranch, opened a steel gate at the opposite end of the alley to admit the cows to a holding pen. The rusty hinges groaned. The calves trotted after their mothers. But Salazar darted across the alley, swung open a second gate, and hustled the calves into a separate pen.

As the men repeated the weaning process with several dozen more animals, the mother cows bunched up, lowing, in one enclosure. The fuzzy-headed calves milled around in the other, griping, urinating, and occasionally knocking against the steel fence with a clang. The calves, born on the range the previous spring, had had scant contact with people before this roundup. Now they would be sold to a stocker operation. They would graze on rich, green Texas wheat fields for a year or so, then get trucked to a feedlot where they'd fatten up on grain before the final trip to the slaughterhouse.

Beside the old corral, a pair of massive black bulls faced off, still and silent: forehead to forehead, they leaned into each other with all their might, oblivious to the commotion of the calves. Half a dozen Blue Lacy herding dogs—temporarily spent from a couple of hours of sprinting after cattle—lolled in the shade of a pickup truck beyond the stone stock pond. Halfway through the autumn roundup, the athletic gray dogs had begun to wear thin.

Hurt's day had started before the November sun crept over the Little Hatchet Mountains, where the U.S.-Mexico border jogs south to form the Boot Heel. He had loaded five horses into a trailer hitched to his two-ton pickup truck and driven more than seventy-five miles to this pasture. Then, with the ranch helicopter wheeling overhead and Salazar and four other riders at his side, he had cantered across the vast pasture of grama grass and creosote bush, herding a hundred animals toward the rusting corral.

It was a ritual the red-bearded Hurt had performed hundreds of times, and one his father and grandfather had known as well, raising beef cattle on this arid landscape over the past century. Lawrence's grandfather Erastus Hurt, a stonemason from Virginia, had homesteaded the family place east of Deming in 1909, digging a well and housing his wife and babies in a tent the first year while he built a home of adobe bricks.

"We're the only family on the deed," said Hurt. "Everything there, we built it." Hurt's parents, Jim and Velva, had concentrated on raising row crops—cotton, alfalfa, maize, and pinto beans—until they had money enough to buy more land and expand the ranch in the 1950s. In a country so dry that a square mile produces only enough fodder to support seven or eight head of cattle, ample acreage was essential. So when the four Hurt sons came of age and decided to go into the family business in the early 1980s, they expanded further: buying and leasing property down in the

Boot Heel from the Phelps Dodge Mining Company—which smelted copper there—and the federal Bureau of Land Management. Now the Hurts managed a breeding operation with roughly five thousand Brangus cows (a Brahma/Angus cross) on almost seven hundred square miles of Chihuahuan Desert grassland.

"From the time I was old enough to figure it out, I knew this was what I wanted to do," said Hurt. "We like the lifestyle and our parents instilled a good work ethic, so we're not afraid of hard work. You don't figure you're going to get rich out of it, but you'll make a living."

Elsewhere in the borderlands, ranchers, Indian tribes, and other residents in Arizona, California, and parts of Texas have become accustomed to not only slashed fences and litter but fouled water supplies, break-ins, and theft. On top of that, they have had to contend with hundreds of migrant deaths each year and an increasingly heavy presence of the Border Patrol and volunteer militia groups.

The barriers the federal government has built in heavily trafficked areas to the east and west of the Boot Heel—whether with scores of miles of double-layer steel fencing or with a "virtual" fence of lights, cameras, motion detectors, and radar—could well channel future illegal immigrants and drug smugglers right across this fragile open country at a greater rate than ever. "A fence is only as good as its weakest point. Wherever is the weakest point, that's where they'll target. It's the same for people as it is for cattle," said Hurt. "I feel for these people leaving their homes and coming north to better their lives, but I wish they weren't so disruptive." When smugglers cut a pasture fence and a herd that had taken three days to round up got loose, Hurt calculated he was out nearly $5,000 in helicopter fuel, labor, and materials.

Building a partial fence along the 1,952-mile border "is like funneling cattle into a corral," observed Wendy Glenn, a longtime border rancher just over the state line in Arizona, who was acquainted with the Hurts. "It's going to push more people into the area without a fence."

Glenn and a group of neighboring ranchers in the hills east of Douglas, Arizona, hired a man to work full time picking up the tons of trash left behind on their lands by illegal immigrants. She saw how the border fence that runs between Douglas and Agua Prieta reduced illegal crossings after it was built there in 1996. And she worried that the migrants were trampling the fragile habitats of endangered frogs and rattlesnakes. But Glenn was no fan of walling off the border. Her husband, Warner, had twice encountered jaguars—almost unheard of in the United States in the past century—roving north from their breeding grounds two hundred miles distant in the Sierra Madre of Sonora. The Glenns, both third-generation ranchers, wanted these stately beasts, as well as pronghorn antelope, bobcats, cinnamon bear, and bighorn sheep, to have room to roam.

Warner and Wendy Glenn were part of an unlikely experiment at the border: a group of cattle ranchers in southeastern Arizona and southwestern New Mexico who were also committed conservationists. They had banded together in the early 1990s to preserve open space for ranching and wildlife against the encroachment of suburban subdivisions. The Malpai Borderlands Group, which includes several dozen landowners, had obtained conservation easements to protect hundreds of thousands of acres. They were restoring grasslands by allowing fire to burn woody brush, controlling erosion, restoring watersheds, protecting endangered species, and encouraging scientific research on the land, all with an eye toward keeping cattle ranching economically viable and minimizing government interference. The centerpiece of the Malpai effort was the Gray Ranch, a five-hundred-square-mile reserve in New Mexico that straddled the Animas Mountains, just west across the Boot Heel from the Hurts' land. Still a working ranch, it was purchased in 1990 by the Nature Conservancy and then sold—with the condition that it be permanently protected as open space—to a foundation set up by the Hadley family, heirs to the Anheuser-Busch fortune, who had ties to the area. But the region's fragile ecosystem of high desert flora and fauna would be threatened if it became the new migrant highway.[1]

The region was the traditional home of the Chiricahua Apaches. It was part of Mexico until the Gadsden Purchase of 1853, a border adjustment following the Mexican-American War. To establish a clear boundary between the United States and Mexico, a binational team surveyed the line here in 1855, marking it with mounds of loose stone. In the early 1890s the border was resurveyed in an effort to improve the accuracy of the boundary, and the surveyors installed a series of six-foot-tall iron obelisks on high points along the line—intended so that a person standing at one marker could see to the next one.[2] Most are still standing today. In the 1930s officials added a barbed-wire fence. Local property owners say that the federal government used to give them the materials to maintain the fence but that in recent years they have borne the full responsibility for keeping this demarcation of the international boundary intact.

A couple of times a week, Lawrence Hurt's older brother, William, flew over the southernmost corner of the ranch in his Cessna 172 propeller plane. From the air, the landscape of southern New Mexico and northern Chihuahua appeared as one continuous swathe of tawny grass. The Antelope Wells port of entry was a small blip on a dirt road. Across the wire fence, Mexican cattle ranches and cotton fields fronted the Hurts' property. Indeed, more significant than the international border here was the boundary created by the north-south Animas ridge. Rising to 8,500 feet, it formed the Continental Divide, separating the watershed flowing toward the Pacific Ocean from that emptying into the Atlantic. As he glided above red-tailed hawks and banked around the Alamo Hueco Mountains where he had built his home, William scanned the border fence and his own pasture fences, looking for places where the wires had been snipped—either by drug smugglers, who typically packed their loads through on mule or horseback, or by *coyotes* transporting migrant workers by van or truck.

"From here north, it's a smuggler's paradise," he said, swinging the Cessna over Monument 53, where the border turned the corner and headed north from the southeast corner of the Boot Heel. "They're cutting this fence here constantly. We find the cattle running everywhere. . . . By the time they get to Highway 9, they've cut as many as fifteen fences."

William Hurt, fifty, was all for securing the border, but he was skeptical that the multi-billion-dollar wall would prevent illegal immigrants from crossing. And with the border region's steep mountains, and canyons prone to flash floods, he doubted such a fence could ever be built to stand. Better, he said, only half joking, for the government to pay border landowners to keep the boundary secure. For the right sum, he cracked, "Hell, I'll even keep the jackrabbits on the other side."

William didn't hesitate to call the Border Patrol when he spotted people coming overland from the border, and he had confronted at least one smuggler face to face, warning her in confident Spanish never to drive her loads of migrants past his house again or she'd risk being shot by William's wife. He steered clear of the drug runners, though, whom he sometimes saw passing through on horseback with a couple of laden mules and an armed outrider. "I don't want to get involved in a gun battle," he said. And William had no truck with the Minutemen, a dozen of whom had spent a month in the nearby hamlet of Hachita and had succeeded only in diverting immigrant smugglers right through his side yard. "I don't want them on the ranch," he said vehemently. "They come in and stir up the hornet's nest and leave me to deal with it."

At the border, ranchers know their neighbors in Mexico almost as well as they know the family down the road. Over the years, William had herded cattle with his Mexican neighbors and they had helped him in kind. Ranching operations are similar on both sides of the border, and cattlemen in Chihuahua and Sonora often sell their calves to buyers from the United States. Corrals are built into the border fence itself to facilitate the transfer of livestock—under the supervision of agricultural inspectors—from one country to the other, a practice that dates back generations.

Hector Morales, a Sonoran cow-calf rancher with a herd of a thousand mother cows along ten miles of border fence just south of Douglas, Arizona, had similar problems with migrants tramping across his pastures and leaving water bottles and other trash behind. But he tolerated the nuisance because, he said, "The majority are going out there to make a living. They don't need to be hassled any more." When the drug trafficking got too intense, he said, he invited the army to come camp on his land.

Mexican cowboys, or *vaqueros*, predate the U.S. variety, and they have a long history of working the border ranches in the American Southwest. The Hurt brothers all spoke fluent Spanish, learned in the saddle over a lifetime.

Mexico was a constant presence here. But the family's cross-border connection had become most tangible in recent years. A confirmed bachelor after a divorce, William told Oscar Chávez, a cowboy who had worked for the Hurts for two decades, that he was looking for someone to keep his house. Chávez introduced William to Lupe Regalado, his girlfriend's niece in Chihuahua, and soon a romance blossomed. William courted Lupe in Mexico and eventually began the laborious paperwork necessary for her to legally immigrate to the United States. On a spring day in 2004, they were wed right on the border at the sleepy Antelope Wells port of entry, he standing on the American side and she on Mexican soil. Careful to comply with every intricacy of immigration law, they said their "I dos" before she stepped across into the United States.

Taking a midday break from ranch work, William dandled their five-month-old son David, as two-year-old James scooted across the kitchen on his toy tractor and Lupe salted great slabs of Hurt ranch beef and laid them on the grill for lunch. Petite and dark haired, she bantered with her red-bearded bear of a husband over what would accompany the steaks.

"William, are tortillas okay?" she asked in Spanish. "No, I want bread," he replied in English. "We don't have any bread," she said firmly. "Well, that's what I want," he insisted, a stubborn twinkle in his eye. "Well, you'll have to go down the road and get some," she shot back in Spanish. "The walk will do you good." In the end, a plate of hot tortillas shared the table with the steaks, salad, and homemade french fries Lupe had prepared. For Lupe, the transition from Ciudad Cuauhtémoc, a city of 135,000 with a growing manufacturing economy at the center of Chihuahua's beef and dairy region, to this remote corner of New Mexico had been a bit of an adjustment. "It's a little lonely," she admitted. "I miss my family. But it's better now that I have the boys."

With an average of two people per square mile, Hidalgo County, where they lived, had more cows than human beings. The county didn't have a decent supermarket, let alone much opportunity for a social life. Lordsburg, the county seat, with three thousand souls, had the remnants of an old downtown facing the railroad tracks, a courthouse, a post office, a couple of bars and restaurants, and a few motels and gas stations geared to travelers passing through on the Interstate. For most of their needs, Lupe and William made the eighty-five-mile drive to Deming, population fourteen thousand. When it came to Christmas shopping or a trip to the mall, they would head on to Las Cruces, 150 miles away, where the Hurt brothers all had gone to college at New Mexico State University.

Deming was also the nearest hospital, so out on the Alamo Hueco Lupe tried hard to keep her children out of harm's way. "There are creatures everywhere here: spiders, crickets, lizards, snakes, mice," she said. "James likes to pick them all up." When she went out to mow the yard one day, she insisted that James stay right by the front door rather than toddle along beside her because she feared that snakes could be hiding in the tall grass. After mowing she began to cut back some weeds that had grown up around the door, but her machete struck a rattlesnake curled up under the leaves, not two feet from where her child was playing. "It started rattling," she recounted. "I grabbed James and called William. He came and killed it."

After the steak and tortilla lunch William took a call from a Border Patrol agent, who alerted him that a vanload of migrants had driven through his property early in the day and asked if he had spotted it. He hadn't, but he spent a couple of hours that afternoon driving out over the dirt tracks to the border fence to try to find where the driver had cut through. He had no luck.

Trucks, the airplane, and a helicopter had become integral tools for the Hurts, allowing them to work these vast acreages more efficiently. In the early morning chill of the fall roundup, Lawrence Hurt rode out to a spot where his helicopter pilot, Hank Hays, had located the cattle and was beginning to drive them in. Lawrence reflected that the morning's job would have taken the same six cowboys three or four days with dogs and horses alone.

Figure 7. On their ranch in the Boot Heel of New Mexico, William Hurt and his son stop beside an iron obelisk along the fence line, which is also the international boundary with Mexico. Photo by Sandy Huffaker Jr.

"The helicopter will never replace the horse, but it's an addition. It's like harvesting grain with a combine," he said as Hays swooped low, urging the animals on in a cloud of dust. "I'm a rancher, not a cowboy," said Lawrence, insisting that he wasn't yoked to some nostalgic idea but sought the best tools to get the job done. Still, as he spoke he looked like nothing so much as a cowboy. Yellow dust packed the crevices of his saddle, and the leather gleamed from years of wear. He cantered comfortably, reins in one hand, the other readying his lariat as he approached a heifer bent on breaking free from the herd. As he passed, a flock of doves rose, twittering, from the grass.

In addition to Hays, the Hurts maintained a core staff of four. A couple of neighboring ranchers pitched in on the labor-intensive roundups in spring and fall, and the family's teenagers helped out on weekends. But hired labor was getting harder to find and keep, they said, and the crew was smaller than in years past. In response, the family had mechanized the operation as much as possible, investing in the airplane and helicopter, a road grader and backhoe, cattle-hauling trailers, a hydraulic squeeze chute, walkie-talkies, and cell phones.

When the crews had been bigger, Norma Pennell had prepared meals for the Hurts' cowboys. But there were no longer enough of them to justify a cook, so a few years back she had signed on as a ranch hand herself. A miner's daughter, Pennell, forty-five, was married to a Phelps Dodge boilermaker. He had worked at the smelter in the Boot Heel until it shut down in 1999. Since then, the closest job Pennell's husband could find was at the copper mine in Morenci, Arizona, three hours away. He stayed there during the week and came home weekends. Pennell's three kids used to help her in the kitchen, she said, but once they learned to ride they were more interested in ranch work. "My kids started out vaccinating and then they progressed to castrating," she said. "The girls were out riding just like the guys. The boys used to tease them until my daughter said, 'I can castrate faster than you can.' And she could." But since they didn't have a ranch of their own, the rural Boot Heel couldn't hold them, and the kids, now in their twenties, moved on to Denver and Tucson. Pennell, tanned by the high desert sun, with a thick ponytail of sandy brown hair and hands as calloused as the men's, was still riding. Through the long quiet winter, she would check every fence on the ranch, put out salt for the cattle, and make sure the windmills were pumping water as they should. She'd gotten wary, though, as the number of migrants and drug smugglers had increased. "It used to be I'd ride and not think too much about what was out there," she said. "Now I'm more careful, I'm very alert. I take my dogs and my gun with me."

The other three cowboys were Mexican: Salazar, Chávez, and his younger cousin, Socorro Chávez. Mexico had long been a reliable source of affordable manual labor for the United States, the Hurts said, and shutting that relationship off would be a mistake. At sixty-eight, Velva Hurt, the family's gentle matriarch, kept the company's books and cultivated a garden of grapes, figs, walnuts, and apples on the old home place. She could remember participating in the Bracero Program, which had brought Mexican agricultural workers onto U.S. farms and ranches on seasonal contracts from 1942 to 1964. "It really worked smooth," she said. "I sure would like to see something like that again. There needs to be a legal program to protect everybody."

William had learned firsthand through sponsoring Lupe for a green card, or lawful permanent resident status, how tough it could be to immigrate to the United States. The process entailed hundreds of dollars in fees and repeated trips to El Paso to meet with lawyers and government officials. And he knew a visa was a lot easier to get if you wed a U.S. citizen than if you were a low-skilled worker. "People say these Mexicans should come over legally, but there's no way, short of marrying someone," he said. "You can't blame the Mexicans for wanting to come over and better their lives. And you can't blame the Americans for wanting to get the job done as cheaply and as well as possible." Like his mother, William favored giving "illegals" guest worker status in the United States, and also like her, he was wary of offering permanent residence to the nation's twelve million undocumented immigrants. "We need the labor they provide," he said. "If you give them amnesty, where they can go do any job they want, they're going to vacate these hard labor jobs." After the Immigration Reform and Control Act in 1986 offered legal residence to undocumented immigrants and made it a crime for employers to hire unauthorized workers, the Hurts helped a dozen of their Mexican employees apply for green cards, said William. Of those, only Oscar Chávez remained. Chávez, forty-eight, had grown up on a Chihuahuan *ejido,* a communally owned farm, about three hundred miles south, and had begun coming across the border in the early 1980s. He had worked harvesting chili peppers near Deming until Jim and Velva Hurt hired him on as a ranch hand. "*Estaba más fácil en esos días,*" he said. "It was easier to cross back then. You just walked over. It's a lot harder now." As he spoke, he measured out syringes, preparing for a day of branding and vaccinating calves with Socorro and Avery, the youngest Hurt brother.

The day after Lawrence's cattle were rounded up, along with a second batch from a pasture at Avery's place, they were corralled at the homestead east of Deming. The calves would be prepared for market and the cows checked to see if they were pregnant before being turned back out to pasture for the winter. With the comfortable efficiency of a practiced team, the men roped the youngest calves—born since the spring branding roundup—and marked their hides with the red-hot branding iron. As the smell of singed hair dissipated, Socorro held the little animals still while Oscar gave each one a couple of shots in the armpit. With a sharpened penknife in his blood-streaked hand, Avery notched their ears and castrated the bull calves, deftly slitting the scrotum and squeezing out the testicles. Within a minute each calf sprang to its feet and trotted out of the pen into a larger corral. The *cojones* were tossed to the dogs lingering nearby—except for the first pair, which Socorro set to grilling by the gas fire where the branding irons were heated. "*Están ricos,*" he said. "They're tasty."

Socorro Chávez, a burly thirty-eight-year-old in a sweatshirt and base-ball cap, worked half the year in New Mexico, then returned home to

Figure 8. Chihuahua native Oscar Chávez herds calves through a corral on the Hurt family's homestead in southern New Mexico. Photo by Sandy Huffaker Jr.

the city of Chihuahua, where his wife looked after their three small children and his aging mother. In Santa Fe, Socorro could earn $12 an hour as a roofer, but the noxious chemicals irritated his eyes and skin. He preferred riding and considered ranch work safer, though it paid less and he had been thrown from a horse, breaking his clavicle, a couple of years back. So he returned to the Hurts' ranch for the roundups each spring and fall. A green card, acquired during a previous marriage to an American citizen, allowed him to cross the border freely. But it pained him to see his countrymen converted into illegal immigrants, trudging across the borderlands.

"*Está muy feo,*" he said, his eyes darkening. "It's ugly. It's sad. I know because I did that for years. Back when I was a teenager, we used to ride above the wheels of the train." Socorro herded the larger calves, those too big to wrangle by hand, into a crowding pen, then released them one at a time into the squeeze chute, where Oscar and Avery continued to castrate, brand, and vaccinate. "They can build a wall and it won't matter," said Socorro. "We Mexicans will cross however we can."

Mexicans have been crossing the border for generations, and absent a means to enter the United States legally, they have come without authorization. U.S. immigration officials have tended to look the other way in times of prosperity and then crack down on illegal workers when the U.S. economy is contracting and political resistance to foreign workers is high.[3] Traditionally, immigrants from Mexico settled in the American Southwest—Texas, New Mexico, Arizona, and California. But beginning in the 1990s, Mexico's labor surplus, combined with a concerted pull by American employers, drew migrant workers beyond the border states to jobs cleaning hotel rooms in Nevada, gutting hogs in Iowa, harvesting Christmas trees in the mountains of North Carolina, or pouring concrete in the subdivisions of Georgia.

As immigration from Mexico to the United States has increased and spread, the experience of the border has extended from Chiapas to Chicago. And as the border itself has hardened in recent years, making the crossing tougher, undocumented immigrants have chosen to stay put in the United States and send for family members, rather than return home after seasonal stints of work, the traditional pattern of "circular migration" from Mexico.[4] Of the roughly twelve million unauthorized immigrants in the United States, an estimated 60 percent are from Mexico.[5] And given Mexico's physical proximity to the United States, the long history of interaction between the countries, and their current linkages through NAFTA, Mexican migration is likely to continue. Some analysts believe it merits special treatment under immigration law.

One in three immigrants in the United States was born in Mexico. They are transforming U.S. communities with the customs and language they bring north and at the same time reshaping their hometowns with the financial remittances and American ways they send back to Mexico. Their arrival has come as a bit of a shock in communities that have not previously had big immigrant populations. And the culture clash has been intense. In places where the growth of the migrant population has been swift, established residents have frequently reacted with bewilderment, resistance, and even outright hostility. Though border residents get fed up with the aggravations of illegal immigrants passing through their communities, the most vociferous immigration restrictionists are in states far from the border, where Mexicans are seen as foreigners rather than as more or less familiar neighbors.

The immigration debate playing out among U.S. lawmakers and in communities across the country pits opposing conceptions of the United

States' economy, culture, and even nationhood. Do immigrants stimulate the economy with their hard work and ingenuity or undercut U.S. workers by accepting inferior wages and working conditions? Are immigrants enriching American culture with their cuisines, customs, and languages or fragmenting national unity by an unwillingness to assimilate? Are immigrants who enter the country without authorization merely taking the logical next step in regional economic integration or threatening national security by flouting U.S. boundaries and laws? How Americans answer those questions largely determines where they fall on the issues of immigration reform and border enforcement.

The U.S. government's response to high levels of illegal immigration has been to ratchet up border enforcement. Yet serious questions remain as to whether the strategy has been effective. Apprehensions have fluctuated between 700,000 and 1.7 million per year from the early 1990s to the present day. But the annual number of arrests was almost the same—1.2 million—in 1992, before the launch of Operation Hold the Line and Operation Gatekeeper, as in 2005, when the Border Patrol had four times the budget and manpower. Meanwhile, perhaps a third of the illegal immigrants in the United States didn't hike or swim across the U.S.-Mexico border but entered the country on legal visas and overstayed their welcome.[6] Most troubling, as border enforcement made the illegal crossing more difficult, the number of migrant deaths ballooned. The number of people who died trying to enter the United States increased 800 percent from 1995 to 2005. Every day, more than one person dies in the attempt, on average.[7]

The number of arrests or "apprehensions" at the border dwindled in 2007 and 2008, and Homeland Security officials were quick to attribute the decline to an increase in border fencing and staffing. Indeed, the sharpest dropoff occurred in the Yuma, Arizona, sector, where the Border Patrol had built forty-five miles of a solid steel wall, twenty feet tall. There arrests declined from 119,000 in fiscal year 2006, to 38,000 in 2007, to 8,000 in 2008. But in the past, barriers in one area have merely pushed migrants to cross in other places. And immigration analysts have long correlated the rate of illegal immigration more closely to the vigor of the U.S. job market than to border enforcement. "The reason we're seeing a decline in apprehensions right now is that we're seeing a decline in the economy," said University of San Diego professor David Shirk in 2008. "It's that simple."[8]

The Obama administration, while it has backed away from fence building, has continued to put resources into border enforcement. But the emphasis has begun to shift: from deterring illegal immigration to combating drug trafficking, and from intercepting migrants at the border to tackling the U.S. economy's appetite for unauthorized labor. In the first six months of President Obama's term, U.S. officials also held numerous cabinet-level meetings with Mexican leaders, emphasizing a more bilateral, and potentially more holistic, approach to the border, immigration, and related issues than characterized the Bush administration.[9]

In time, immigration pressures from Mexico will decrease on their own. The fertility rate of Mexican women has been declining steadily: from 6.8 births per woman in 1969 to 2.4 in 2008.[10] Over the next couple of decades, Mexico's birthrate is expected to drop even further, making it easier for the Mexican economy to meet the employment needs of the country's workforce. But the linkages between the United States and Mexico, especially at the border, are here to stay.

Migration has deepened the interpenetration of the two countries. But it has also contributed to dislocation in scores of Mexican communities. In the United States, it has sparked tensions that have manifested in the passage of laws denying public services to illegal immigrants and in outcries against day labor hiring halls and other places where undocumented immigrants are visible. As communities throughout the United States and Mexico grapple with the wide-ranging effects of this labor migration and the larger globalization of which it is a part, the exchange of trade and traditions is well established in the borderlands. And the circumstances that have led to illegal immigration remain in play.

Across the borderline in Agua Prieta, Sonora, seventy miles southwest of the Hurt ranch, half a dozen travelers made up their bunks at a twenty-bed migrant shelter behind the Holy Family Catholic Church. One man, Roberto Valenzuela, threw his powerful baritone into the old Mexican folk song "Cielito Lindo." *"Ay, ay, ay, ay,"* intoned Valenzuela, his salt-and-pepper whiskers glinting on his jaw. *"Canta y no llores!"* (Sing and don't cry!) The other migrants in the dormitory paused to listen as twilight fell outside. They were hundreds, some of them thousands, of miles from home, bedding down for the night among strangers. Most had landed here after being caught by the U.S. Border Patrol and returned to Mexico, but they would attempt the perilous trek again. Many of the migrants had come to this small city just across the line from Douglas because they had heard that, though more heavily patrolled, the crossing routes here were less treacherous than those of the punishing Sonoran Desert of western Arizona, which had become the most trafficked—and most deadly—illegal entryway to the United States, accounting for half of the migrant deaths in recent years.

"I've been caught twice. It's very well patrolled," said Valenzuela, forty-seven, a Sonoran native who was on his way to Phoenix and Los Angeles to sing and play guitar with mariachi groups for a few months, the way he had made a living for years. "Next week I'll try again, maybe further east by New Mexico. If I can't cross, I'll go back to my village for a while."

For the others, the stakes were higher. They had ridden buses, hitch-hiked, or hopped freight trains from the south of Mexico and beyond, intent on reaching the United States in the hopes of earning some decent money to better support their families back home. A slight, mustachioed man from Chiapas, too nervous to give his name, said he had sold his small plot of land to get here. But he had been promptly snagged by Border Patrol agents after slipping into Arizona. He struggled to control his anxiety, for he had a wife and five children to feed and he would not return to them empty-handed.

Another man at the shelter was Luis Enrique Guido Ruiz, thirty-nine, who had bundled his short frame into an oversized red down parka, creating a sort of protective cocoon for himself, though the November night was not particularly cold. Guido's right cheek bore an angry scar where he had been slashed by a knife during a mugging while he was passing through Veracruz. He had been beaten so brutally that he had been hospitalized for fifteen days, he said, and he had stitches inside his mouth. But as soon as he was able, he had continued north. "We're migrating because the poverty in our countries gets worse every day," said Guido, after a dinner of soup and tortillas. A carpenter and bricklayer from Masaya, Nicaragua, he had left his wife and eight-year-old daughter a month before. He had paid bribes to border guards along the way and entrusted his fate to providence. "Whenever I cross a border, I always ask God for protection," he said. "I ask for the strength to get to my destination." Others in the shelter that night were from Oaxaca, Guerrero, and Veracruz, poor states in southern Mexico that had been hard hit by economic liberalization policies—including the elimination of protective corn tariffs and changes in land tenure laws—that had dispossessed two million Mexican peasants.[11]

There weren't enough jobs in Mexico, or enough of a social safety net, said Father Cayetano Cabrera, the priest who had run the shelter for a dozen years. "It's brute capitalism, that's what's propelling the migration," he said in his cluttered office. "They say the economy is stable and growing slowly, that we're paying down the foreign debt. But the reality for most poor Mexicans is more difficult every day. Free trade in agriculture is worsening things for farmers. And we're seeing more migrants from the cities: higher-educated people, even professionals, jumping the fence because there's no work."

As the United States clamped down on the border, he said, the migrants he was seeing had endured greater hardships than in the past. "Before, they used to try crossing again right away, but these days they have suffered more. They've walked further. They're sick. The increased vigilance means they have to hike longer distances," he said. "Many are going to Sasabe [further west], but there's more violence there. Some of those who are deported say that next time they will try crossing into New Mexico."

There were some who might not get a second chance. Alone at age fifty-one, María de la Cruz had left her home in a mining town in Zacatecas, bound for Chicago, where her three sons had settled six years earlier. A smuggler had guided her and about thirty other migrants across a mountain near Naco, Arizona, under cover of night earlier in the fall. "At about four in the morning, the helicopters came and the *coyote* told us to run," said de la Cruz, one of a growing number of older women trying to follow their children and grandchildren to the United States. "We didn't know the terrain and I broke my foot. The Border Patrol caught us all." With a two-month convalescence still ahead of her, she passed her days on the shelter's worn plaid sofa, crocheting scarves for the staff. "I feel terrible not to be able to get to my sons," she said, tugging loose a length of orange yarn from the skein on the wheelchair where she had propped her injured foot. "But in the state I'm in, I can't try again. Once I heal up, I'm going to try to find work here in Agua Prieta. I just have to be patient."

In the decades after the Mexican-American War created this border, residents of northern Mexico and the southwestern United States continued to move back and forth across the line, pulled by work and family ties, and with only a gradually developing sense of a division between the two countries. As early as the 1880s, about the time a railroad line was built from Mexico City to Ciudad Juárez, there began a modest but "continuous flow of migrants to the United States from Mexico's densely populated central plateau."[12] However, Mexico was still overwhelmingly rural, with many peasants tied to the land through peonage. The vast majority lacked much in the way of transportation, let alone news of opportunities in foreign parts.

That began to change with the economic and social upheaval of the Mexican Revolution, beginning in 1910, when thousands of Mexican families crossed the Rio Grande into Texas to escape the turmoil of war. Labor migration from Mexico picked up during World War I, when the

United States faced a wartime labor shortage. Employers turned to private labor contractors, or *enganchadores,* to deliver Mexican workers. The process continued through the 1920s, despite growing nativist sentiment in the United States and increasingly restrictive policies limiting immigration from Europe and Asia.[13] When Congress set permanent immigration quotas in 1924, sharply restricting the number of immigrants by country, Mexico and Canada were exempt. During the Great Depression, however, as U.S. jobs dried up, Mexicans became scapegoats for the country's economic ills, and the government embarked on a massive deportation campaign, arresting and removing almost half a million Mexicans between 1929 and 1937.[14] Migration north slowed to a trickle. The majority of those who did cross the border during the early decades of the twentieth century settled in the Southwest, particularly Texas, where historical ties and agricultural employment were strongest. (In California, during those years, most of the immigrant farmworkers came from Asia.)[15]

With the outbreak of World War II came a new labor shortage, and the two governments established the Bracero Program in 1942 to deliver Mexican workers to U.S. farms (and later to railroad jobs) on short-term seasonal contracts. Migration pathways began to stretch deeper into both countries, drawing workers from broader reaches of Mexico and delivering them further into the United States. Even during the Bracero years, however, there was plenty of unauthorized immigration from Mexico, with many American growers preferring to hire outside the government contract system. One million undocumented Mexicans were deported under President Eisenhower's Operation Wetback in 1954.[16] Nor did the end of the Bracero Program in 1964 end labor migration from Mexico, just the legal avenue by which such workers could enter the country.[17] Today the H-2A and H-2B programs provide temporary visas to tens of thousands of low-skilled foreign workers in agriculture and other fields.[18] Beyond that, there have been scant legal opportunities for such laborers from Mexico or anywhere else to enter the United States for jobs.

Many braceros stayed on and settled in the United States, summoning their families from Mexico, while others returned home with a new sense of mobility that they passed on to their children. The ties thus formed shaped migration routes that would endure for several decades to come. Levels of Mexican migration to the United States since 1990 have correlated closely with the U.S. employment rate, rising as U.S. job growth has risen. Indeed, that correlation has been even closer than the relationship between Mexican emigration and trends in the Mexican economy.[19] Owing to a lack of legal avenues for low-skilled workers to enter the United States, more than 80 percent of Mexican migration in recent years has been unauthorized.[20]

Immigration laws governing movement across the U.S.-Mexico border have not always been so restrictive. Early enforcement along the Mexican border was aimed primarily at catching unauthorized Chinese immigrants, whose entry by legal means had been curtailed. Not until 1929 did the U.S. government make it a misdemeanor to enter the country other than through a formally designated "port of entry." And around 1934 the U.S. government made border-crossing cards available to Mexican citizens living in the border region, in recognition of their long-established cross-boundary ties. Immigration restrictions have tended to get more stringent when the U.S. economy has been in a downturn.[21] The recession of the early 1970s stimulated a nascent anxiety about undocumented immigration and an increase in border enforcement, though by 1980 the Border Patrol's budget was still just $77 million, less than half that of the Philadelphia Police Department.[22]

In 1986, with the unauthorized population numbering between three and five million, Congress enacted the Immigration Reform and Control Act, which gave legal permanent residence to roughly three million undocumented immigrants living in the United States, more than 75 percent of them Mexican. It also applied criminal penalties to employers who hired undocumented workers, in the hopes of reducing the "job magnet" that contributed to unauthorized immigration. But the law's employer sanctions were hardly enforced, and IRCA did not create any new legal avenue for low-skilled workers to enter the country, so illegal immigration continued. By granting legal status to many Mexicans in the United States, the 1986 measure also allowed the new permanent residents to sponsor immigration to the United States by their relatives in Mexico, further cementing family networks across the border.[23]

The wage differential between the two countries is clearly an important factor in motivating Mexican migration to the United States. But the portrayal of undocumented immigrants as lawbreakers—a common theme among U.S. restrictionists—tends to emphasize that migrants are making individual (and unlawful) decisions to cross the border to maximize their incomes. That's true as far as it goes. But the reality of Mexican immigration is a much more complex interplay of economic, cultural, and technological forces, argue Douglas Massey, Jorge Durand, and Nolan Malone in their book *Beyond Smoke and Mirrors: Mexican Immigration in an Era of Economic Integration.* "Migration is a natural outgrowth of the disruptions and dislocations that occur in this process of market expansion and penetration," they write. "The international migration of labor generally parallels the international movement of goods and capital, only in reverse."[24]

As Mexico's economy shifted from subsistence farming to market-based production, the countryside became increasingly linked to cities, and Mexico linked to its northern neighbor, by trade relations and consumer goods and by infrastructure, including roads and railroads, and later telephones, television, and the Internet. These links facilitated migration when farmers found themselves displaced by the often-jarring transformation of the economy. Credit and insurance have long been scarce in Mexico, and that has also led households to diversify their sources of income by sending a member abroad to work for a time and accumulate savings, whether to cope with a crisis or make a major purchase. "In effect, migration is the poor Mexicans' MasterCard," Massey has said.[25]

At the same time that Mexico's economy has not been creating the number or quality of jobs needed to provide for its growing workforce, the U.S. population has become older (on average) and more highly educated than it was a generation or two ago. In 1960 the median age was twenty-nine and just over 40 percent of American adults had high school diplomas. By 2000, the median age had risen to thirty-five and more than 80 percent of the adult population had a high school degree, according to U.S. Census data.[26] Consequently the United States has a smaller proportion of people willing to fill low-skilled service and manual jobs and a greater need for service workers as its citizenry ages. Further, the more that Mexicans put down roots here over time, the easier it has become for their families and friends back home to learn about crossing the border, finding a job, and making their way in the United States.

By the early 1990s, border arrests of unauthorized migrants were increasing, especially in California, while the state was experiencing a serious recession. Immigration restrictionists, with California governor Pete Wilson in the lead, ratcheted up political pressure on Washington, D.C., and the federal government responded with increased border enforcement. Operation Hold the Line was launched in El Paso in 1993 and Operation Gatekeeper in San Diego in 1994. They formed the basis of the Border Patrol strategy that continues to the present.

The buildup made it more difficult to jump the fence in those urban areas where, once across, migrants could blend into the mass of population with relative ease. But rather than discouraging people from crossing, that difficulty propelled border crossers to try alternate routes through smaller cities like Calexico, Nogales, and Douglas, as well as Laredo, McAllen, and Brownsville. As those places in turn became fortified, migrants shifted to the vast, unpatrolled expanses of the Sonoran Desert. The hardening of the U.S. border also strengthened the hand of entrepreneurial smugglers who have come to control the majority of crossings.[27] In early 2006, those smugglers—*coyotes* or *polleros,* chicken herders, as they are known south of the border—were charging $2,000 to guide their customers across the rugged wastelands of southern Arizona, $3,000 to smuggle them through a port of entry, and $5,000 to cross them at a port of entry with false or borrowed papers.[28]

As the Arizona desert became the route of choice, the Border Patrol stepped up enforcement there in the early part of this decade, and the buildup continued, with ever more agents, fencing, and high-tech equipment—from aerial drones and all-terrain vehicles to infrared cameras and buried motion detectors. And so—with the underlying economic forces that impel migrants northward unchanged, and binational family ties stronger than ever—the migration routes appear to again be shifting. Meanwhile, a growing number of Central Americans, displaced by distressed economies and linked to the United States by their own historical ties, have been joining the ranks of the U.S.-bound migrants.

Border Patrol arrests, a crude reflection of the number and location of unauthorized border crossings, dropped from one million in 2006 to seven hundred thousand in 2008. But some observers believe migrants are increasingly smuggled through at ports of entry. Scholars who have interviewed migrants at length on the Mexican side of the line say that the number of people crossing the border may have dropped off but that their numbers in the United States have remained steady because the difficulty of the crossing has encouraged permanent settlement in the United States. Many potential immigrants are arrested repeatedly before they make it across or give up trying. Even if an immigration reform law provides a legal avenue for Mexicans and other foreign-born workers to come to the United States, the government's emphasis on border enforcement will almost certainly continue, with an increase in staffing and high-tech monitoring.

One night in Columbus, New Mexico, the border town due south of Deming, the Border Patrol arrested a pair of young men from the southern Mexican state of Veracruz. The men were hiding out in the Pancho Villa State Park (named to commemorate the Mexican revolutionary leader's 1916 raid on the town). They were waiting to meet the smuggler who would take them north. Sitting on the asphalt of the park's parking lot under the beam of squad car headlights, Israel Laguna, twenty-eight, said he had left a job as a nurse to come north. He hoped to spend a year working in the United States and socking away money before returning to his wife and young daughter. "I came here because people in Juárez told me it was easier to cross here," said Laguna. "But this is the second time I've been caught."

After Laguna and his companion were processed and locked in a holding cell, Border Patrol agent Adrian Aizpuru continued cruising the dirt roads outside town, where new vehicle barriers, infrared cameras in mobile surveillance towers, and troops from the Georgia National Guard supported his efforts. An agent for fourteen years, Aizpuru has seen migration routes shift when enforcement has increased in one area or another. "Once they started tightening down in Arizona and California," he said. "We started getting them."

Aizpuru was born in El Paso and raised there by his Mexican-born mother. His father, who lived across the river in Ciudad Juárez, came over frequently to visit. Aizpuru's mother worked as a seamstress sewing Levi's jeans in an El Paso sweatshop. But her ability to get a raise was undercut by the fact that a crew of undocumented workers would come in on the second shift and do the same job for half the pay, he said. Seeing this as a young man, Aizpuru grew increasingly frustrated and became determined to join the Border Patrol. (Those U.S. garment manufacturing jobs, however, have since been outsourced to Mexico, Central America, and various parts of Asia, where workers can be found who will accept even lower wages than illegal immigrants in the United States.)

Aizpuru was proud of the Deming station's success in reducing border crossings, crediting it in part to a temporary program of sending all arrestees before an immigration judge for formal deportation rather than allowing them "voluntary return" to Mexico, which carries no penalties. But he had seen a growing number of migrant deaths over the years and an increase in parents bringing their small children along as they attempted the thirty-five-mile trek from the border to Deming. That was a phenomenon he found particularly distressing now that he had a two-year-old daughter of his own. "I don't know if people really understand how bad it can go, crossing with your family," he said.

"I think we're more effective now," said Aizpuru. "But what we're doing can never control the border without fixing things in Mexico. There's no reason why a man or woman shouldn't try to better their life, especially when there's no light at the end of the tunnel. And that's why people cross. The way Mexico is now, you can build whatever kinds of walls you want [and people will still try to cross]. I would do it. I would cross. It would take several things to make the problem manageable: we should make it harder to cross illegally, easier to come in legally, and give people some reason to stay home."

That approach made sense to Hank Hays, though he called the idea of a seven-hundred-mile fence "hilarious." Hays, who had retired from the Border Patrol after a twenty-nine-year career, took up flying the Hurts' ranch helicopter. He went to work for the Hurts in 1998 after Velva's second son, Ernie, who had been the pilot in the family, died in a helicopter crash. Though he had retired from the Border Patrol, Hays kept up on agency gossip through former colleagues and his son, who was also a Border Patrol agent. Hays, fifty-nine, had spent nine years patrolling the Boot Heel back when there were just five agents assigned to the Lordsburg Station. Lately there were closer to three hundred agents, and most were from outside the area and still wet behind the ears, he grumbled. "They have to stop everybody on the road because they don't know who the local people are," he said. "There's a lot of smuggling going on, but the smugglers beat them because the agents don't know the area." Not only that, said Hays, but the agency's accelerating growth over the past decade meant that new agents were hired without sufficient background checks. He had heard from knowledgeable friends that the Department of Homeland Security was looking into hundreds of cases of corruption among its staff on the Mexican border. "That's what happens when you dump so many people in so fast," he said. "It's a mess."

After the Hurts and their crew finished branding their calves on the home place, they moved on to pregnancy-testing the cows. Silver City veterinarian John Wenzel, who tended to livestock all over southwestern New Mexico, arrived before lunch, wearing green coveralls with one sleeve cut off. Socorro and Norma guided each cow into the squeeze chute, and Lawrence's younger brother Avery levered it shut, immobilizing her. Quickly, Oscar vaccinated and Doc Wenzel moved in from behind, plunging his bare arm, swathed in a long plastic glove, down the animal's rectum to palpate her uterus. With a red grease pencil, he striped the cow's haunch: one mark if she was in her first trimester of pregnancy, two for the second, three for the third. Wenzel was also eyeing each cow's brand, as he did on every ranch, to be sure the Hurts were her rightful owners, and checking her udder to see if she was lactating. At his side, Avery kept a running tally on a clipboard of the pregnant cows.

"If she's dry, she didn't bring a calf to market this year. She might have calved but the dogs or the coyotes could have gotten it," Wenzel explained. "Two years of that in her life and she's culled. A rancher down here can't afford to have a cow eating feed if she's not producing a calf." Soon came a young cow that fit that description: for the second year in a row, she wasn't pregnant. But, noted Avery, she was a special case. "This is Princess, a dogie that my daughter raised after its mother died," he said. "She should be sent to slaughter, but . . . maybe I should consult a higher authority," he laughed to Wenzel, and the cow was spared until Avery could talk the matter over with his teenager.

In addition to the family's 4H brand, each of the Hurt brothers had his own. And as their kids came of age, they all applied for their own branding marks and raised a handful of their own cattle, banking the profits when the calves sold. Giving the teenagers a stake in the family business helped cultivate a legacy that Wenzel found striking. "To have these brothers work this close together on a daily basis and still like each other, that's a big deal," said the vet, who had known the family for twenty years. "And their kids will do the same thing. They'll encourage them to get an education, but they'd be disappointed if the boys didn't come back to the ranch."

Part of the Hurts' success, said Wenzel, was their cohesion, which had increased after Ernie's death in 1998: "They're unbelievably close. I've never seen them mad at each other." Part of their success was that all of the brothers had gone to college. "They're info savvy," said Wenzel, whose work took him to all sorts of ranches. "A lot of ranching is done by tradition. We have people down here doing things exactly the way their grandfather did. But the Hurts are willing to change. They want to stay on top of the industry. They're very good producers." And part of it was their willingness to roll up their sleeves. "Their secret is, they're not afraid to work," Wenzel remarked. "Most of the bigger outfits, the owner tends to be involved with the cows themselves but not the daily operations, not the mechanical work. The Hurts do their own windmills, they assemble the sprinkler pivots themselves, they do their own electrical work, work on their own vehicles. They've got a well-equipped shop. If Lawrence needs something, he makes it."

The Hurts had thrived in this corner of the Southwest—proud, independent, self-sufficient—though more than fifteen years of drought had taken a toll. They were competing now too with hobby ranchers who inadvertently pushed up the cost of doing business because they had other income and could afford to pay more for an acre of land or a day's labor. And living at the border brought its own set of challenges. "They've got drug runners, illegal aliens, Minutemen . . . a lot of issues that other ranchers in other areas don't have to deal with," said Wenzel. "The border also raises a concern about bio-security. The foot traffic from a set of shoes that's been in, say, Brazil, which has foot and mouth disease, that's really concerning, being a border area. We just hope that when it does cross we can stop it or localize it quickly."

At the end of a long, dusty, bloody morning in the corral, the crew of Mexican and American cowboys settled down in the shade of the cottonwoods on the green lawn beside Velva's ranch house and ate lunch, conversing laconically in both English and Spanish. Afterward Lawrence Hurt wandered through the junkyard down the lane, which looked like a museum of twentieth-century farming and Hurt family history. Rusting tractors, plows, and hay rakes sat alongside a derelict chuck wagon and the remains of a horse-drawn hearse. "I used to get my dad out here whenever I could to tell me about all these things and how they worked and what they were used for," he said. Hurt had passed those stories on to his son and daughter: the secrets to the tools that, over a century, had helped their family extract a living from this arid place in the borderlands. His teenage son, Remington, was showing an interest in the family business. But with the cost of feed and fuel rising dramatically and the price for cattle dropping, Hurt sometimes felt the future was bleak. "The income is so marginal, it may not exclusively be ranching for them," he said. "We've been talking to some solar energy guys about either selling some land outright or leasing it." The Hurt brothers were working to pay down debt and diversify their income, while hoping that the United States and Mexico could resolve the problems of the border region before they got more disruptive. "We need to look at the legacy," he said, "at passing it on."

FOUR

Nogales / Nogales

"If they get sick here, we care for them"

MAKING HIS ROUNDS THROUGH THE HOSPITAL GENERAL, in the growing border city of Nogales, Sonora, internist Enrique Contreras stopped beside a bed where a stout nurse was bathing a badly injured patient with a washcloth. The patient, Hugo Llanos, a twenty-year-old peasant from Oaxaca, had spent a week in this public hospital, drifting in and out of consciousness, after being transferred by ambulance from St. Joseph's Hospital in Phoenix. Border Patrol agents had found his body crumpled near some railroad tracks in Arizona, his hands and face smashed and bleeding, and guessed that he had jumped or fallen from a freight train. "He's lucky to be alive," said Contreras. "He fell on his head and he's got a big brain hemorrhage."

Every week Contreras, the Hospital General's deputy director, received three or four Mexican patients transferred from medical centers in Arizona. In the brutal heat of summer, when hundreds of northbound migrants perished in the desert, there could be up to four a day. Many, like Llanos, were not natives of the border region but migrants from much further south, and their presence here had burdened northern Mexico's health care resources. But the transfers were a point of pride for Contreras: Mexico could take care of its own. They were also a manifestation of a sensibility shared by medical providers in the borderlands: that their responsibility to care for the ill and injured didn't stop at the border but linked their work across the region.

The number of cross-border transfers has increased in recent years as American health care providers have begun aiding Mexican border hospitals in improving their capacity to treat critical cases. In Arizona, several hospitals have pooled their resources and donated and helped maintain medical equipment, assisted administrators in applying for grants, and shared training and skills with Mexican hospitals.

For U.S. hospitals near the border that have borne the cost of caring for uninsured Mexicans, improving health care in Mexico and transferring patients back to their home country makes financial sense. A few years back, Llanos probably would have been kept at the Phoenix hospital until he recovered, at a cost of tens of thousands of unreimbursed dollars. American doctors, bound, like all physicians, by the Hippocratic oath, would have been concerned that sending him home to an underfunded hospital could endanger his health. But with improvements in Mexican care, they had become more confident that they were doing the right thing morally as well as fiscally.

For Llanos, the move to the Sonora hospital marked the first step in getting reconnected with his family in Mexico. Llanos had left home in the early spring, three months earlier, and joined a brother in California's Central Valley. He had planned to work for a season, as he had done once before, save some money, and then return to Chazumba, the Mixtec Indian village of his birth. The brothers were harvesting fruit one day when *la migra,* the U.S. immigration authorities, raided the fields and the men took off running. Some days later, Llanos's sister Clementina and her husband, Erasto Juárez, phoned California to see how things were going. Llanos had left for Tucson, the brother told them, and nothing more had been heard from him.

Alarmed, Juárez began calling hospitals along the border, employing the English he had picked up on a six-month stint in a Stamford, Connecticut, restaurant kitchen. Finally a doctor at the hospital in Nogales, Arizona, helped him track Llanos to the Hospital General. Juárez immediately boarded a bus from Mexico City, where he and Clementina lived, and arrived in Nogales hoping to take his brother-in-law back with him. Getting to Llanos's bedside was easier than it would have been if he had remained in the United States, but as it turned out, taking the injured man home proved trickier than Juárez had anticipated.

Like many Mexican hospitals, the Hospital General in Nogales, Sonora, has not been well equipped to handle trauma or other acute problems, even though almost half the residents of the sprawling city of more

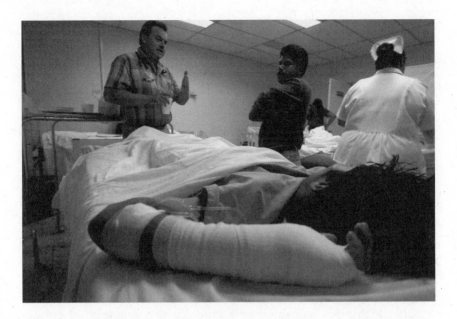

Figure 9. Dr. Enrique Contreras consults with Erasto Juárez about Erasto's brother-in-law, a migrant worker who was injured in Arizona and is recuperating in the public hospital in Nogales, Sonora. Photo by Chris Stewart/San Francisco Chronicle.

than a quarter million and all the surrounding countryside rely on it. The single-story, concrete-block hospital has a busy outpatient clinic, where the city's poorer citizens receive immunizations, neonatal care, and routine medical exams under a government-run "popular insurance" program. The thirty-bed hospital has a five-bed emergency room with one trauma bay and a single-bed intensive care unit. When serious cases arise, doctors have had to transfer patients by ambulance two and a half hours to the trauma center in Hermosillo, Sonora's capital, or over the border to Arizona.

The first stop in the United States is Carondolet Holy Cross Hospital in Nogales, Arizona. Contreras and the staff of the Hospital General have formed a close relationship with Holy Cross, just a mile away over the rusting border fence. The Arizona hospital, built by Mexican nuns in 1960, is hardly any bigger—with thirty-one inpatient beds and a six-bed emergency room (along with a forty-nine-bed nursing home).[1] But the population it serves—the forty thousand residents of rural Santa Cruz county and parts of the nearby Tohono O'odham Indian Reservation—is a fraction the size of the Mexican hospital's load. And though it lacks the full array of specialists and trauma surgeons, the private Catholic hospital's resources, just by virtue of its location in the United States, are greater. "Mexico has highly competent, well-trained physicians, but they don't have the same access to technology," said Richard Polheber, director of Holy Cross. "The only CT scanner over there [in Nogales, Sonora] is in a private clinic."

Before the U.S. government erected a two-mile-long, fourteen-foot-tall steel wall in 1994 between the two Nogaleses (Ambos Nogales, as they're known locally), the towns used to share annual parades and a sense of civic and cultural unity.[2] Even with the wall and a thirty- to sixty-minute wait to pass through it, the two communities have remained intimately connected. "Go back a few years and Nogales was one community," said Polheber. "One of the things we're trying to do in health care is blow up the wall."

Just past the turnstiles and the customs officials on the way into Nogales, Sonora, the first blocks of shops are crammed with pharmacies, advertising their wares in English. It's the same in just about every other Mexican border town. The cost of prescriptions is much lower in Mexico, and many Americans, lacking prescription drug coverage, buy their medicines here. In fact, U.S. residents along the border make ample use of all sorts of health services in Mexico. Dentistry is cheaper, and doctors often have a more personal touch, pointed out Polheber's assistant, Dina Sánchez, who is Mexican American. "You still have in Mexico a way of thinking, a way of being treated, that includes home visits, house calls," she said. Polheber agreed: "Some of our staff prefer care in Mexico. There's no managed care there, so a visit with the doctor can be an hour, not thirteen minutes. The wait for a specialist might be one or two days, not four to six weeks. Some people are willing to pay cash for care in a private hospital."

Holy Cross replaced much of its high-tech medical equipment at the turn of the millennium in preparation for the threatened Y2K computer glitches, then found itself with a lot of expensive—and still perfectly functioning—surplus machinery. "We got talking to the Department of Health Services and the University Medical Center [in Tucson], and we said, 'Why don't we consider donating it to the Hospital Básico across the way?'" Polheber recalled, using an informal name for the Hospital General. "We gave them monitors, defibrillators, anesthesia machines."

The donated equipment, said Contreras, the Sonoran physician, "has allowed us to improve the quality of care we provide." The contributions added up to $1 million worth of equipment. And twice a year, technicians from the Catholic hospital network that includes Holy Cross visited the Hospital General to repair and recalibrate the donated machines. In addition, a $365,000 grant from the U.S. Agency for International Development (USAID), obtained with help from former U.S. Rep. Jim Kolbe, an Arizona Republican, helped build a new wing—including the trauma unit, two operating rooms, and a neonatal intensive care unit—for the Hospital General. Another USAID grant, for $1 million, would pay for a CT scanner, which creates detailed x-rays, in another new wing being built mainly with funds from Mexico's federal and Sonoran state governments. The push to improve the hospital also stimulated charitable donations from Mexican business leaders and some of the companies that operate maquiladoras in Nogales.

The collaboration to improve the Hospital General built on longstanding ties that had linked medical professionals across the border for decades. At the heart of the relationship were Dr. Adolfo Felix, a Mexican surgeon, and his wife, Barbara Felix, an American hospital administrator with a background in nursing, who had spent their professional careers nurturing links between health care providers in Arizona and Sonora.

Forty years ago, when the dean of the University of Arizona medical school visited the Hermosillo hospital where Adolfo Felix practiced, the doctor and his wife hosted him in their home. "We had a relationship treating patients back and forth even then," said Barbara Felix. Later she became the international patient services coordinator at University Medical Center (UMC) in Tucson, where she tracked the care of foreign patients, the vast majority of them Mexican, including transfers back to Mexico when appropriate. Her husband taught at the medical school in Tucson, though they still maintained a home in Hermosillo.

Over the years, the medical school and the affiliated medical center in Tucson have built a continuing medical education program for physicians, nurses, and paramedics from Mexico. A telemedicine link connects UMC with Hermosillo's Hospital General. And medical professionals participate in joint research and training efforts across the border. In addition, Arizona and Sonora doctors maintain regular contact through meetings of the U.S.-Mexico Border Health Commission, a government-created binational forum.

Cross-border efforts by Arizona hospital administrators to equip Mexican hospitals began in 1999 with the outfitting of a neonatal intensive care unit at the Hospital Integral in Agua Prieta, Sonora, the border town just south of Douglas, Arizona.[3] After the clinic was created—with funding from University Medical Center and Tucson Medical Center, as well as the state of Sonora—the infant mortality rate in Agua Prieta dropped from 17 percent to 2 percent. And the number of ill and premature infants transferred to UMC—at a cost of about $75,000 apiece—dropped from fifteen a year to zero, according to UMC chief financial officer Kevin J. Burns.[4]

Caring for undocumented immigrants who lack health insurance and are ineligible for public assistance such as Medicaid has become a significant cost in recent years for hospitals along the border and in U.S. cities with large immigrant populations. In 2005, Holy Cross provided $500,000 in unreimbursed care to foreign nationals, while UMC spent $5 million on such care. "It's $5 million which has no revenue attached," said UMC's Burns. "We have to cover it in other ways." A 2002 study by the U.S.-Mexico Border Counties Coalition estimated that American hospitals in the twenty-four counties along the border spent $200 million in 2000 for unreimbursed emergency care for illegal immigrants.[5] Further from the border, hospitals in Phoenix, Los Angeles, Houston, Jersey City, New York, and Philadelphia, among other cities, have also struggled with the burden.

California hospitals spent an estimated $700 million in 2006 on charity care for illegal immigrants, said Jan Emerson, a spokeswoman for the California Hospital Association. That amounted to 10 percent of the $7 billion in total uncompensated care the state's hospitals provided that year, she said.[6]

The federal government dictates that hospital emergency rooms must treat and stabilize all comers, regardless of their ability to pay. Holy Cross, because it is a Catholic hospital, also has its own historical mission of caring for the poor, said medical director Dr. Ross Luther. Those imperatives underpin the charity care the hospital provides uninsured Mexicans, but they don't make the trade-offs easy if it means limiting care for uninsured Americans. "Right now there's a patient in Tucson who's critically ill, running a 107 degree fever, he's a migrant who was found dehydrated in the desert and brought here. We get folks who jump the fence and have bad fractures; we feel ethically and morally bound to get them the kind of care they need," said Luther. "We're not differentiating between U.S. citizens and foreign nationals. As a human being, you see a sick neonate and you don't care if it's a foreign national. But at the same time, there's the American clerk earning $8 an hour who can't afford a gastroenterologist for her kid."

Immigration opponents, angry at the government's failure to seal the border, have seized on the toll of these medical expenses, which are eventually absorbed by taxpayers and those who pay private health insurance premiums. The Web sites and blogs of immigration restrictionists have long been full of stories of hospital bankruptcies and closures blamed on the cost of caring for illegal immigrants. The reality is more complex.

Urban and rural hospitals in the United States have indeed faced economic crises in recent years, and in many cases unreimbursed care for immigrants is one part of the problem, but it is only a part. Six emergency rooms in Los Angeles County closed over the course of fourteen months in 2003 and 2004 (reducing the number of emergency rooms in the county to seventy-nine), casualties of the growing population of uninsured residents, regardless of immigration status.[7] The nonprofit Tucson Medical Center closed its trauma unit in 2003, citing annual losses of $5 million. Restrictionists were quick to blame the deficit on illegal immigrants, but officials attributed the problem to dwindling revenues on a variety of fronts, from low payouts by health maintenance organizations to shrinking Medicare payments.[8]

The little Copper Queen Community Hospital in Bisbee, Arizona, six miles north of the border, began treating more than its share of ill and injured Mexicans in the late 1990s, when federal border enforcement started channeling illegal border crossings through southeastern Arizona. The fourteen-bed hospital even shuttered its skilled nursing facility and maternity ward to cut costs. The situation was exacerbated by the Border Patrol's practice, when encountering a sick or injured undocumented immigrant, of calling an ambulance without arresting the person. The cost of care becomes a federal responsibility only if the migrant is in custody, so the Border Patrol has ended up shifting the responsibility to the local hospital, frequently a small, rural hospital, like Holy Cross or Copper Queen, or an overburdened urban one. "The more free care we give, the more we have to ration what's left," Copper Queen's chief executive officer Jim Dickson told *Time* magazine in 2004. "If you make me treat someone, then you need to pay me. You can't have un-funded mandates in a small hospital."[9]

While unreimbursed care for immigrants did cost the Copper Queen as much as $300,000 a year for several years, Dickson told a federal committee on rural health issues that beyond his overcrowded emergency room and growing load of uninsured Mexican patients, the biggest problem imperiling his hospital was a severe crisis in malpractice insurance.

Dickson's testimony at a 2002 meeting of the National Advisory Committee on Rural Health and Human Services is summarized in the minutes:

> As a direct result of the losses incurred in the re-insurance market by the September 11 tragedy, more than 40 percent of the malpractice insurance carriers pulled out of the market, leaving Arizona physicians scrambling for malpractice insurance. . . . Consequently 80 percent of the physicians in Cochise County lost their malpractice coverage and were forced to pay huge sums for "tail coverage." . . . Four family practitioners who offered obstetric care had their insurance carriers pulled from the market, and the new insurance carriers increased their rates 500 percent over a 3-year period. These physicians have been forced to cease obstetric coverage immediately, thus virtually shutting down maternity services at the Copper Queen Community Hospital. This malpractice problem has also had a severe effect on other specialty providers. Two general surgeons who currently serve the Copper Queen Community Hospital are considering leaving their practices because the cost of malpractice insurance increased to $80,000 a year. Their departure would eliminate general surgery from the surrounding 4,000-square-mile area.[10]

Multiple factors, then, have contributed to the financial pinch in which hospitals like the Copper Queen find themselves. Insufficient Medicare and Medicaid reimbursements, the sky-high cost of malpractice insurance, rural hospitals' difficulty in retaining staff, and the overwhelming expense of treating the nation's growing population of uninsured patients all combine with the real costs of caring for people from across the border—whether they are in the United States legally or illegally, temporarily or permanently. When the Border Counties Coalition tallied the cost of emergency care for the undocumented, it found that such care consumed just one in four of the dollars border hospitals spend on emergency care for the uninsured overall. Administrators at individual hospitals have come up with comparable estimates. The UMC in Tucson says care for foreign patients makes up 25 percent of its unreimbursed care. The Maricopa Medical Center in Phoenix puts the figure at 10 percent.[11] And in Nogales, right on the border, caring for uninsured foreign patients at Holy Cross constitutes about 30 percent of all charity care.

The challenge of treating uninsured people in general is much greater than the burden of treating illegal immigrants in particular, said Polheber, quick to put the matter in perspective. "While it's a problem, it's no more of a problem than providing care to the uninsured," he said. "Here in Nogales, we have a lot of uninsured patients. The workers in the produce warehouses here typically don't have health benefits through their jobs."

In addition to illegal immigrants, the Mexicans whom American border hospitals treat without reimbursement are typically legal visitors to the United States or those who have received "compassionate entry" waivers because they arrived at the border already in critical condition. At Tucson's University Medical Center, Barbara Felix said the hospital has long considered that "the population of northern Mexico is part of the population we serve."

"There's a lot of confusion; people think all these people just jumped over the wall last night. But people come and go daily, and if they get sick here and decide to present, we care for them," she said. "There are families where part of the family lives in Arizona and part lives in Sonora. There's nothing unusual about this. We have had families who traditionally came here from Mexico who are very good clients and paid their bills. We said, 'These are our people. We want to work with them.'"

In 2005 the federal government implemented a four-year, $1 billion plan to defray unreimbursed emergency costs incurred by hospitals and ambulance companies attending illegal immigrants, the Federal Reimbursement of Emergency Health Services Furnished to Undocumented Aliens. The money covered only a fraction of actual costs and could be a headache to claim, especially because most hospitals refused to ask patients directly about their immigration status, feeling it would scare off undocumented immigrants in need of medical care. But the money helped. As of 2008, however, the funding had not been renewed.

U.S. and Mexican health care providers at the border, meanwhile, have become adept at cutting through red tape, making direct personal contact, and working out solutions without waiting for federal help. Rich Polheber has hosted evening social gatherings to help the doctors of Ambos Nogales get acquainted. And Holy Cross may even be able to use its border location to improve its bottom line. "We're trying to get an orthopedic surgeon [and other specialists]," Polheber said. "If I build a new modern facility, there are people who can pay, who will come over the border to us."

In Nogales, Sonora, Enrique Contreras was already seeing the benefits of the cross-border collaboration. In the primary care clinic of the Hospital General, he weaved his way between knots of waiting patients and through swinging doors into the new wing. He showed off the trauma room and two surgical theaters outfitted with equipment donated by the American hospitals. "Not even the private hospitals have this," he said.

Mexico's private hospitals generally offer superior care. But they serve only 5 to 10 percent of the population: people who either can afford to pay out of pocket or have private insurance, which is rare. Many private sector employees are covered by the Mexican Social Security Institute, which is financed jointly by employers, employees, and the federal government. Public employees, members of agricultural cooperatives, and retirees, along with their families, get health coverage through the Social Security and Services Institute for Government Employees, which has its own network of hospitals and clinics across Mexico. Neonatal care and immunizations of children are publicly funded and free for all Mexicans.[12] But as many as 40 percent of Mexicans were not covered until President Vicente Fox launched a basic Seguro Popular insurance, on a sliding scale up to $200 per family per year, to cover the poor.

Contreras beamed most broadly as he entered his hospital's new intensive care unit for newborns, where a mother nursed her twelve-day-old preemie and a father sat attentively beside a day-old infant on a child-sized ventilator. "Before we built this, we had to send premature babies to Hermosillo or Tucson. And U.S. hospitals never sent the babies back to us," he said. "Now they can, and we are very pleased and proud to be able to receive them."

Contreras stepped outdoors to a vacant lot where the second new wing was to rise over the next few years. Diesel buses rumbled loudly past on the city streets, and the dusty lot was filled with street vendors and schoolchildren. But Contreras could picture in his mind's eye the new addition, which would double the number of inpatient beds to sixty and make room for specialty clinics handling obstetrics, internal medicine, surgery, and ear, nose, and throat care.

An internist by training, Contreras had spent nine years at the Hospital General, but his ties to this place dated back to 1984, when he had worked at the hospital for a year after medical school to repay the government for his education. He went into private practice for a while, then moved to the United States, studying English and passing his boards in hopes of practicing medicine there. But with a foreign medical degree he was unable to land a job in a U.S. hospital, and he returned to Sonora after three years and rededicated himself to working in the local community.

Becoming a doctor in the first place fulfilled a family dream, said Contreras. He had grown up in Cananea, in the mountains just to the east, one of seven children of a hard-rock copper miner. "My father worked fifty years in the mines," he said. "He had to spend one month's wages to pay for one semester at private school. But he wanted me to get a good education. Before my mother passed away I made a promise to her that I would use my education to become a doctor."

Contreras and his wife, a pediatrician in private practice in Nogales, Sonora, lived just over the border in Arizona with their two children, ages six and twelve. Though they both worked in Mexico, they had chosen to settle on the U.S. side, he said, for the same reason his own parents had scrimped: to give their children access to the best schools around. Knowing that his command of English had helped him advance professionally and build ties with American doctors, he found satisfaction watching his kids growing up perfectly bilingual. "Education is the best legacy you can leave your children," he said.

A lot of his time was spent at the port of entry, though. "I cross the border two or three times a day," he said. "Is it a long wait? Not really. It's psychological: you listen to music or read the paper, and in half an hour, forty-five minutes, you're across."

Contreras had high hopes for his little hospital, but for the time being the Hospital General was still scrambling for resources and the worst trauma cases continued to flow north. A Mexican ambulance would typically deliver a patient to the U.S. port of entry, and border officials would call the Nogales, Arizona, Fire Department. The paramedics would alert Holy Cross Hospital that a patient was en route, hustle to the border in their own ambulance, and deliver the patient to the emergency room, five minutes away. "We're the first responders for care," said Polheber. "Sometimes we're dealing with zero information, with someone who's scared, who may not speak English or even Spanish. We don't always know what kind of testing or procedures they've had in Mexico."

Because Holy Cross, too, was a small hospital and lacked the full array of specialists and the most advanced technology, it stabilized patients but often transferred them on to Tucson or Phoenix. "You can't keep as many patients as you'd like, so you burden the urban center, which is already overburdened," said Luther, the medical director. "We'll send 50 to 60 percent of our admitted patients to the urban center."

One summer night, paramedics whisked a fifteen-year-old boy injured in a car crash in Sonora into the Holy Cross emergency room. Tony Meras, a Nogales emergency medical technician, delivered an envelope of x-rays to the nursing station as his partner lowered the boy onto a gurney

Figure 10. Paramedics whisk a teenager injured in a car crash in Sonora into the emergency room of the Holy Cross Hospital in Nogales, Arizona. Photo by Chris Stewart/San Francisco Chronicle.

and wheeled him into the building. The teenager's mother hovered near him anxiously. He already had casts on an arm and a leg.

The emergency room had been busy all evening, and the beds, plus a couple of gurneys in the hallway, were full—with a vomiting preschooler, a cardiac patient with a malfunctioning pacemaker, a pregnant woman with abdominal pain, a child with a broken arm, a dehydrated old man, a feverish infant, and a schizophrenic woman with a mysterious swelling in her throat and great bruise-like blotches down her legs. But John Díaz, the on-duty emergency physician, didn't miss a beat. He had spent a long career in Arizona emergency rooms, the last fourteen of them here in Nogales.

As nurses bustled around checking the patient's blood pressure and temperature, Díaz took a quick look at the x-rays. Then he examined the youth and questioned him in a calm, neutral voice. "Do you have any headache? How about chest pain? Stomach pain? Do you have difficulty breathing?" He checked the boy's vision and asked him to wiggle his toes. Then Díaz headed for the telephone at the nursing station. As he walked, he directed a nurse to order two units of blood to stabilize the boy's blood pressure. "This guy's going to get a new hip. His femur is sheared off. This is a *bad* injury," remarked Díaz. "I have to find him a hospital bed in Tucson. It's always difficult."

The boy's mother had moved outside and was talking urgently into a cellular phone. The family was from Tucson, Díaz said, but had been on a road trip in Mexico to visit relatives. About four o'clock that morning, they had crashed on the highway. The teenager, sleeping in the back seat of the Jeep, had been thrown from the vehicle. Though he didn't yet know it, his father had been killed. His younger siblings, five and nine years old, had been injured but were in stable condition at the Hermosillo hospital and would eventually be transported north. Díaz and his colleague, Dr. Julie Wolters, started working the phones, an all-too-familiar routine.

"Can I have the ER please?" the wiry, gray-haired physician asked, trying to infuse his voice with a little warmth to cover the strain. "Hello? This is Dr. Díaz from Holy Cross Nogales. Can I speak to Dr. Porter or whoever's on call for trauma? I've got a fifteen-year-old male. Motor vehicle accident. Right hip fracture. Left leg fracture." He waited. "Okay." Díaz hung up, spoke quietly to Wolters, dialed the phone again. "Can I have the ER please? I just talked with Dr. Porter about a transfer. Who's this? Lisa? Oh, Lisa from Baboquivari!" He laughed, and for a moment the distance and the bureaucracy melted away in small-town familiarity. "Yes. He's fully alert and oriented. Dr. Porter said he'd take the patient. We're calling a helicopter. The chest x-ray is not the best quality, but it looks okay. I'll probably repeat it here."

Soon the Lifeline helicopter landed in the darkness outside the hospital. The flight medics rolled in their gurney, and Díaz briefed them on the case. As they carefully shifted the youth into the chopper, the pilot, Jack Cunningham, commented on the cost of the growing number of undocumented immigrants with injuries. "We see the Border Patrol chasing their vehicles and then there's a rollover and it's four, five, six patients," he said. "It's something you can't say no to. But your flights would be cheaper if we didn't have to do so many free ones." The crew made room for the boy's mother to kiss him goodbye. "He'll be there in twenty minutes," someone assured her. Then the helicopter revved up, creating a fearsome wind. Its doors closed, its lights blinked on, and the chopper lifted off into the night sky, leaving a swirl of gravel and leaves around a hospital statue of the Virgin Mary cradling her infant son.

Inside the emergency room, the evening's work was far from over. Díaz was back on the phone, trying to get some expert help for the schizophrenic woman with the unexplained bruising. Tests that Díaz had ordered came back with normal results, and he couldn't see what was wrong. The addled woman's sister and sole caretaker, Sandy Ramírez, sat by her bedside and spoke soothingly. She had brought her ill sister into the emergency room after a scheduled appointment at a health clinic had been postponed because the clinic was overfull. "Not to get help at the time you need it, that's hard for me. I could lose my job," said Ramírez, a home health aide who lacked health insurance herself and said she just tried not to get sick.

"Look, do you have any monitor beds?" Díaz asked into the telephone, with increasing impatience. "She's pretty stable. But she has purpura and her voice has changed dramatically." He hung up in frustration and prepared to try another hospital. "It's getting more like this over the years," he said with a sigh.

In the darkness outside, beyond the glow of the emergency room's lights, the steel border fence could just be made out past the dumpsters in the back parking lot at the edge of hospital property. Border Patrol agents cruised quietly by in their white and green SUVs, circling Holy Cross Hospital on their nightly rounds.

While border hospitals scramble to deal with the need for acute medical care, public health officials on both sides of the line have focused on infectious and chronic diseases. The region is growing fast, and people are continually crossing back and forth, carrying microbes with them, so the health secretaries of the two countries signed off on the United States–Mexico Border Health Commission in 2000. The binational agency has brought together health care providers to monitor tuberculosis, ameliorate asthma, and educate residents about AIDS and cancer prevention. They've held joint trainings and set up early-warning systems to prepare for potential cross-border epidemics and other public health emergencies, whether from an earthquake or a bio-terrorist attack. Every autumn, Bi-National Health Week provides medical screenings and health education to hundreds of thousands of Mexican immigrants in the United States, many of whom lack insurance and regular health care.

In the U.S.-Mexico border region, where hundreds of thousands of people have attachments in both countries, contagious diseases such as swine flu have ample opportunity to spread in both directions. Germs don't know borders.

Health care providers in the San Diego–Tijuana region have been especially concerned about AIDS transmission. Recent epidemiological studies by University of California researchers discovered high rates of HIV infection in the border area. A 2006 study, conducted by UC San Diego's Division of International Health and Cross-Cultural Medicine, estimated that Tijuana's HIV infection rate could be three times the national average in Mexico.[13] And a 2002 investigation by the Universitywide AIDS Research Program found alarmingly high infection rates among young men who had sex with men in both San Diego and Tijuana.[14] Many of the men surveyed in the 2002 research reported having sex with women as well as men, and few of them said they practiced safe sex. In Tijuana, intravenous drug use was also rife among survey participants.

Though she emphasized that the study focused on a very high-risk group, eighteen- to twenty-nine-year-old men recruited from gay cruising areas, Dr. Maria Luisa Zúñiga, a UC San Diego epidemiologist who follows border AIDS issues, said the findings—a 19 percent infection rate in Tijuana and 35 percent in San Diego—were worrisome. "There's a high percent of the men in the study who reported having partners on both sides of the border," she said. "Just because someone says they're a resident in one place doesn't mean that they don't have a life, including a sexual life, on the other side too."

The reasons behind the high rates of infection at the border are a complex combination that includes a lack of education about how HIV is transmitted, a widespread resistance to condoms, and a persistent stigma attached to homosexuality and AIDS among U.S. Latinos and Mexicans. "I see a lot of married men coming in for services that have sex with other men," said Rosana Scolari, director of Casa, an AIDS service center in San Ysidro, on the California side of the border. "They have a stable family and have not told their wives, but they're living this other life that is very risky.

"I grew up in this culture and I know how strict it is," added Scolari, who was raised in San Ysidro and went to school in Tijuana. "Culturally, sex is something you don't talk about. Having sex with other men is something of course you don't talk about. And then being HIV-positive is something you really don't talk about. So there are three levels of denial."

Tijuana's long-standing reputation as a party town attracts Americans, including legions of San Diego college students, to its bars and nightclubs and flourishing red-light district, where as many as nine thousand women and an unknown number of men work in the sex trade.[15] The city also draws migrants from elsewhere in Mexico, many of them intent on crossing into the United States to work. When they can't make it over, they

Figure 11. Juan Manuel Sánchez, a volunteer for an AIDS-prevention group, distributes condoms to transsexual prostitutes in the nightclub district of Tijuana, where tourists frequently cruise for sex. Photo by Julie Plasencia/San Francisco Chronicle.

find themselves in an unfamiliar city without jobs or family ties, and some turn to prostitution to earn some money. Mexicans and Americans who pass through Tijuana and San Diego can end up carrying the virus further into the United States and Mexico.

"We're right here on the border, but HIV doesn't know borders," said Juan Manuel Sánchez, a gay Tijuana man who distributed condoms and AIDS information in gay bars and discotheques, focusing especially on the transsexual prostitutes who he knew faced the greatest danger of contracting the disease. "A lot of young people and gays come down here [from California] to cruise. The people who are at greatest risk are those who come from farther south in Mexico. They're less accustomed to condoms, but they're at greater risk in Tijuana because we have a higher infection rate."

In response to the crisis, UC San Diego and other institutions, including USAID, have launched a variety of prevention and training programs, designed to reach out to high-risk groups on both sides of the border and to improve the capacity of Mexican public health officials to improve AIDS research, prevention, and treatment. Mexican doctors say the need is still great. "We get support from the government, but the resources don't stretch to cover all the patients," said Dr. Jorge Alvelais, director of the AIDS clinic at Tijuana General Hospital. "Here we have a little more access to treatment than in other parts of Mexico, but we need more beds, more medicines, more trained staff. With this epidemic, the resources are never sufficient."

In addition to cross-border public health efforts, hospitals and insurance companies have been experimenting with a variety of binational approaches to covering patients at the border in recent years. In San Diego, which lacks a public hospital to take indigent patients, a private company founded by an employee of the Scripps hospital chain has begun transferring uninsured Mexican patients in San Diego hospitals to a private Tijuana hospital once they are in stable condition. The company, called Nextcare, had contracts with five U.S. hospitals in 2003 to provide treatment on their dime at its Tijuana facility, Hospital Inglés, for patients who consented to be transferred. The hospitals pay a fraction of what it would cost them to care for the patients themselves. But some U.S. physicians have questioned whether the quality of care is equivalent at the seventeen-bed Tijuana hospital, which is more like a skilled nursing facility, though it lacks full-scale rehabilitation services.[16]

Two U.S. health insurance companies, Blue Shield of California and Health Net, have begun offering low-cost insurance in California to workers willing to receive their medical care in Mexico, where services typically cost less than half what they would stateside. The cross-border health maintenance plans primarily enroll Mexican citizens working legally for U.S. employers in places like California's Imperial Valley. The fact that the premiums and co-payments are much lower than in American plans has made health insurance available for the first time to some workers. And for some, receiving care in Spanish in Mexico is more comfortable and familiar. Under California law, the Mexican facilities providing care must be audited by the American HMOs they serve for sanitary conditions and staff training levels.[17]

The Mexican government, meanwhile, working with the California Endowment, a publicly funded health care philanthropy, has begun developing plans for a health insurance arrangement to ensure that Mexicans working in the United States, regardless of their immigration status, have health insurance coverage. "We can build a new model for attention to the health needs of Mexican workers here," said José Angel Córdova Villalobos, Mexico's health secretary under President Felipe Calderón. On a

2007 visit to California, Córdova said he hoped to craft a basic health insurance policy that would be jointly funded by the worker, his or her U.S. employer, and the Mexican government, as an extension of Seguro Popular. Mexico would eventually offer migrants a system of universal health care that the Calderón administration hoped to develop, he said.

Hugo Llanos, the migrant farmworker from Oaxaca who fell off the train in Arizona, had no such insurance plan, so the costs of his care were picked up by the hospital in Phoenix and then the Hospital General in Nogales, Sonora. His brother-in-law Erasto Juárez paced the small ward in the Hospital General where Llanos lay. "Sometimes I ask him my name and he tells me. Sometimes he doesn't even recognize me. He's talking a lot about the job in California and his friends there," said Juárez, a bricklayer. He and Clementina had been beside themselves with worry; he had telephoned her back in Mexico City as soon as he had arrived at the hospital the day before. "She was very upset," he said. "I felt so bad to see him. I feel so bad to think that my wife will see him in this condition."

Finding Llanos so damaged from his foray into the United States caused Juárez to reconsider his own priorities. He himself had crossed the border a year earlier and worked for a while, earning money for his wife and two small children. But he had missed them terribly and returned home after half a year. Now he was even less inclined to take the risk.

"I might never go back to the United States after seeing this," he said, regarding Llanos's bruised face and bandaged hands. "We have no papers, so we have to walk across the border. It's very dangerous. I walked for two or three days through the mountains outside Tijuana. I don't want to go back. It's not worth it."

For the present, he had a new challenge. Though Llanos had more relatives back in Oaxaca, Juárez and his wife had decided they should take him home to Mexico City, where they could find better medical care than in the family's rural village in the south. Above all, Juárez didn't want to leave his brother-in-law here at the border, among strangers. The identification paper over the patient's bed even misspelled his name—Hugo Llamas, it said—exacerbating Juárez's fear that he was unknown here and would not be treated properly.

Juárez waited for Contreras to return to Llanos's bedside, then planted himself firmly in front of the tall, confident doctor and stated his case. "What I need to do is transport him to Mexico City because I don't live here," said Juárez. "It's very difficult. I need to get home and work and take care of my family."

"Fine," retorted Contreras, looking down at his patient. "If you've got the money, hire yourself an ambulance." Juárez, of course, didn't have money like that, so Llanos had to stay put. It would be a couple of months before he recovered enough to make the journey by bus. The hospital had no public ambulance available to take a patient 1,200 miles to Mexico City, much less a medical helicopter.

Efforts to bridge the health care needs of the border region have drawn on the creativity and goodwill of medical providers in both countries, but the disparity of resources between Mexico and the United States has remained glaring. Despite the help from neighboring hospitals to the north, financial strain was still evident everywhere at the Hospital General. One patient's jury-rigged oxygen helmet, a cumbersome plastic box, was held together with gaffer's tape. "We make do," said Contreras, glancing at the repair job with a wry chuckle. "We've got a term we use when we fix things that way: we say it's *mexicanizada*."

FIVE

Sells

"O'odham first and American or Mexican second"

DRIVING THE RED CLAY ROADS of the Tohono O'odham Indian Reservation, Harriet Toro passed an adobe house with a fence of dried ocotillo stalks and jounced over a cattle guard set into a wire fence that marked the border with Mexico. Toro was heading south from the tribal headquarters in the town of Sells, Arizona, to pay a visit to an O'odham man just over the border in northern Sonora.

This place—which today is the borderlands—was home to the Tohono O'odham, or Desert People, long before the international boundary was scrawled across it in 1853. Over thousands of years, O'odham hunted deer, harvested cactus fruit, and raised corn and beans on this unforgiving high desert we know as northern Sonora and southern Arizona. It was the same land then as it is now, but it was understood as one place, not two separate countries.

For generations after Mexico ceded this swath of southern Arizona to the United States, the tribe, once known as the Papago, was little disturbed by international politics or even by very many non-Indians. But that has changed, and perhaps never as dramatically as in the past decade. The border used to be marked by a few strands of barbed wire. But the federal government is building a waist-high concrete and steel barrier intended to prevent smugglers' vehicles from cutting through. Here the border is not only an international dividing line; it has come to divide a people.

The Tohono O'odham Nation has wound up on the front line of the battle over drug and immigrant smuggling. And that has cost the tribe scarce resources, impeded its members' ability to move freely across their ancestral land, and threatened the tribe's very identity. Tribal members have been caught in the cross-fire of shoot-outs between drug smugglers and federal agents. Some have gotten lured into the drug trade themselves. They have stumbled on the decaying corpses of dead migrants. And they have often encountered difficulties crossing the international line for family visits, ceremonial pilgrimages, or trips to the doctor.

The cattle guard, known as the San Miguel Gate, sits on a wide plain dotted with mesquite, creosote bush, and prickly pear cactus. Off to the east rises the jagged ridge of the Baboquivari Mountains (Waw Kiwulik, in the O'odham language, in which *w* is pronounced like a Spanish *b* or *v*, and *l* like a Spanish *r*). To the southwest, a smaller range breaks the horizon. As Toro drove across the cattle guard, a Border Patrol agent in a white and green SUV sat sentry on the north side of the fence. To the south, two men crouched in the bushes, scouting for their chance to dart across the border. A pickup truck emerged from Mexico in a cloud of dust, received a wave from the agent, and continued north.

"When you live down here they get to know your vehicle," said Toro, fifty-eight, a resident of Chukut Kuk, this border-hugging district of the nation, who worked for the tribal government. Though the gate is not an official U.S. port of entry, it is one of three long-used Indian crossing points still honored by federal authorities. Tribal identity cards entitle enrolled members of the Tohono O'odham Nation to pass back and forth between the United States and Mexico informally. Indians in the Mexican state of Sonora seek treatment at the tribal health center in Sells. Residents on the Arizona side visit relatives and go to cemeteries and other sacred sites in Mexico. And a few Mexican O'odham children wait each morning at the San Miguel Gate for the nation's school bus to take them twenty-five miles north to school in Sells, the reservation's hub. But the border has become a harder boundary than ever.

After ten minutes' cautious driving over the bumpy dirt road, Toro pulled up at Harry Noriega's compound—three small houses surrounding an outdoor kitchen under an open-walled sunshade (known in Spanish as a *ramada*, in O'odham as a *watto*) outfitted with chairs, tables, an unplugged refrigerator, and a bedstead. Noriega, a wiry sixty-nine-year-old, had just climbed into his pickup, intending to buy some ice at the nearest settlement, six miles north in Arizona. But he stepped back down and ushered Toro and her friend and traveling companion Rosemary López, deputy director of the tribe's department of human services, to seats under the shade of the *ramada*. The three chatted softly in a mixture of English and O'odham, a breathy, sibilant speech, punctuated by *k* and *t* sounds. Around them, cicadas chirred in the mesquite trees and the heat climbed toward 110 degrees this late June day.

"I've spent half of my time on this side and half on the other side," Noriega said, a quick smile lighting his leathery face. "I was born right where the road crosses over the border. All that's there now is a hump of dirt."

Noriega had returned to his family's place in Sonora after decades as an itinerant farmworker, picking crops around Tucson, Phoenix, and Yuma and as far away as California's Salinas Valley. He had lived fourteen years in Sells with his wife, Irene, but alcohol was getting the better of him there, he said, and he made the decision to move home. The structures on the home place included a wattle-and-daub house Noriega had built half a century earlier, a tin-roofed shack, and a contemporary stucco home. During the heat of summer, though, he preferred living under the *ramada*, as his ancestors had, cooking on a mesquite-fired stove and sleeping beneath the stars.

"I'm glad I came back. I would've been dead if I had stayed [in Sells]," said Noriega. But he added: "There aren't too many people around here anymore. Most of them passed away or they're moving to the other side. They like the other side better because they've got running water and electricity. Some are working, some are drawing welfare, but they get help there. On this side, they don't give you nothing."

Noriega offered his guests a drink of water from a galvanized bucket with a lid and a ladle. He didn't mind chopping wood and pumping water. But he depended on frequent trips to "the other side," to visit his wife on weekends, to see the doctor at the health center, to haul barrels of water when his well went dry, or to fetch a bag of ice to refrigerate his groceries.

Those trips were no longer as simple as they used to be. As border controls had toughened in urban areas of the United States, illegal immigration and drug smuggling had shifted to this remote land, and the U.S. Border Patrol responded with more enforcement here to try to stem the flow of marijuana and human beings. The Tohono O'odham Police Department had to devote more than a third of its time to border-related problems—from drug busts to death investigations.[1] Tribal police sergeant Vincent García appreciated the help of the Border Patrol and accepted their presence. But he knew many O'odham people disliked the Border Patrol because newly arrived agents would often follow their cars, stop them, ask for their papers, and shine flashlights in their eyes, treating them as if they were criminal suspects. "Citizens get upset. They feel they're being harassed by the agents," said García. "The agents are just being law enforcement in a place with two different countries. But people don't see it that way. They see themselves as O'odham first and American or Mexican second."

If not for his tribal identity card, Noriega would have been in a bind. "Us O'odham, we're lucky they're letting us register over there," he said, referring to the United States. "If the O'odham over there hadn't helped us, we wouldn't be able to cross." Many O'odham people, though, especially those born at home who lacked a birth certificate, have had difficulty proving their nationality and their tribal identity. Noriega's own mother had been born in Tucson, but she lacked papers confirming her U.S. citizenship because the record of her baptism had been destroyed in a fire at a Catholic church there, he said.

Even with the ID card, it wasn't always so easy to enter the United States, Noriega had found. "One day my wife and I came across and a policeman stopped us and told us, 'Next time, go through Sasabe,'" he recalled, referring to the nearest town with a port of entry. That's a 140-mile journey, most of it over rough dirt roads—a long way for a bag of ice.

Toro, a mother of six and grandmother of nine, with straight salt-and-pepper hair falling to her waist, visited the border often in her work for the tribal government and on the Chukut Kuk district council. She had been raised by her Mexican-born maternal grandparents, learning to speak O'odham first, then some Spanish, and English only after she started school. Much of her childhood had been spent off the reservation in a cotton camp south of Tucson, where her grandparents worked in the fields. Toro had gone off to the Phoenix Indian School, a government boarding school, as a teenager. López was sent all the way to Santa Fe, New Mexico. "At boarding school, we'd find kids to talk to in O'odham," said Toro. "That was fun. But they'd punish us for it." Though her Spanish was rusty, Toro felt an affinity with those, like Noriega, whose lives straddled the line, as her own family did.

The O'odham terrain once stretched from Hermosillo, more than 150 miles south of where the border is now, all the way north to the Gila River in Arizona and from Tucson west to the Colorado River. Today the reservation is a 2.8 million acre chunk of Arizona the size of Connecticut, set aside in increments between 1911 and 1940, as the Papago pushed the U.S. government for the legal right to their aboriginal lands. But the irrigable river valleys and land with mineral deposits remained in private or federal hands.[2] Almost half the tribe's 28,000 enrolled members live on the reservation. Roughly 1,800 O'odham in Mexico are enrolled members of the tribe, while another 3,000 have applied for tribal recognition.[3] Because Mexico does not offer special status or governmental autonomy to its indigenous people, in 1979 the Papago tribal council (as it was called then) agreed to enroll Mexican Papago in the Arizona tribe to share the benefits of tribal membership with all O'odham people.[4] In light of escalating border tensions and land disputes in Mexico, the tribe stepped up its efforts in recent years to extend membership to O'odham living south of the border.

Toro and López were checking in with Noriega after a recent summit Toro had organized at Noriega's compound for Mexican O'odham to meet with the tribal leadership. "We have to have our meetings in O'odham, English, and Spanish," said Toro. "It takes forever." Indeed, O'odham community decisions have traditionally been made slowly, through a deliberative process. In generations past all the men of a village would gather each evening at the council house, and they wouldn't take action until the older men all reached agreement.[5] At the meeting at Noriega's, López had gotten approval to conduct a health assessment among the O'odham in Mexico, and tribal chairwoman Vivian Juan-Saunders had listened to the problems her people faced south of the border.

The most urgent concern on the Mexican side has been encroachment of non-Indians on traditional O'odham land. In 1928, the Mexican government set aside a modest *ejido* of 7,600 acres around the village of Pozo Verde for the Papago.[6] But there are nine identifiable Tohono O'odham communities still in Mexico, and scant recognition of ancestral land rights. At one point, decades back, Mexican surveyors came through while most of the Papago were off in the mountains at their winter camps, according to Gary Nabhan, a naturalist and writer who taught at an O'odham school in the late 1970s. Finding the Indian settlements empty, they declared the land abandoned and deeded it to new owners.[7]

In recent years some Sonoran ranchers, perhaps more familiar than the rural O'odham with land tenure laws, have been trying to get title to lands near Noriega's place through the Mexican legal system. The Indians have found themselves handicapped because they haven't always had documents proving their ownership. "O'odham have lived here for ages. Why would we have title to the land? It's ours," said Toro. "We used to have an O'odham office in Mexico and we're trying to revive it. We're trying to recover some traditional O'odham land."

Curious about her own roots in the area, Toro asked Noriega about a nearby house she remembered from childhood, where her grandfather's sister used to live. "It's collapsing," he told her. But early memories, family stories, and ancestral history remain layered on the landscape. Pointing south, Toro said, "The places where we would traditionally pick our saguaro fruit are on the other side of that mountain there, *Shoigak.*"

The fruit of the saguaro cactus ripens in late June or early July. O'odham women and children traditionally decamped to a cactus grove for a few weeks to harvest the juicy red fruits. They would knock them from the tops of the tall cacti using a *qwipat*, a long-handled tool fashioned of dried saguaro ribs, and cook them down to a syrup that they could carry home in jars. Every family contributed some syrup to a communal pot that would be fermented into wine for a village wine feast or *n'awai't*. The event, called a "sit and drink," marked the O'odham New Year and included songs, poems, and dances, as well as ritual drinking, to summon the rain clouds.[8]

"Most families maintain separate territories for picking cactus. These territories are not fixed, like ranches and fields—they are not fenced—but they are meant to be respected. In the midst of a family's territory is a simple camp; an open-walled sunshade (ramada or watto), a fireplace, and little more. These, however, are somebody's place just as surely as a house is," explained anthropologist Ruth Underhill.[9]

When the saguaro fruits ripened, López said, she hoped to find time to go gathering with her family. "I'd like to go out, but we have to check our schedules," she said. "Now we live on schedules." The O'odham consider the saguaro plant, with its bent-elbowed arms, to be human, magically transformed by "elder brother," the god-like I'itoi, into a rooted plant. "A boy was fighting with his brother and I'itoi heard him and told him the O'odham don't fight with their siblings," López repeated the legend. "The boy wouldn't stop. He ran toward I'itoi. And I'itoi made him into a cactus." Another O'odham woman told Nabhan, the naturalist, that the stately plants must be treated with reverence: "The saguaros, they are Indians too. You don't *ever* throw *anything* at them. . . . You don't do anything to hurt them. They are Indians."[10]

The saguaro wine feast was one of several rituals that marked important events in the yearly cycle of the seasons, including an autumn deer hunt and an annual pilgrimage O'odham men used to make to the Sea of Cortez to gather salt. When the summer rains came, monsoonlike, the O'odham would plant corn, beans, and squash. They collected rainwater in *charcos,* or excavated ponds, and irrigated their fields with the water. After Jesuit missionaries introduced livestock in the eighteenth century, the ponds also provided a water source for cattle and horses. When the *charcos* dried up in the autumn, the O'odham moved from their villages on the plains up into the mountains, where springs served as a water source and hunting, along with their dried corn and tepary beans, provided the food supply. "Every family had a regular winter home near some spring and generally the people of a whole village moved together, so each village was really in two places," wrote Underhill in a 1941 report for the U.S. Bureau of Indian Affairs.[11]

Hunting and farming were supplemented by foraging for wild foods, including amaranth greens, cholla buds, wild onions, prickly pear fruits, mesquite pods, piñon nuts, and acorns. In that way the O'odham eked out a living from this dry and unforgiving land. Subsistence required a lot of territory to feed a modest number of people.[12] The seasonal wild harvests also provided a chance to socialize and work at a different pace, as some O'odham recounted to Nabhan. " 'Oh, that was such a good time,' Maggie laughed, recalling the acorn harvest up in the mountains near *Ali Wak.* 'I guess it was like our vacation, getting away from our houses to go where it is cool. We went up to *Waik Wiyo:di* and all us ladies would just sit and talk and gather those *wiyo:di* all day long. It wasn't even like work.' "[13]

During the 1920s and 1930s, the federal government dug deep wells and installed pumps on the Papago Reservation, allowing the tribe access to a steady supply of water from the underlying aquifer.[14] It eased the hardship of life for the Tohono O'odham, but it began to transform age-old seasonal subsistence patterns. The tribe's name also translates as "thirst-enduring people," and O'odham parents long admonished their children to "drink only a little water."[15] The wells provided a permanent water source for homes in the alluvial valleys, reducing the people's dependence on the rain for agriculture and thus diminishing the importance of the wine feast. It also ended the need for a winter migration to mountain spring settlements. Toro had never lived in a winter village, though her mother had. "My mom used to be the messenger between our summer village and our winter camp. She'd ride her horse back and forth when she was just a little girl," said Toro. "I still have an aunt, she's eighty-four, who's one of the last people that live up there. Too many rattlesnakes up there for me."

Over the twentieth century the Tohono O'odham gave up farming their own flood-watered fields, and many worked for wages on irrigated lands, especially in the cotton farms that boomed in southern Arizona beginning with World War II. According to Nabhan, the O'odham grew roughly ten thousand acres of crops with traditional runoff farming in 1913; that number fell to one thousand acres on the reservation by 1960, and by 1982 O'odham farmed fewer than one hundred acres using floodwater irrigation.[16]

Today a handful of O'odham people are trying to revive the farming of traditional crops, like the drought-resistant tepary beans, not only for their environmental soundness but for their nutritional benefits and their cultural importance. Terrol Dew Johnson and Tristan Reader, co-directors of a nonprofit organization called Tohono O'odham Community Action, have reported that the beans and other traditional O'odham foods help regulate blood sugar and can stem diabetes. Their group has launched a community farming project on the reservation, along with a basket-weaving festival and a project that links children with tribal elders who can teach them O'odham songs, stories, and cultural traditions. It's all part of an effort to revive O'odham *himdag*, or the desert people's way.[17]

There's an urgency to the quest. Today adult-onset diabetes afflicts more than half of the O'odham, and obesity and gall bladder disease are rampant. The increase in processed foods, some of them introduced by the U.S. government in the form of surplus agricultural commodity handouts, and the decline in physical activity over the last few generations are partly to blame.[18] In 1941 Underhill wrote, "In olden days no woman went out without her carrying net [a cone-shaped burden basket]. She ran at a jog-trot and she declared that the load on her back pushed her on. Old women now say it is hard to walk without the load, but the young women laughingly call the cars which their husbands buy their 'carrying nets.'"[19]

Nabhan noted in 1982 that the diabetes problem was not a consequence of the Papago gorging themselves. "Diet studies in the villages have indicated that the average O'odham today consumes about the same number of calories, and the same amounts of carbohydrates and fat, as the average U.S. citizen. The real problem may just be that the Papago *do* eat like the average European-American. Their metabolism may be adapted to an altogether different diet."[20] Native foods, both wild and cultivated, were rich in complex carbohydrates, protein, fiber, and a wide range of vitamins and minerals, but their availability fluctuated tremendously through the course of the seasons, he found. "Because some of these wild foods do not lend themselves to long-term storage, the Desert People take advantage of them while available. They have relied on their own bodies to store this energy," Nabhan wrote. The O'odham metabolism, so well adapted for seasonal variety, may not handle a year-round uniform diet too well.[21] Researchers with the National Institutes of Health believe they've identified a "thrifty gene" that evolved over generations in people like the O'odham, to store fat during times of famine.[22]

Even after the U.S.-Mexico border was laid down, the O'odham used to range across the land without regard for international boundaries, moving between their summer "field villages" and winter "well villages," traveling to family saguaro camps, taking hunting expeditions, and—before the tradition faded out at the end of the nineteenth century, when salt became commercially available—making an annual pilgrimage to the Gulf of California to collect sea salt. For O'odham in the United States, that journey entailed crossing into Mexico.

The salt pilgrimage, like many O'odham rituals, was a transformative journey—as much a spiritual rite of passage as it was a functional errand. A group of young men, with an experienced leader, would walk or ride for days, nearly fasting, until they reached the shore. "A man must suffer in equal measure to his desire," the leader would explain. At the gulf they would not only gather salt but run the length of the beach and immerse themselves in the ocean, absorbing its power. On their return, just as they did on returning from a hunt or a battle with Apaches, the men would live apart from the community for several days, integrating the experience and taming its magic before it was considered safe for them to return to their wives and families.[23] In many cultures, "the feeling is that when a man has done a brave act he should be given praise and gifts," wrote Underhill. "Very few people take the attitude of the Papago, that the hero should be humble and should, in fact, be afraid of his power until he has tested himself and is sure he can use it well."[24]

The arrival of Catholicism added new rituals, including the celebration of saints' days, which necessitated their own journeys to holy places. And these travels also often took O'odham people on routes that, after 1853, required crossing the international border.

Spanish colonial rule reached the area in the late seventeenth century as Jesuit priests moved north through New Spain, converting Indians and establishing mission outposts. The first of the missionaries to arrive in the Papaguería, as the Spaniards called the Papago territory, was the German-trained Tyrolean priest Eusebio Kino in 1687. Kino and other missionaries brought new foods and animals, metal knives, plows, and wagons with wheels, but also a new belief system that the O'odham adopted alongside their traditional religion. The Jesuits established missions all the way up to Tucson, and they were followed by Spanish military garrisons and ranchers who took possession of land granted them by the Spanish crown. Franciscan missionaries succeeded the Jesuits in the 1760s, replacing the first modest missions with their own more opulent churches.[25]

Centuries of Spanish, and later Mexican, presence meant that the O'odham adopted the Spanish language and many Hispanic customs and traded with Mexico. Many O'odham intermarried with the settling Spaniards and, later, with *mestizo* Mexicans. In many ways, their lifestyle came to resemble—and in turn to shape—northern Mexican peasant culture. After the Southern Pacific Railroad was completed in the 1880s, Tucson became connected to the national U.S. market, and the Papago and others in the region began to purchase goods manufactured in the United States. The new U.S. orientation came at the cost of long-time Sonoran suppliers and trade routes that had tied Arizona to Mexico.[26] But the O'odham sense of connection to Mexico continued. "As late as 1900 there were still enclaves of Papago miles north of the border who thought of themselves as Mexican," Nabhan wrote.[27] To this day, Spanish names persist among the U.S. O'odham, and the Mexican ranching diet based on wheat, beef, and cheese, including the *tortilla grande de harina,* a huge flour tortilla, translucent with lard, is prevalent across the region.[28]

Catholic missionaries summoned the O'odham to settle in the missions and adopt European ways. But many of those who heeded the call sickened with contagious diseases and died in the missions. After Mexican independence in 1821 missionary work among the Indians dwindled. But the religion had taken hold, and the O'odham continued to travel to churches in Mexico during the winter to have their children baptized and to study Christian doctrine.[29] Returning to their villages, they built small adobe chapels, and devout women who had memorized the rosary and perhaps some scripture would recite for congregations of their relatives.[30] Thus the O'odham became "strikingly self-reliant Catholics,"[31] practicing a distinctly Indian-inflected worship known as Sonoran Catholicism.

These days the O'odham celebrate feasts for San Juan and other saints, often at little chapels on the reservation or in remote Mexican *rancherias.* By far the most important Catholic ritual for the O'odham is the annual pilgrimage to celebrate the October 4 feast of St. Francis in the Sonoran town of Magdalena de Kino. The holiday, celebrated there for two centuries, honors St. Francis of Assisi, the patron saint of the Franciscan order. For the O'odham the statue of St. Francis in the church in Magdalena also represents St. Francis Xavier, who was introduced to them by the Jesuits. And the ritual celebrates the revered Father Kino, whose remains are buried in Magdalena. The O'odham go to ask St. Francis for help, to give him thanks, and to let him recharge the religious objects they have brought from home. But they also partake in the secular market and fair on the plaza, eating and drinking, shopping and dancing through the night.[32]

In her work for the tribal government, Toro hired extra staff and began making arrangements with U.S. and Mexican officials two months before the feast day to smooth the way for the O'odham to join the pilgrimage to Magdalena. "Hundreds of our people are going down," said Toro. "Many will go through that gate and walk to Magdalena. We'll have staff to help with paperwork. Those who go by car have to go through Nogales. We work with the Mexican government to find places where people can camp around Magdalena."

As they ended their mid-afternoon visit with Noriega, Toro and López asked him for directions to a little church nearby. Worried the women would lose their way, Noriega led them there instead, driving slowly over the meandering dirt tracks that criss-crossed the desert hardpan. Then he sped north to run his errand in Arizona. The whitewashed chapel of Our Lady of Mt. Carmel was tucked in a clearing in the scrubby brush. Agave plants and a great brass bell flanked the wooden door. "There used to be mass here all the time, but not any more," said Toro. Residents were getting scarcer on this hot, dry plain between the Mexican towns of Sasabe and Sonoyta. But the church door was always left unlocked, and local people kept the quiet stucco sanctuary clean with a corn-straw broom propped in the corner. The door opened to the east in the tradition of Sonoran Catholicism. The altar was decorated with tissue paper flowers, magenta streamers, and an arc of plastic roses over a statue of the Virgin Mary. Three wooden benches served as pews.

Outside the church, a concrete slab set in the ground functioned as a dance floor for the all-night dances to Chicken Scratch music (*waila* in O'odham), the Indian take on borderland polkas and cumbias, which often accompanies O'odham religious rituals. "The best time is when the sun is coming up," said López, with a grin. "It's beautiful, and the music sounds even better."

"The last time we were here, you could tell a lot of IAs had been here from the little things they left on the altar," Toro said, using the tribe's

Figure 12. Harry Noriega pauses inside a small Catholic chapel near his home on the ancestral land of the Tohono O'odham in northern Sonora. Photo by Chris Stewart/San Francisco Chronicle.

shorthand term for illegal aliens, as she closed the chapel door quietly. Many migrants stop to pray before starting the perilous hike through unknown terrain into the United States and across the reservation.

Small numbers of Mexican migrants seeking work in the United States have trekked across the reservation for generations, and the O'odham people have a history of offering aid and hospitality to passing travelers. But in recent years members of the tribe have grown weary of the increasingly large groups of migrants and the more aggressive tactics of the *coyotes.* One band recently stopped at Toro's home. "They wanted food and we were eating, so we gave them a couple of plates," she said. "We thought they'd be on their way, but they grabbed a bag of clothes on the way out. They want to dress like Americans to blend in, so they stole my grandson's clothes right under our noses."

Gloria Chávez, who lives down the road from Toro, about five miles from the border, was alarmed to find her home invaded by a pair of illegal immigrants one night. "It was just me and my son, who's nine. We had gone to Tucson, and when we came back I was so tired I put away the groceries and fell asleep on the sofa," she said. "All of a sudden I heard something and woke up. I saw a man walking in the hallway. He came around and stood here in my living room and bent over me lying on the couch. I reached up and yelled. He fell back and then he ran out the door.

"His body odor stayed in my nostrils a long time," she added, shuddering.

Chávez, who drove the O'odham school bus and picked up the Mexican pupils at the border, found that the intruders had broken a window and entered through a back bedroom. She put bars on her windows and got a couple of dogs to guard the place. But she still encountered migrants camped by the *charco* where she watered her cattle. And she feared her pickup truck could be stolen someday while she was out making her rounds in the school bus. It was not a pleasant way to live.

In the morning, before Toro visited Harry Noriega, she had led Sgt. García through a mesquite grove behind her house to show him a pair of immigrant encampments she had discovered there. First they saw trash: empty tuna cans and Gatorade bottles, discarded toothbrushes and deodorant, abandoned blue jeans, brassieres, and backpacks. The travelers had collected some of their debris into plastic trash bags, but more was scattered across the ground. Then Toro pointed out a pair of low shelters built of branches, just big enough for a clutch of migrants to hide from Border Patrol helicopters. "It's funny," said Toro. "They look kind of like our traditional homes."

García, a burly forty-two-year-old in his seventeenth year on the tribal police force, said he had begun spending more and more time coping with illegal incursions in 2003. "Sometimes I'll stop a group of illegals and I'll call the Border Patrol, but they'll say they won't have anyone available until the next shift in six hours," he said. "So I'll let the people go and tell them which way to Phoenix. I try to estimate the kilometers for them." Dead and dying immigrants had become a common sight, especially during the brutally hot summer months, when desert temperatures could reach 120 degrees. "Yesterday we picked up a dead illegal alien," said García, shaking his head. "He was probably seventy-five yards from a residence."

The Tohono O'odham Reservation fronts the border for seventy-five miles, less than 5 percent of the entire U.S.-Mexico frontier. But a third to a half of all migrants who died trying to cross were found in the stretch of Arizona that includes the reservation, according to the Border Patrol. In 1995, the Mexican Interior Ministry recorded sixty-one deaths of unauthorized immigrants at the border. A decade later, the agency's tally was

Figure 13. Harriet Toro and Sgt. Vincent García hold open a gap in a fence for Gloria Chávez as she takes them to the *charco* behind her house on the Tohono O'odham Indian Reservation near San Miguel, Arizona. Photo by Chris Stewart/San Francisco Chronicle.

eight times as high, at 516 fatalities. The cumulative death toll from the start of Operation Gatekeeper through March of 2007 reached 4,235, based on the Mexican count. A 2009 report by the American Civil Liberties Union and Mexico's National Commission of Human Rights, put the number of bodies recovered at up to 5,607 over fifteen years, well over the number of American fatalities in the war in Iraq.

The Mexican government records the deaths only of Mexican nationals, not of the Hondurans, Salvadorans, and others who perish on the northward trek. The U.S. Border Patrol tracks migrant deaths regardless of nationality. But the agency doesn't include in its count people whose bodies were found in Mexico, skeletal remains whose cause of death is impossible to determine, or those who die at some distance from the border itself, such as the nineteen migrants who suffocated in 2003 in the back of an unventilated tractor trailer in Victoria, Texas. Consequently, the Border Patrol's numbers are almost always lower than those of the Mexican government. Human rights advocates are convinced that the actual number of people who have died trying to cross the border is higher than the figures kept by either government. The deaths, they say, are preventable, and the fact that the U.S. and Mexican governments allow them to continue, and largely ignore them, is a moral stain on both countries.

One particularly poignant death took place near the Tohono O'odham Nation. On the first day of summer in 2005, a fifteen-year-old Mexican migrant, Jesús Buenrostro Domínguez, sat helpless beside his mother as she died of heat prostration in the Arizona desert, near Baboquivari Peak. When Border Patrol agents found Jesús four days later, wandering in a daze, severely dehydrated, he wanted only to reach his mother's body again. Instead, the boy was deported to Mexico. He contacted his grandfather in Zacatecas and returned to the border town of Nogales, Sonora. Jesús's grandfather, Cesario Domínguez, equipped with a visa, took the bus to Tucson and began to search for his daughter's body. For more than three weeks, aided by humanitarian volunteers, Domínguez traversed the area where Jesús had been rescued, photographing the landscape as he went. At the end of each day, he crossed the border and showed his grandson the pictures until at last the boy recognized familiar landmarks. In that way they narrowed the search and eventually found the bones of Lucrecia Domínguez Luna, identifying her by the three distinctive rings still on the skeletal remains of her hands. Along the way, Cesario and his friend José Lerma, who joined the search, found numerous lost and desperate migrants and the bodies of three other people who had died as Lucrecia did. "Who knows how many others are out there," wondered Lerma.[33]

Like an increasing number of Mexican families, Lucrecia Domínguez Luna had made the trip with her children (Jesús and his seven-year-old sister Nora) to be reunited with her husband, who had spent the previous two years working in Texas. As U.S. border enforcement has become increasingly tough, undocumented migrant workers have become less likely to return to Mexico at the end of each year, opting instead to send for their families and settle more permanently in the United States. Village friends traveling with the Domínguez family did succeed in delivering Nora to her father, but in the process she lost her mother forever.[34] Lucrecia's parents buried her body in their village in Zacatecas.

More than one thousand of the migrant dead have never been identified but were buried in paupers' graves in places like Holtville, California, a parched town in California's Imperial Valley. In those cases, family members have not learned their loved one's fate or had a body to put to rest.

And countless migrants who died crossing the desert have never been found, their remains left to the elements and the vultures.

Writer John Annerino crossed the Sonoran Desert himself several times, with migrants and Border Patrol rescue trackers, to fully understand the danger of the desert and the toll it could take. In his book *Dead in Their Tracks: Crossing America's Desert Borderlands,* he wrote: "Some say one death is too many. Others: 'They're just Mexican.' . . . If a Mexican dies trying to cross the deadliest desert in North America, or eighteen Guatemalans vanish, and no one sees them, did they ever really exist in our national conscience? Mexico's ruling elite may be willing to sacrifice a poverty-stricken populace . . . but how many Mexican lives will it take for American policymakers to take notice that they're still dying to work for us—and that they're dying on American soil?"[35]

At the Mexican consulate in Tucson, Deputy Consul Enrique Muñoz charted the locations of Mexican nationals who have died trying to cross the border. The number of fatalities in his jurisdiction had increased more than twentyfold in the sixteen years he had been on the job. A grim map on the wall behind his desk showed that the deaths were overwhelmingly concentrated on the reservation, where sources of water and assistance were few and far between. At seven o'clock one evening, Muñoz's phone rang. It was Robin Hoover, an immigrant rights activist from a group called Humane Borders. He had been alerted to a small group of migrants newly arrived in Tucson and in need of help, one of them a teenage Mexican girl. "They escaped from a *coyote*," Hoover told the consul. "She doesn't know what to do. I don't have a phone number for them, but a taxi is going to take them to the church." Muñoz told Hoover to call back once he had met the girl and could put her in touch with the consulate directly. "It's like this twenty-four hours a day," he sighed, hanging up. "When I came here we didn't have deaths. We didn't have illegal immigrants crossing the desert."

The deaths of migrants—an average of seventy a year—and the suffering of the many others who are found injured, exhausted, and dehydrated have put a psychic strain on the O'odham.[36] "It takes an emotional toll to see people so hungry and thirsty they can't make it to your front door," said Toro. "Sometimes they'll have infants and children with them. In years past you hardly ever saw that." The stress has been particularly acute for those charged with serving the medical needs of the tribe. The small, outdated tribal hospital in Sells, where López once worked as a nurse and Toro was a candy striper many years ago, is the only source of emergency medical treatment between Tucson, sixty miles to the east, and Yuma, 170 miles west. While Border Patrol medics can stabilize some of the border crossers they find in distress and airlift them to a larger hospital, the most critical patients are treated in Sells. "It's very traumatic for our clinicians, because the patients are practically dead on arrival," said Indian Health Services staffer Robert Price.

In addition, treatment for the growing number of undocumented immigrants has strained the health service's already scanty resources. For several years, the number of undocumented immigrants receiving care there skyrocketed, according to the hospital's clinical director, Dr. Peter Ziegler. "It further erodes the resources that are meant for tribal members," said Price. "The hospital is not adequately staffed and funded to handle the things we see every day." A volunteer emergency physician at the Sells hospital described it vividly in a 2005 essay in the *Los Angeles Times Magazine.* "I must cut short my evaluation of a 73-year-old Tohono O'odham grandmother with abdominal pain in order to care for the UDIs with heat exhaustion and dehydration in the next two beds," wrote Dr. Fred Leonard. "I do not have the antibiotic I want to treat a 3-year-old Tohono O'odham boy with bloody diarrhea. It's not on the hospital formulary because it is too expensive. I request a specialist's evaluation for a Tohono O'odham man with facial paralysis. A month later he still hasn't been seen. Emergencies must be taken care of—and paid for—first, and there are many emergencies involving undocumented immigrants in this small hospital."[37]

The upsurge of drug and immigrant smuggling has affected the already-compromised health of many O'odham people in more subtle ways as well, creating a climate of insecurity. "I really encourage people to exercise for their diabetes," said Ziegler. "But patients will say, 'I used to love to walk in the evening, but now I don't trust going out.'"

Profoundly distressing is the way the drug trade has overtaken the Tohono O'odham's land and people. Week after week, Border Patrol agents have reported discoveries of marijuana—more than a ton at a time, in some cases—stashed in homes and sheds on the reservation or in vehicles abandoned there. One November day in 2007, for example, agents discovered 2,400 pounds of pot, stacked in shrink-wrapped bundles, in the backyard of a home in the O'odham village of Little Tucson. Less than three weeks later, they sniffed out another 2,500 pounds stashed in an abandoned building in the same village.[38]

A federation of Mexican drug cartels based in the state of Sinaloa has made Arizona the principal route to transport marijuana into the United

States. Border agents at U.S. ports of entry have lately seized more than half a million pounds of marijuana a year, but specialists say that because the drug is bulky and has a pungent smell that's hard to conceal, most of it is smuggled across the border in remote regions between ports of entry. In 2007, the Border Patrol reported seizing 1.8 million pounds of pot. Half of that was captured in the agency's Tucson sector, which runs along the Arizona border and includes the reservation. The 900,000 pounds was three times as much as agents had picked up in the sector just five years earlier.[39] Those quantities are estimated to be just a small fraction of the drugs that make it across.

Traffickers recruited unemployed Indians on the American side to run carloads of dope to Tucson, luring them with the promise of money, García said. "These are kids who've never had more than a couple of hundred dollars, so when they get $3,000, they'll do it again," he said. "They get hooked. You see a house that's poor and it has a new car in the driveway, a big-screen TV . . . They know you know. But things get so bad out here."

The Tohono O'odham Nation has augmented its own modest budget with revenue from two casinos it began operating in the 1990s and a third that opened in 2007, but the tribe has continued to struggle. Though the tribal government has preferred not to open its books to the public, an analysis by the *Arizona Daily Star* newspaper estimated that the casinos grossed close to $200 million in 2006. With the proceeds in recent years, the nation has built a special dialysis center, a new health clinic on the western part of the reservation, a nursing home for aging members of the tribe, a cultural center, and five new youth centers, and it has upgraded the offerings of the Tohono O'odham Community College and funded college scholarships. Every couple of years the tribal government has made a distribution of cash, about $2,000, to enrolled members of the tribe from the casino revenue. But poverty is still endemic. Food stamp usage averages 23 percent for the O'odham. Jobs on the reservation are few and far between. The unemployment rate was 18 percent in 2007. In 2000, the tribe's median household income was just under $20,000, less than half the national average, and just two-thirds the median for all tribes combined, according to the U.S. Census Bureau. Fewer than half of all O'odham adults have completed high school, the lowest rate for all U.S. Indian tribes, and the dropout rate at Baboquivari High School was 26 percent in 2006, according to the Arizona Department of Education. In recent years gang activity has taken hold, luring kids away from school and into trouble.[40]

In traditional O'odham society, grandparents took responsibility for much of the guidance and upbringing of their grandchildren because the parents were busy with planting and foraging, hauling water and gathering firewood, making pots, baskets, ropes, clothing, and tools—all the work of living, according to Underhill. Every morning before dawn, or in the evening around the fire, a grandfather would talk quietly to the children and explain their duties and traditions. They must always work, they must never be idle, he would tell them, because it was only by work that people kept alive.[41] But in recent generations those ties to tradition have weakened, and the prospects for O'odham youth in the modern world sometimes seem bleak. Several generations of Indians were shipped off to government-run boarding schools to be educated and "Americanized." The schools cut young people off from not only their culture but their families, and many Indians raised in boarding schools never learned parenting skills because they didn't grow up with their parents, observed López.

The problems of crime and poverty hit home for García when his own brother was arrested trying to move a load of marijuana across the reservation with his wife and kids in the car. The brother spent a year in federal prison and was serving five years on probation. "He wanted the easy money," the sergeant said. García himself could have followed a similar road, he reflected. As a young man he was living in Tucson with his girlfriend and their baby, going to community college, and working odd jobs. But one night he was mugged and woke up in the emergency room. The violence of the attack, and his own vulnerability, spooked García and impelled him to enlist in the army. He spent seven years as a soldier, then joined the Tohono O'odham police force and moved back to the rez. "I think if I had not joined the service, I'd have been killed or I'd be in prison or I'd be home being a bum, like my friends from my village are doing," he said as he patrolled along a dusty border road.

The drug syndicates prey precisely on those down on their luck, on both sides of the border. But the ruthlessness of the drug runners has taken a fearsome toll in the isolated communities of the O'odham Nation. Then-tribal chairman Edward D. Manuel told a congressional committee in 2003 that "smugglers are armed with automatic assault-type weapons, have armor-piercing bullets and have sophisticated communications equipment to detect our law enforcement presence. . . . They recruit our children to transport the drugs, they lure our teenagers to experiment with drugs such as cocaine, heroin, and crystal meth, drugs that never before were found in our communities. When our kids become addicted, we have no services to treat them, no residential care, and no detox beds."[42]

Tribal officials described incursions by men in uniform, apparently Mexican troops or their impersonators, armed with machine guns and protecting loads of drugs crossing the border. Fern Salcido, who was a member of the nation's legislative council and a resident of Menager's Dam in the Gu Vo district, which sits on the border in the western part of the reservation, told the congressional panel about a pair of disturbing incidents that illustrated the way Indian people were on the front lines of the border battle and suggested that Mexican troops were collaborating with drug smugglers.

> At about 7 pm, well after dark, someone knocked at my door. I opened the door and found a man dressed in a Mexican military uniform carrying a machine gun. A Humvee vehicle was parked in my front yard and four other uniformed and heavily armed men stood next to the vehicle. The man at the door asked for a man I did not know. It was obvious to me that the men at the door were looking for a lost drug load. My children were in the house and I was very scared for our safety.
>
> Last summer, federal agents and the Tohono O'odham Police Department surrounded my neighbor's house about 200 yards from my house. As the law enforcement officers moved in on the house, a drug runner tried to escape, driving out of the property at high speed. The man was shot by Customs agents and crashed his vehicle into my shed. Several shots were fired in the direction of my home. Again I was very fearful for the safety of my children, my grandchildren, myself and my community. Unfortunately, incidents like these two occur regularly in our community and they put us all at grave risk.[43]

In 2007, tribal police seized sixty-four thousand pounds of marijuana and made 109 drug-related arrests. Each year the tribe's police department has spent between $2 million and $4 million on such cases, money for which it was not reimbursed by the federal government.[44]

Border crime and alarming, unpredictable violence have interrupted the rhythms of life for tribal members, but reminders of O'odham traditions remain embedded in the landscape, which stretches from Sonora into Arizona. Looking east toward the mountains, Toro recalled the stories her mother and aunt would tell about the family's winter camp near Baboquivari Peak, the sacred mountain that is the mythical home of I'itoi, who led the O'odham people up from inside the earth and gave them the gift of the crimson sunset. In the late afternoon, she drove back into the United

States. A roadrunner scurried in front of the car—a sign, the O'odham say, that you have forgotten something.

Toro had a meeting with the chairwoman back in Sells, but she made a detour to the home of ninety-year-old Jesús Antonio López and his daughter Mariana, whose flour tortillas were known as the best on the reservation. Toro and Rosemary López knocked on the kitchen door of the modest ranch house set among mesquite and creosote bushes just yards from the border. "Any tortillas today?" Toro asked in O'odham. The elder López turned and translated the question into Spanish for his middle-aged daughter. Mariana spoke neither English nor O'odham, having lived most of her life in Hermosillo. She shook her head. "Sorry, they've all been sold," her father told his visitors. But Mariana also had cold drinks for sale, and the women gratefully accepted cans of grape soda and seats in the kitchen, where a ceiling fan provided some respite from the still-hot day. The conversation started flowing, with translations from O'odham to Spanish and back. "Which side of the border are you from?" Rosemary asked the old man, who spoke little English himself. "When I'm on this side I'm from here, and when I'm on the other side, I'm from there," he answered with a wry chuckle. Before long, with country hospitality, Mariana was serving her guests a meal of refried beans, Mexican cheese she had brought back from a visit to Hermosillo, and a plate piled with the last of the day's tortillas, the ones she had set aside for her own family.

On the drive back to Sells, nighthawks swooped past, chasing insects in the waning light, and storm clouds began spitting the first summer rain on the dry land. Dusty and tired from a day on the road, Toro entered Juan-Saunders's office, where baskets woven from strands of yucca and devil's claw depicted I'itoi walking through the maze of life. Toro sat down heavily. The chairwoman, too, looked weary.

The tribe had approved the installation of vehicle barriers along the border on the western part of the reservation, she said, because that's where the drug runners and cattle rustlers from Mexico crossed most often. But she didn't want to wall off the reservation. "We have concerns about the needs of tribal members to go across," she said. "There are sacred sites and cemeteries that people need to have access to. . . . Right now we have no choice: we need the Border Patrol. But we have to balance that with respecting the sovereignty of the nation, our land, our people. It's a sensitive balancing act."

Lightning flared across the dark desert sky outside. "The border is not going to go away. We didn't ask them to place it here, and we were not consulted," said Juan-Saunders. "All we ask for is a seat at the table on policies that affect the border."

A fence, like the fifteen-foot-high steel walls the federal government has erected in some places, could further reduce the incursions that have plagued Tohono O'odham police officers like García. But he wasn't in favor of dividing the land that way either. "As far as my job goes, it would be easier, but I like to think about the environment," he said. "I wouldn't like to keep the wildlife from doing what they do naturally." García learned to hunt when he was a boy, and he liked to take his own children hunting. He wanted to ensure that the deer and rabbits could still move freely across the land.

The reservation was becoming increasingly militarized, however. Drug cartel scouts had encamped on the slopes of mountains, keeping lookout for law enforcement patrols.[45] National Guard and Border Patrol helicopters circled over at night, shining spotlights on formerly quiet Indian villages.

The tribal leadership eventually agreed to allow the U.S. government to install a vehicle barrier along the length of the reservation's border. And in the spring of 2007, the Border Patrol began constructing the barrier of waist-high steel poles, set a couple of feet apart and sunk in concrete. The aim of the barrier was to prevent cars and trucks from crossing but not impede the movement of people, wildlife, and flowing water. But drug smugglers soon learned they could mount metal ramps on the poles to drive their vehicles over. The new obstacle has slowed their traffic but not stopped it.

Meanwhile, some O'odham traditionalists decried the barrier. "We don't agree with this wall," said tribal elder Ofelia Rivas. "It's like a knife in our mother [earth]. These metal things are going to go in our mother and we can't pull them out."[46] The construction of the barrier also unearthed human remains at two Indian burial sites dating to the twelfth century, according to the tribal government. The graves were among eleven archeological sites the tribe identified in the path of the fence. Tribal officials said the remains had been handled respectfully, in accordance with a protocol the tribe and the U.S. government developed, put into safe storage, and later reburied. But some O'odham families were outraged and called the removal of the dead a desecration. "They didn't ask us when they took them away, and they are our people," Julia Acunia told a Reuters reporter through an interpreter.[47]

The Tohono O'odham people are in a bind. After a century of dislocation many tribal members want to reclaim their traditional ways and strengthen their connection to the land. They have struggled, like many

American Indian tribes, with the scourges of poverty, poor nutrition, and a lack of jobs and educational opportunities. But here on the Arizona-Sonora border, the O'odham feel invaded from both sides, by drug cartels and illegal immigrants on the one hand and Border Patrol agents and Homeland Security dictates on the other. The problems of drug and migrant smuggling can't be resolved at the border itself. But until they are resolved, the violence and trauma take a terrible toll here on a people who already know better than most the damage wrought by dividing the land and those who live on it.

Ned Norris Jr., the tribal chairman who succeeded Juan-Saunders, said the new barrier was making it more difficult for smugglers to move their cargo across the Tohono O'odham Nation. "There was a time when 1,500 people were crossing each day onto the nation's land. Now [the Border Patrol] are telling us it's 500 to 800 people a day," he said. "Though that has decreased, it's not without a cost. The cost is the fact that we have a militarized zone because of the increased number of agents. . . . The United States needs to take more of an interest in addressing the economic situation in Mexico to have a long-term effect on this problem. Until we do that, this is what we're going to grow accustomed to living with."[48]

A few months later, Norris traveled to Washington, D.C., and told the U.S. Senate that his nation was facing new troubles. Not only was the Tijuana cartel vying with the Sinaloa cartel for control of the reservation, but because drug runners had been blocked by the vehicle barriers from driving through, they were increasingly recruiting O'odham people as mules to transport their cargo north, off the reservation. "More and more of the Nation's members are getting involved in the illegal operations. . . . Our children are routinely exposed to the drugs, violence and death," he told the senators in a plea for aid. "Should this type of activity occur in any town or city in the United States it would be considered a crisis. The Tohono O'odham Nation is in the midst of this crisis."[49]

SIX

Mexicali
"The wind doesn't need a passport"

A PAIR OF FORTRESSLIKE POWER plants looms on the empty desert plain outside Mexicali, just a few miles south of the U.S. border. On a calm September morning, three men tromped around the perimeter of one of the plants. They peered through the chain-link and barbed-wire fence and took note of a sharp chlorine smell where water from the plant's cooling towers burbled out of a concrete drainage pipe into a discharge canal shaded by tamarisk and bulrushes.

Two of the three—brawny men in cowboy boots—were Imperial County air pollution agents, who had driven by pickup truck from their little office in rural El Centro, California. They had come to survey this newest source of emissions in the heavily polluted inland basin that includes both the Imperial Valley in California and the Mexicali Valley in Baja California. The third man was an earnest, tenacious engineer from San Diego with wire-rimmed glasses and a trim mustache. The engineer, Bill Powers, had become a leader in a fledgling binational movement that has challenged an emerging cross-border energy network producing power in Mexico for U.S. consumers.

Here in the desert borderlands, industry, agriculture, and human populations have burgeoned, but the regulations governing development are written by each country in isolation, though the ecological effects are felt across the airsheds and watersheds shared by both. In response, Mexican and American scientists and environmentalists have undertaken their own grassroots monitoring of the impacts and have been pressuring their governments and industries to be more mindful of human health and environmental impacts.

Powers trained his video camera through the fence onto the sprawling complex of condensers, steam turbines, and fuel tanks. The natural gas-fired plant, built in 2002 by the Massachusetts-based energy company InterGen, exported half of its output to the United States over power lines that hook it to the Imperial Valley Substation. The second plant, just across the road, was owned by Sempra Energy of San Diego. It sold 100 percent of its electricity into the U.S. market.

"To drop plants two or three miles across the border where you get cheaper labor, quicker permitting, and lower standards is a slap in the face to the people who live on the border," said Powers, who had kept a watchful eye on the plants, which he called "energy maquiladoras," since they were first fired up in 2002. "They're getting full advantage of the U.S. market on the cheap."

Powers was spending the day examining energy projects in Mexico and touching base with colleagues on both sides of the border who were part of his network of environmental watchdogs. In the fragile desert of the western borderlands—where the natural environment has borne the brunt of intensive human use, and binational bureaucracy and the profit motive have hindered solutions—a loose network of politically savvy and scientifically knowledgeable Americans and Mexicans has forged cross-border alliances, convinced that the welfare of their region can be safeguarded only if they work together across the international boundary.

The two power stations are building blocks in a new and growing complex that crisscrosses the U.S.-Mexico border and includes a variety of other energy sources due to come on line over the next several years. The network stretches 150 miles west to Ensenada, on Baja California's Pacific Coast, where Sempra has built a massive terminal for importing liquefied natural gas, known as LNG. It reaches north along high-tension wires and gas pipelines into California and Arizona, where most of the energy consumers reside. And it would potentially extend 250 miles south along the Sonoran shore of the ecologically delicate Gulf of California, where another American company is planning its own LNG terminal. Energy executives say the network is essential to meet the growing demand for power created by population pressures in both the American Southwest and northwestern Mexico.

Population growth and economic development increase the consumption of fossil fuels and the emissions from smokestacks. But they have other environmental impacts as well. Water is a scarce commodity here in a desert that receives just a few scanty inches of rain a year. On the U.S. side, thirsty farms and suburban subdivisions suck about 90 percent of the water from the Colorado River. The U.S. releases Mexico's required allotment of water south across the border, but next to nothing is left for the Colorado's once-vast delta or the Gulf of California beyond. On the Mexican side, meanwhile, factories and mushrooming shantytowns discharge raw sewage and industrial sludge into the Tijuana and New Rivers, which both flow northward across the border.

The populations of California, Nevada, and Arizona, the three U.S. states that constitute the so-called "lower basin" of the Colorado River, grew by almost a third between 1990 and 2007, and the population of Sonora and Baja California, which flank the Colorado in Mexico, increased by fully 50 percent between 1990 and 2005.[1] All together more than thirty million people and four million acres of farmland in the United States and Mexico now depend on the Colorado River's water. Meanwhile, the region is in the grip of a persistent drought that began at the turn of the twenty-first century and appears to be worsened by global warming.[2] As the two countries wrangle over water rights and pollution responsibilities, the natural environment lacks a seat at the negotiating table.

Mexico has welcomed investment by foreign energy companies, including Sempra and InterGen, even if they produce primarily for U.S. consumption.[3] There has been little capital in Mexico to invest in energy exploration or the construction of new plants to fuel that country's own growing industries and increasing consumer demand. At the same time, in the United States—which has three times as many people but consumes ten times the oil, thirteen times the natural gas, and twenty-one times the electricity of Mexico[4]—conservation campaigns have been slow to take hold despite rising concerns over global warming.

"There was a need for new capacity somewhere, and because electricity has no borders we built it there," said Michael Niggli, a Sempra executive who was head of the company's electricity division, in an interview at the company's high-rise headquarters in San Diego. "Our power goes into the U.S. and can be sold from there to the southwestern states or back to Mexico."

But for Brad Poiriez, one of the Imperial County air agents, the worsening air quality that resulted from power plant emissions was not only a professional concern but a personal one. "Imperial County has one of the highest asthma rates in the country. My son, he's eleven, he's one of them," said Poiriez, whose family raised vegetables on irrigated farms on both sides of the border. "We oppose the power plants. We wanted them to be held to the same standards as power plants in California. . . . There are no big fans blowing the pollution back into Mexico." Mexicali was already the third most polluted city in Mexico, after Mexico City and Guadalajara, added Poiriez's colleague, Mexican-born Reyes Romero. "But it's not one of the biggest cities," he said. "Tijuana's air is clean by comparison, because it's near the coast."

In the borderlands, air and water move without heed for political boundaries. And the environmental consequences on one side have inevitably affected communities and habitats on the other. Federal agencies in the two countries have attempted to negotiate solutions, but often they've been bound by bureaucracy or hamstrung by diplomatic stalemates. Instead, environmental activists and local officials, including Powers, Poiriez, and Romero and their counterparts in Mexico, have tried to reach across the border and fill the breach.

On the dusty plain west of Mexicali's sprawl, Powers waited alongside Mexico's Highway 2 for a couple of semi-trailers to hurtle past, then darted across the road for a better look at the Sempra power plant. With video camera in hand, he walked the fence line, examining the facility's layout for evidence that the operation could be made less damaging to the environment. Powers believed, for example, that the plants, rather than using scarce water for cooling, could install air cooling systems. Reducing environmental impacts was vital, Powers and the air pollution agents said, because the plants were setting precedents for the region's new energy network, especially if additional power lines and gas pipes would be routed through the area, as energy companies have proposed.

"Our concern is that—with the new line coming through and all the natural gas you could want—this is the breeding ground for more power plants down here," said Poiriez. "We want to make sure we don't have to fight the same battles all over again that we've fought with these two plants."

The cross-border energy connections began more than two decades ago with power lines that linked Baja California, geographically isolated from the rest of Mexico, into the energy grid for California and the southwestern United States. In 2000, when Mexico's electrical utility decided to convert a particularly dirty, oil-fired power plant at Rosarito, south of Tijuana, to cleaner-burning natural gas, Sempra engineered the conversion and built a gas pipeline from San Diego to Rosarito, and later a longer pipe across northern Baja to import natural gas from Arizona. The Bajanorte pipeline in turn made it feasible for Sempra and InterGen to build their gas-fired power plants outside Mexicali in 2002. Then, because the plants were right near the border, it was easy to build a connecting spur to tie them in to the Southwest Power Link, a five-hundred-kilovolt transmission line running from Phoenix to San Diego.

Sempra Energy, the parent company of Southern California Gas and San Diego Gas and Electric, which formed in 1998 when the two utilities merged, has emphasized that its Mexicali plant was built to California standards. The fact that in Mexico the company secured the permits to build the plant in just five months, a fraction of the two-year average wait it would have faced in California, was just a fringe benefit, said Niggli. In addition, he and his colleagues said, by piping natural gas into Baja the company has actually improved air quality over the past decade by allowing dirty industries to shift away from fuel oil.

Nor are the plants the only polluters in the region. Poor, rural, and remote, Imperial County has California's highest rate of hospitalized asthma. Pollution in the Mexicali Valley is worse. Dust kicked up from dirt roads and bare fields in both countries contributes, as do pesticides and agricultural burning. Wind-borne silt blows off the parched Colorado River Delta to the south. When the wind comes from the west, it brings sand from the Yuha Desert. On the Mexican side of the border, soot from brick kilns mixes with acrid smoke from trash incinerators and a smoldering heap of tires. Noxious vapors escape from gasoline pumps. Cars spew exhaust as they idle at the U.S. port of entry, waiting to cross the border. Poiriez and Romero have to contend with all these sources of pollution, many of which are outside their control, as they struggle to bring their county into compliance with federal environmental standards and keep the air breathable for their own children.

In the Imperial and Mexicali valleys, the prevailing winds carry pollution from north to south two-thirds of the year. The rest of the time, they blow it from Mexico to the United States. "They say the wind doesn't need a passport or a visa," said Margarito Quintero, a professor of environmental sciences at the Autonomous University of Baja California in Mexicali. "We share a neighborhood, we share an atmosphere. Without the plants, there would still be a [pollution] problem, but they're adding to the problem. . . . I don't see much benefit for Mexico."

Energy executives insist they are providing benefits for the environment and the economy. The two Mexicali plants exceed Mexican environmental requirements, provide clean power, and meet the demands of the growing energy market in both countries. Getting them to comply with American clean air standards has entailed some heavy political and legal pressure, however.

As the plants were being built, the environmental law firm Earth Justice and the Border Power Plant Working Group, a grassroots group started by Powers and clean energy advocates on both sides of the border, sued the U.S. Department of Energy to force it to require the plants to meet U.S. standards by putting pollution scrubbers on their turbines to reduce smog-producing gases. Under federal rules governing cross-border facilities such as electrical transmission lines, the companies had to obtain U.S presidential permits, whose terms were set by the Energy Department, in order to import their electricity into the United States. Sempra voluntarily installed the scrubbers on its 625-megawatt plant. InterGen, which sold half of its 1,065-megawatt plant's power on either side of the border, promised to install them on the two turbines producing energy for the United States. When Powers discovered that the company had not done so, he complained loudly to regulators and policy makers, and in consequence the U.S. government shut the generating unit down for several months until pollution controls were installed. California senator Dianne Feinstein subsequently persuaded the company to put pollution controls on all four turbines, threatening legislation to ban the importation of all power from the plant if it did not.[5]

InterGen's plant was originally intended to serve only the Mexican market, explained Sarah Webster, a spokeswoman for the company, which started out as a joint venture of Bechtel Corp. and Royal Dutch Shell Group Companies, before it was sold off to a Canadian teachers' pension plan. The company didn't decide to expand the plant to produce power for both markets until the California energy crisis hit in 2001. Operating on the border has presented both benefits and challenges, she said: "There's increased demand for the power you produce. Any time you're dealing with a national boundary, though, it will add a dimension of complexity."

Had the plants been built in California, say their critics, they would also be required to compensate for the more than 1,600 tons of pollution they are estimated to produce each year.[6] The companies could meet that obligation by reducing emissions from other polluters in the region, for example, by paving dirt roads. Mexico, however, has no such requirement that new projects minimize their impact by offsetting other sources of smog and particulate matter.

Imperial County supervisor Joe Maruca said the companies could have improved both pollution and the job picture in his county, one of the poorest in California, by locating there. "I said, 'Come on and build up here. It would be good for our economy,'" said Maruca, a former school superintendent, who said he was particularly pained watching childhood asthma rates climb. "'If you build your plants in Imperial County, I will be your biggest proponent because there would be no pollution.' Everything they emit, they would have to offset."

On top of that, though the companies say they monitor the emissions from their stacks, Mexican law doesn't require them to disclose the information, said Steve Birdsall, Poiriez and Romero's frustrated boss. "We've asked for that data," said Birdsall. "If they were on the U.S. side there would be continuous emissions monitors and we would be getting all that data."

The two south-of-the-border power plants would not be the last components of energy infrastructure to serve north-of-the-border consumers. Sempra had been lobbying for a new power line (dubbed the Sunrise Power Link) that would run from Imperial County to northwestern San Diego County and that could hook up with power lines to the Los Angeles area, facilitating the flow of more electricity generated in the borderlands. The company had also sought to build a second, parallel, pipeline to double the amount of gas it could move across the border. That's because Sempra had built an LNG terminal near Ensenada—the first on the Pacific Coast of North America—to receive and re-gasify LNG shipped from Indonesia. The $875 million terminal was equipped to receive one billion cubic feet of LNG each day, with the capacity to expand to 2.5 billion cubic feet a day. A quarter of the new gas supply was to be sold in Mexico, but the majority would go north to the United States through the same Bajanorte pipeline that had been used to import gas to Baja from American sources.[7]

"The world has a lot of gas, and as [domestic supplies] decline, our next best option is to import gas," said Darcel Hulse, the head of Sempra's LNG division. "Anybody on the West Coast could get access to this gas. This is one of the new sources that will enable all customers on the system to benefit."

Once it is pumped out of the ground from reserves around the world, natural gas is liquefied by being chilled to minus 260 degrees Fahrenheit so it can be transported by tanker. At a destination terminal, it is warmed again and moved through pipelines in its gaseous state. The United States has four natural gas terminals, all built in the 1970s on the East Coast and the Gulf of Mexico. Numerous proposals over the last several years to build facilities on the California coast have foundered on community opposition. More recently, developers have turned their attention to Oregon, but there too, progress has stalled on concerns over environmental impacts and fears of spills, explosions, and even terrorist attacks. In 2004 an explosion at an LNG plant in Algeria killed twenty-seven people and injured fifty-six others.[8]

"With LNG you've got to come to a coastline, and in populous areas where the gas needs are, you don't have coastal areas available to be developed," said Hulse. "We'd love to be able to put one in San Diego Bay or Los Angeles Harbor, but those are much more difficult to permit. Thank goodness for Mexico allowing us to do it."

Business people and energy analysts say economic growth in the United States and Mexico requires more energy production, and natural gas is a cleaner alternative to coal and oil, which Mexico relies on most heavily. "You've got plants there burning fuel oil and dirty, combustible stuff," said Jeremy Martin, energy director at the Institute of the Americas, a San Diego center that promotes private sector involvement in Latin American development. "Their plans are that all the plants are going to be natural gas fired. If you look at the increase over the next ten years, it's phenomenal." Mexico's federal electricity commission already has a contract to purchase a quarter of the fuel Sempra would import through its new terminal, called Energia Costa Azul.[9]

Even some analysts accustomed to thinking first of the environment have taken a practical view of the energy dilemma. "North America is in an energy straitjacket," said Neal Elliott, industrial program director for the American Council for an Energy Efficient Economy, a research institute in Washington, D.C. "We haven't been building up storage capacity, and we may be in a real problem. We're short of coal, we're short of heating oil, we're short of gasoline, and we'll be short of natural gas as well."

California responded to this impending shortage in 2005 with $2 billion in conservation measures, including rebates to customers who installed insulation and energy-efficient appliances. That move was followed by the passage of the California Global Warming Solutions Act of 2006, which aimed to reduce the state's carbon emissions to 1990 levels by 2020, a 25 percent reduction. Policy makers hoped the combination would replace fossil fuels with energy from renewable sources and reduce the need for new energy production overall. "We can either increase the supply or reduce the demand," Elliott said. "Our experience is that it's cheaper, faster, and more beneficial to the economy to go out and reduce the demand."

But energy executives have insisted that conservation can't compensate for rising demand, and Sempra's Hulse said importing natural gas was a hedge against a decline in U.S. domestic reserves. The California Energy Commission has said that the West Coast needs at least one natural gas terminal so that the state does not remain at the very end of the country's natural gas pipeline, according to commission spokeswoman Claudia Chandler.[10]

Despite the avowals of some energy companies that imported LNG would be cheaper than piping North American gas to the West Coast, Powers and other environmentalists say it has become not only more expensive but riskier because of the questionable state of domestic security in source countries like Russia and Indonesia. On top of that, they argue, LNG is more polluting than domestic natural gas because it requires more energy to move to American markets.

To have a look at the construction under way on Sempra's LNG terminal, Powers took his leave from the air pollution agents in Mexicali and drove west. He planned to have lunch with Carla García Zendejas, a Tijuana environmental lawyer and fellow founder of the Border Power Plant Working Group, then head down the coast with her. But halfway to Tijuana, on a rugged plateau studded with pine trees and wind-sculpted boulders, Powers stopped the car and hopped out to look around the outskirts of La Rumorosa, a town named for the constant murmur of the unremitting wind. The video camera captured the desolate landscape and wind-blown trees as Powers made his case. This is where energy companies ought to be focused, he said, collaborating with Mexico on wind farms rather than shipping hydrocarbons halfway across the globe.

Sempra would eventually try doing just that, not as an alternative to its fossil fuel plans, but as an addition—and, once again, not to serve Mexico's needs, but to export across the border. In July 2007, company officials signed a deal to provide Southern California Edison with 250 megawatts of power from a wind farm they planned to build at La Rumorosa that could be expanded to produce 1,000 megawatts.[11] The company also planned another cross-border electrical transmission line to link the wind project to power lines in the United States.[12] Spanish and Mexican firms also began exploring wind energy projects there after the state government of Baja California broke ground on its own small wind farm at La Rumorosa.

Situated in San Diego, Sempra has had an especially close perspective on energy developments in Mexico and has come to consider doing projects across the border a business imperative. "Baja is growing faster than the United States," said Niggli. "That's one of the reasons Sempra has worked in Mexico for decades. We're on the border, so we understand their needs and we have good relations with Mexico."

After weaving through Tijuana traffic, Powers reached García Zendejas's home, a whitewashed condominium built into a coastal hillside south of Tijuana, where tourism is a mainstay of the economy. As García Zendejas made ham sandwiches, she looked out her picture window at the dramatic, rocky forms of the Coronado Islands. The Chevron Corporation had made its own proposal to building a floating LNG terminal in the lee of the largest of the islands. With tanker traffic and lights blazing around the clock, the facility had threatened to obscure the scenic island for Mexicans and tourists alike. But García Zendejas said she had initially preferred that proposal to Sempra's onshore terminal because of safety concerns. Then she visited the islands with a group of environmental scientists. "We said, 'Maybe we could live with it ruining our view.' But then we learned about the richness of the Coronado Islands, the marine life, the migratory birds." The scientists sued under the North American Free Trade Agreement, charging that the terminal would imperil the largest known colony of the endangered Xantus' murrelet, which breeds on the islands. In the end, Chevron abandoned the plan, thwarted in part by the environmentalists' pressure but also by changes in the market: Sempra had made it to the finish line first.

Powers and García Zendejas joined forces in 2001, combining his engineering expertise and her knowledge of the Mexican legal system, along with the energy and savvy of activists and academics from the United States and Mexico. García Zendejas grew up in Tijuana but had attended school in San Diego. She had received her law degree at the Autonomous University of Baja California and had gone on for a master's in international law at American University as a Fulbright scholar. She had first met Powers, a mechanical engineer with a private consulting business, through his wife, Lorena, who was Mexican and also worked in environmental protection. Bilingual and bicultural, Powers and García Zendejas were uniquely positioned to tackle cross-border environmental issues that sometimes stymied the governmental authorities in the two nations, saddled as they were with the intricacies of bureaucracy and international diplomacy.

Hiking out across the chaparral north of Ensenada to get a glimpse of the construction under way, Powers and García Zendejas were aghast. Sempra had chosen the location because it was undeveloped and shielded from

Figure 14. San Diego engineer Bill Powers, Tijuana attorney Carla García Zende-jas, and Ensenada golf resort employee Rodolfo Palma survey the construction of a liquefied natural gas receiving terminal on a formerly pristine stretch of the Baja California coast. Photo by Chris Stewart/San Francisco Chronicle.

the coastal highway. But those features had also helped make the spot an ecological treasure. Now the pair saw a landscape bulldozed in preparation for a gigantic pair of steel and concrete storage tanks. "This was completely untouched," said Powers, turning his gaze from the dump truck–demolished sagebrush to the base of the cliff where a crane loomed over the undulating brown kelp beds. "They've totally destroyed all of it. It's just nuked." Offshore, construction of the concrete jetty, dock, and pipelines had displaced fishermen and surfers. Meanwhile, gray whales had long passed through these waters as they migrated down the Baja coast to their calving grounds. Sempra said it had spent $1 million researching the whales' habits and designing a sonar system to warn them away from the LNG terminal,[13] but environmentalists worried that the migration would be disrupted and the animals' breeding patterns threatened.

As it became clear in succeeding months that the Sempra terminal would be completed in spite of community opposition, García Zendejas turned her attention to yet another LNG proposal, this one slated for the

Figure 15. The first liquefied natural gas terminal on the west coast of North America is constructed by San Diego–based Sempra Energy in Baja California. Photo by Sandy Huffaker Jr.

Sonoran town of Puerto Libertad on the shore of the Gulf of California. The $1 billion project—a joint venture of El Paso Corp. and DKRW, a Houston company run by former Enron executives—would import LNG for both the Mexican market and customers in Arizona, 130 miles north. Mexican president Felipe Calderón had said the project would diversify Mexico's gas suppliers and reduce its dependence on U.S. natural gas. Company officials hoped to have the plant operating by 2011.[14] But García Zendejas and other lawyers and marine biologists working with a small Mexican nongovernmental organization reviewed the company's request for a permit from Mexico's environmental protection agency, SEMARNAT, and raised questions with the agency. "A lot of information was lacking," she said. "It didn't show the ship routes, it didn't include inventories of the marine mammals. . . . It's a very fragile area, and these humongous tankers have to go through the Sea of Cortez. There wasn't a real assessment of 'What is your mitigation for not affecting these whales, these migratory birds, these reptiles?' It's a beautiful, bio-diverse area."

The Mexican environmental agency did issue a permit for the LNG terminal, but—in a sign that Mexican regulators were becoming more responsive to public input—SEMARNAT imposed a series of conditions requiring the company to correct problems in its proposal. Even more surprising, a federal court in late 2007 granted the environmental group, Defensa Ambiental del Noroeste, legal standing to challenge the permit and then threw out a SEMARNAT requirement that the group post an $8 million bond in order to get an injunction to temporarily prevent construction of the LNG terminal, said García Zendejas. "It's a wonderful decision," she said. "Of course the company will appeal, but this is completely unprecedented. It's becoming a legal nightmare for the company." García Zendejas believed that court rulings like that one—she had seen others in Mexico recently—were impelling greater transparency and ethics in government agencies and were partly a consequence of a maturing of civic engagement on the part of Mexican nongovernmental organizations. "They're not just standing in front of the municipal building saying, 'This is wrong.' They've gone much further in professionalism and scientific assessment. There's an evolution in NGOs and activism that's palpable all through Mexico," she said. "This would not have been possible even five years ago."

The same species of birds and fish and marine mammals that could be threatened by an LNG terminal on the Gulf of California have already been stressed for decades by the lack of fresh water flowing down the Colorado River to the sea. The totoaba, a fish that can grow to four hundred pounds, and the vaquita porpoise, the world's smallest cetacean, live only in the Upper Gulf. Both are on the brink of extinction. Mexico created a "biosphere reserve" in the Colorado River Delta and the Upper Gulf of California in 1993 to protect endangered species and their habitat.[15] In hopes of calling attention to the unique ecosystem and the continuing strain it suffers, the United Nations in 2005 designated part of the gulf a World Heritage Site.

Even more stressed than the gulf is the delta of the Colorado River. It was once a verdant oasis the size of Rhode Island that sliced across the desert south of Yuma, Arizona, but 90 percent of it has dried up over the last half century, a consequence of the numerous dams that have diverted the river's water from its natural course.[16]

In his classic book on water in the western United States, *Cadillac Desert,* Marc Reisner compared the Colorado River to the Nile for the way it watered a desert landscape and to the Mississippi for the great volume of

sediment it carried before it was dammed.[17] It is today an intensely engineered and regulated river, physically controlled by more than twenty major dams and hundreds of miles of canals, and legally controlled by a system of rigid protocols, rules, laws, and treaties.[18] For eons before the dams
and the legal compacts, however, the wild Colorado tumbled down from
the Rocky Mountains, chocolate brown with silt, then meandered across
the plains to the sea. "The virgin Colorado was tempestuous, willful,
headstrong," Reisner wrote. "Its flow varied psychotically between a few
thousand cubic feet per second and a couple of hundred thousand, sometimes within a few days. Draining a vast, barren watershed whose rains
usually come in deluges, its sediment volume was phenomenal. If the
river, running high, were diverted through an ocean liner with a cheese-
cloth strainer at one end, it would have filled the ship with mud in an afternoon. The silt would begin to settle about two hundred miles above the
Gulf of California, below the last of the Grand Canyon's rapids, where
the river's gradient finally moderated for good. There was so much silt
that it raised the entire riverbed, foot by foot, year by year, until the Colorado slipped out of its loose confinement of low sandy bluffs and tore off
in some other direction, instantly digging a new course."[19]

In 1922, as the West, especially southern California, was being developed, the seven states that touched the river or its tributaries divvied up the
water on the basis of an estimate by the U.S. Bureau of Reclamation that
the river's average flow was 17.5 million acre-feet a year. Splitting themselves artificially into two basins, the states agreed that the upper basin—
Colorado, Wyoming, Utah, and New Mexico—and the lower basin—
California, Nevada, and Arizona—would each get 7.5 million acre-feet.
Mexico got 1.5 million acre-feet, and the remaining 1 million acre-feet were
secured by the lower basin. The federal government then pushed forward to authorize the construction of Hoover Dam and the All-American
Canal, the first in a long series of dams and diversions. "It did settle things,
temporarily at least, except for one small matter: the average annual flow
of the Colorado River was nowhere near 17.5 million acre-feet," Reisner
wrote.[20]

It subsequently became clear that the federal authorities had measured
the flow in a handful of exceptionally wet years. Tree-ring studies have
shown that the long-term average is actually more like 14.7 million acre-
feet of water a year.[21] And in succeeding decades, the lower Colorado has
undergone tremendous pressures, the combined result of massive population growth and the beginnings of climate change. The American South-

west and northwestern Mexico have been in a serious drought since 2000. The region has undergone severely dry periods in centuries past, but scientists believe the current drought is being extended and exacerbated by global warming.[22] In all of this, human uses of the river's water have taken precedence over natural systems. In the Colorado River Delta, stretching south from the border, the stresses on the ecosystem—and on the Mexican farmers and fishermen who depend on it—have been severe. Among those affected are Cucapá Indians, the River People, who have lived along the Colorado for a thousand years or more and who now must purchase water for drinking and bathing. To fish, the Cucapá now drive an hour to the tidal zone at the delta's mouth because the tributaries along which they live have dried up.[23] But perhaps no humans have yet been affected quite so much as the birds and animals whose habitats have all but disappeared.

The Yuma clapper rail is a secretive creature. The slate brown, cinnamon-breasted wading bird hides deep in the rushes and can make itself "thin as a rail" to dart nimbly through narrow gaps in dense vegetation without rustling the plants. Like other western clapper rails, it is listed as an endangered species because human beings keep destroying its marshland habitat.[24] The rails live among the cattails and bulrushes in the isolated patches of marshland that remain in the Colorado River Delta region, south of the border.

To watch the birds, Mexican ornithologist Osvel Hinojosa Huerta sometimes built a blind and hid in it for hours. More often, he and his colleagues detected rails in the marshes by playing recordings of clapper rail calls and counting the responses from live birds hidden around them. He has estimated that the largest community of rails—perhaps four thousand—live in one slough known as the Ciénega de Santa Clara. He has counted another 172 in the Andrade Mesa Wetlands, a hidden marsh surrounded by sand dunes just south of the border.[25] No more than six hundred birds are believed to live on the U.S. side of the border. The U.S. Fish and Wildlife Service concluded in 2006 that the species was still in danger of extinction. Among the pressures facing the clapper rails in the United States are the increasing salinity of the waters where they live, including the Salton Sea; the encroachment of urban development along the Colorado and Gila Rivers; the loss of marshland due to river diversion, dredging, and damming operations; and an ominous buildup of toxic selenium in the Colorado River and ultimately in the rails' food chain that could poison the birds and harm their ability to reproduce.[26]

Before the Colorado River was dammed and its water diverted to agriculture and urban uses, beginning in 1935, the delta of the river was a vast network of wetlands covering nearly two million acres and emptying out to the Gulf of California. "The whole valley was riparian wetlands going into the sea," said Hinojosa Huerta, who is wetlands conservation program director with the Mexican environmental group Pronatura. "In the lowlands there were channels everywhere, riparian vegetation, cottonwoods and willows. In the backwaters there were big marshes and on higher levels, mesquite bosque mixed with arrow weed." From reading nineteenth-century accounts of the region, Hinojosa Huerta learned about the clouds and clouds of waterfowl, the songbirds, marsh birds, and shorebirds. The delta was home to jaguars and mountain lions, bighorn sheep, deer, bobcats, coyotes, beaver, muskrat, and raccoons, he said, but as the water was diverted and the delta dried up, many of those animals vanished. Among the multitude of fish that once inhabited the Colorado River, six or seven native species no longer survive in the desiccated delta.

About the time that the western states were staking their claims to the Colorado's water, in 1922, American naturalist Aldo Leopold canoed with his brother through the Colorado River Delta. Leopold rapturously described the journey in his essay "Green Lagoons." "When the sun peeped over the Sierra Madre, it slanted across a hundred miles of lovely desolation, a vast flat bowl of wilderness rimmed by jagged peaks. On the map the Delta was bisected by the river, but in fact the river was nowhere and everywhere, for he could not decide which of a hundred green lagoons offered the most pleasant and least speedy path to the Gulf." Leopold described the delta as verdant and opulent, with "a wealth of fish and fowl," and game "of incredible fatness" nourished on grainlike grass seeds, wild squash, and the beans of mesquite trees and other native legumes. "We could not, or at least did not, eat what the quail and deer did, but we shared their evident delight in this milk-and-honey wilderness."[27]

Today the desert encroaches and the once-verdant lagoons have given way to miles of barren, salty flats and irrigated fields growing lettuce, scallions, cotton, and alfalfa. The few patches of marshland to be found in the delta of the Colorado today are accidents, fed by leakage and wastewater from agriculture in California, Arizona, and the Mexicali and San Luis Valleys.

In ordinary years, the United States releases 1.5 million acre-feet of water past Imperial Dam and across the border to Mexico. That's the agreed-upon share, governed by a 1944 binational treaty. It represents a small fraction (10 percent, more or less, depending on the snowfall in the Rocky Mountains in any given year) of the river's natural flow. Mexico diverts all of that water for its own farms—six hundred thousand irrigated acres in the Mexicali Valley—and for the cities of Baja California, piping much of it west to Mexicali, Tijuana, and Ensenada. In wet years, the United States has spilled excess water over the border, and that has nourished the wetlands and helped restore cottonwood and willow groves along the river's main stem. But the persistent drought means the river no longer flows to the sea.

"All the remnant wetlands on the Mexican side of the delta are supported by leftovers, refused water deliveries, and leakages from the All-American Canal and the Mexican canal system," said Karl Flessa, a professor at University of Arizona and a colleague of Hinojosa Huerta's who studies changes in the delta ecology by focusing on the fossil record of clam shells at the mouth of the river. "Whenever you're increasing the efficiency of water delivery systems, you're harming wetlands. It's a terrible paradox: nobody wants to waste water, but the water that goes to these habitats is not wasted."

The largest of the accidental marshes is the Ciénega de Santa Clara, a forty-thousand-acre wetland sixty miles south of Yuma on the Sonoran side of the river. The *ciénega* is fed by 110,000 acre-feet of salty agricultural waste water dumped each year down a canal from the Wellton-Mohawk Irrigation District in Arizona.[28] Because of the high mineral content of the soil in the Colorado's watershed, when water used for irrigation percolates down through the soil and back into the aquifer, it picks up large quantities of salts, as well as chemical residue from pesticides and fertilizers. The Wellton-Mohawk water was too saline to use on the fields anymore or (if fed back into the main stem) to count toward Mexico's ration of river water. As a temporary fix, in 1977, the two governments agreed to shunt the wastewater down a side channel toward the Gulf of California. As it turned out, the water wasn't too contaminated to recreate a marsh that has since become a teeming refuge for hundreds of species, including the endangered clapper rails, and a major stopover for migratory waterfowl and shorebirds along the Pacific Flyway. The resurgence of the *ciénega* was the first proof naturalists found that with a modest amount of water, even of poor quality, the parched delta could come back to life.

Arizona water managers had intended to reclaim that water by building an expensive desalination plant at Yuma and pumping the water through it to clean it up enough so that it could be returned to the main stem of the river and counted as part of Mexico's annual allotment. That would free up additional river water for other Arizona uses. But if it were to happen, the *ciénega* would be deprived of its nourishment, receiving instead, a trickle of toxic brine—the desalination plant's residue—that scientists believe would "eliminate most present life."[29] Environmental scientists on both sides of the border put pressure on their governments. And Mexico eventually designated the *ciénega* and most of the Mexican stretch of the Colorado River a federal biosphere reserve. After visiting the *ciénega,* at the encouragement of U.S. environmental activists, Arizona's water officials agreed to find ways to protect the marsh. With a test run of the desalting plant planned for 2010, U.S. officials were helping enviornmental groups locate some replacement water for the *ciénega*. The slough still has no legal right to the water, but the political climate appears to favor it, and environmentalists hope to codify that sentiment in a binational accord guaranteeing a minimum of water to the *ciénega*.[30]

Naturalists have identified various other returning pockets of wetland. The marshes—six hundred acres here, a thousand acres there—where agricultural drainage supports cattails or tamarisk that in turn form habitat for birds and other creatures, were catalogued in a 2005 report by the Sonoran Institute. Occasional floods in the 1980s and 1990s along the river's main corridor allowed native cottonwood and willow trees to reestablish themselves, the beginnings of a vital environment for songbirds such as the endangered Southwest willow flycatcher. A series of manmade ponds outside Mexico's Cerro Prieto Geothermal Plant that receive brackish water used in generating electricity have become an unexpected home for tens of thousands of critically endangered desert pupfish. Another conservation priority, the Río Hardy, a Mexican tributary of the Colorado that subsists on irrigation runoff from the Mexicali Valley. That river recently got help when environmental organizations persuaded the state of Baja California to reserve 30 percent of the water from a new Mexicali sewage treatment plant for the river, rather than selling all the water back to farmers. That extra supply should increase the flow in the Hardy by 50 percent, said Hinojosa Huerta.

Another surprising environmental success was the discovery in 2002 of the Andrade Mesa Wetlands. This pocket of 9,700 acres of ponds, marshes, and mesquite groves was tucked out of sight among the sand dunes west of Mexicali and fed by seepage running under the border from the All-American Canal, an earthen irrigation canal that had carried Colorado River water to the Imperial Valley since 1942. The seepage nourished the Mexicali Valley aquifer, providing water not only for the wetlands but for farmers and residents in this sere stretch of Mexico's borderlands. Hidden by the surrounding desert, the wetlands became a safe haven, especially for the shy clapper rails, and a rest area for migrating birds passing between the *ciénega* and the Salton Sea further north.

But no sooner was this unlikely habitat discovered than it came under threat—with potentially serious consequences for the creatures that depend on it. "These riparian systems are the stepping stones of migration, so if you get rid of them the birds don't have a place to stop and rest and refuel, and they die," said Hinojosa Huerta, who holds a PhD from the University of Arizona. "Most of the mortality is during stopovers in migration, especially when they migrate through the desert regions."

Just as Powers and García Zendejas and other clean energy advocates on both sides of the border have teamed up to challenge transnational power companies and lax government regulators, so environmental scientists and activists in Mexico and the United States have joined forces to study the delta's ecosystem and lobby for its preservation. Hinojosa Huerta and his Mexican colleagues have worked closely with Karl Flessa and other American scientists and conservationists. The fact that patches of the delta have sprung back to life has spurred on their activism. "This place was thought to be completely dead in terms of ecological value, and we found that's not the case," said Hinojosa Huerta, who has documented 368 species of birds in the delta. "The ecosystem is very resilient, and a little bit of water does miracles, even not very good water."

But users of the Colorado's water may not get serious about protecting the environment until they feel it in their pocketbooks, Flessa believes. He has proposed putting a monetary value on the benefits provided by a healthy river—including natural flood control, natural wastewater treatment, and nursery areas for fish and other marine life—as a way to wake people up to the advantages for humans of a well-functioning ecosystem. Society is losing $2.4 billion a year because the Colorado River no longer flows out to the Gulf of California and vital ecological functions are lost, Flessa said in a 2005 presentation he titled "$200 per Acre-Foot: Nature's Services and the Natural Value of Water in the Colorado Delta and Estuary." "The price we pay for Colorado River water should include the cost of lost ecosystem services," he said. "Included in the price of water should be mitigation costs for the environmental consequences of diverting water." He has proposed that those mitigation fees be used to restore the delta.[31]

The demand for water in the region has only increased as the population grows. Meanwhile the water appears to be diminishing, most likely because of global warming. As a result, water managers in the United States and Mexico have been looking for ways to tighten up their systems, whether desalinating wastewater, recapturing spills, or stopping leaks. All those endeavors promise to divert water away from the delta's natural systems. And the first big change is already underway.

In the spring of 2009 water managers in the United States completed work on a new concrete-lined replacement for the All-American Canal. The $300 million project supplanted the original earthen ditch for twenty-three of the canal's eighty-two miles and was expected to recoup sixty-seven thousand acre-feet of water each year, enough for half a million people. Most of the water was to go to the San Diego County Water Authority, with 17 percent reserved to settle water disputes with American Indian tribes in San Diego County. The lined canal would fix "a leak in the hose that delivers California water to California," according to Daniel Hentschke, an attorney for the San Diego Water Authority.

The seven U.S. states that rely on the Colorado River considered the project key to a 2003 agreement that would reduce California's historical overuse of the river's water. In accordance with a 1928 act, California is entitled to 4.4 million acre-feet from the Colorado,[32] but for years it has sucked more than its share from the river. Lining the canal would help the state live within its means and perhaps even help protect the fragile Northern California delta of the Sacramento and San Joaquin Rivers, which is also tapped for Southern California water users, said Hentschke.

But Mexican farmers and some U.S. environmentalists charged that lining the canal would unfairly deprive the Mexicali Valley of the seepage it has depended on for more than six decades, and they filed suit in U.S. federal court. In the spring of 2007, however, the Ninth Circuit Court of Appeals in San Francisco ruled that the new canal could be built "without delay." The court added that the plaintiffs' concerns were made moot by a little-noticed provision in an omnibus tax bill passed in the final hours of the 2006 congressional session.[33] The late-night rider, pushed by several western senators, specified that, "notwithstanding any other provision of law[,] . . . [the government] shall, without delay, carry out the All-American Canal Lining Project." California senator Dianne Feinstein, one of the key legislators in passing the bill, defended the move, saying that "in a time of increasing population and decreasing water supplies as a result of global warming, I believe it is critical to save every drop of water—and this saved . . . water that would otherwise be lost to groundwater seepage."

Figure 16. Until the All-American Canal in California was
lined with concrete, Nazario Ortiz and other farmers in the
Mexicali Valley relied on the water seeping out of the canal
and into Mexico for irrigation and drinking water. Photo by
Sandy Huffaker Jr.

Across the border, peasant farmers were stricken. "It's a catastrophe,"
said Nazario Ortiz, whose farming village depended on the leakage, not
only for irrigation but for drinking water. "The court's drastic decision is
taking away the means to support our children." If people like Ortiz were
pushed out of farming by a lack of water, some observers worried, there

might not be much to keep them or their children from crossing the border as illegal immigrants in search of a viable living. To them, the effort to block the lining of the canal was not just about preserving a habitat for birds; it was an effort to protect the economic vitality of the Mexicali Valley. Indeed, the state of the economy south of the border would have consequences for California, said Los Angeles lawyer Malissa McKeith, who was a lead attorney for the plaintiffs.

"If you could stabilize the border, it could be one example of how our investing in Mexico could stabilize Mexican immigration," she said. "[Also] the people of Mexicali spend about $1 billion a year in Imperial County. So destabilizing Mexicali's prosperity, the demise of that place, has a direct effect [north of the border]." McKeith said she feared that without the diluting effect of good-quality water seeping in from the All-American Canal, the Mexicali aquifer would become so saline that farming would soon become impossible on the Mexican side. "At this point, I don't see Mexicali there in fifty years," she said. "The farms will dry up, the air quality will become unbelievable. It's already hotter than hell. I can't see it having a sustainable economy."

Meanwhile some of the border conservationists who have made headway on habitat protection through persuasion and delicate negotiation were frustrated that the lawsuit not only failed to protect the Andrade Mesa Wetlands but led to legislation blocking environmental review of the cross-border impacts of other U.S. actions related to Colorado River water.[34] McKeith acknowledged that she had ruffled some feathers. But she was unapologetic. "I've been looking at how can you put your fingers in the spokes a little just to make people think a little more," she said. "The environmentalists fear that if you fight the big fight, you can lose. . . . I'd rather have a good fight once in a while and try to make a difference."

In diplomatic relations between the U.S. and Mexican governments, however, the politics of water is just one of a long string of issues on which Mexico has hoped to exert its limited leverage on its behemoth neighbor. But reaching an immigration accord, jointly tackling the border drug war, and facilitating trade are always higher priorities for Mexican officials. The cause of protecting the shared environment and sheltering endangered birds and fish has often fallen off the agenda. Reaching mutually beneficial solutions to delicate environmental issues, however, requires a high level of diplomacy, asserted Mexico's ambassador to the United States, Arturo Sarukhan.

"At stake is the ability of both countries to show they know how to play chess instead of marbles, to reach holistic solutions," said Sarukhan. "How does San Diego save water? It's not just about that. The lack of water seep-age will displace small and medium farmers on the Mexican side of the border, and without a means of livelihood those people are going to cross the border. What's going to happen when that lack of seepage affects the delta? Both governments understand this [the lining of the All-American Canal] is a done deal. But there's a huge impact that a lack of water can have on a very bio-diverse region on the border."

As Hinojosa Huerta watched and waited for those impacts to start tak-ing effect, he worried about the loss of the Andrade Mesa Wetlands. "How long will it take? I don't know," he said. "The surface water will suffer first. . . . With no seepage the lagoons will dry up. The vegetation will re-cede. The cattails will go first. Hopefully some of the mesquite trees with deeper roots will be able to subsist." He rued the outcome of the litigation and poor diplomacy but tried to remain upbeat about the prospects for protecting the steady supply of water for the Ciénega de Santa Clara and winning a bit more for the main corridor of the river, the struggling, scat-tered marshes, and the Gulf of California itself.

"It seems the Arizona Department of Water Resources is not really look-ing to take the water and make the *ciénega* disappear," Hinojosa Huerta said. "Of course they have the pressure of finding more water . . . but there's a very good relationship now between the environmental groups, the U.S. Bureau of Reclamation, and Arizona. There's a willingness to preserve a minimum of water for the *ciénega* while still finding water for Arizona." Then turning sober, he added, "What we know for sure is that there is not going to be more accidental water getting into the delta. Even the seepage and drainage is not secure. What we need to work on is to legally guarantee all these allocations of water for the environment. That's the only way we're going to be able to guarantee the long-term preserva-tion of the delta." To that end, his group, Pronatura, was purchasing water rights in the Mexicali Valley from landowners who had decided to give up farming, creating a "water trust" in order to maintain a minimum flow in the main stem of the river.

Without the commitment of the two nations to work together and con-sider the border region's environment as a single ecosystem, though, the scientists, lawyers, farmers, and environmentalists will continue waging an uphill battle. "The whole Colorado system and the delta especially, we'd be treating it very, very differently were the whole thing in the United States," reflected Flessa. "Look how much money goes into restoring San Francisco Bay, the Everglades, Chesapeake Bay. We as a society recognize the value of restoring those habitats. But because [the delta is] on the other side of the border, we don't feel the same obligations. . . . The whole area has been transformed into agriculture and cities, and every little bit of habitat matters at this point."

The borderlands along the Colorado River Delta form a single watershed and a single airshed too. They are a habitat not only for birds and fish but also for people. The community has become more bifurcated in recent years, though, by Homeland Security concerns and a sense of economic competition. So while transnational energy companies plotted their next projects, governments jockeyed for position, and regulators deliberated, local environmentalists continued reaching out to their allies across the border. They were looking for opportunities—even little ones—to protect children's lungs from asthma or safeguard patches of reeds where a marsh bird could lay her eggs.

"It is David and Goliath, but that's a role I don't mind playing," said Bill Powers, the engineer, as he crossed the border from Baja back to San Diego, heading home to tuck into bed his two young daughters, children of both Mexico and the United States. "This region deserves as much consideration as any other region. We'd like to put up a little fight and ensure that if they come, that Mexico isn't being used for a race to the bottom."

SEVEN

Jacumba
"The border is a sham"

BRITT CRAIG BACKED HIS OLD brown van gingerly off the dirt road and parked under a piñon tree in the dry, rocky hills of eastern San Diego County. As he waited for night to fall, he made camp in this clearing on a ridge, a scant quarter mile from the Mexican border. He opened the van's rear door, and his two portly black cats, Janie and Homegirl, hopped out to explore the lay of the land.

Craig, fifty-six, a decorated Vietnam veteran, had driven 2,500 miles from St. Augustine, Florida, to join a little band of Minuteman volunteers patrolling the border for illegal immigrants here outside Jacumba, California. It was the third time he had made the journey in six months, nursing the 1986 Ford Econoline van across the miles. He had lost one cat along the way, brother to the remaining pair, but the drive had given him plenty of time to reflect on his life and the sense of purpose he had gained from joining the Minutemen.

"The increase in the level of illegal immigration has gotten exponential in the last couple of years," said Craig, who was drawn to the first, highly publicized Minuteman muster in Arizona in April 2005 by a call for citizens to do the job the government was neglecting: protect the homeland from illegal incursions. "We have heightened the awareness of the fact that the border is a sham. It's dysfunctional. A border is like your skin. There's

Figure 17. Vietnam veteran Britt Craig keeps a vigil beside the U.S. border fence in eastern San Diego County and awaits nightfall, when he and his fellow Minutemen will scout for illegal immigrants. Photo by Sandy Huffaker Jr.

got to be a place where you stop and something else begins. A nation can't exist without a border for long."

Just down the hill from Craig's campsite, the ten-foot-tall border fence of welded steel landing mats gave way to a five-foot-tall section, low enough to look across at the hilly Mexican hamlet of Jacume. At this low point in the fence, families with members living on either side have customarily met for informal cross-border exchanges. This day a daughter drove up on the Mexican side to receive a package of prescription medicine from her father across the corrugated barrier. They chatted for a few minutes, then exchanged a kiss before driving off. Later—it was Mexican Independence Day—a small but jolly binational party of Mexicans and Mexican Americans assembled to share a supper of *carne asada* over the fence and reenact the *grito,* or rallying cry, that commemorated the start of Mexico's battle for liberation from Spain. But Craig was not involved in, or even aware of, the celebration. For him, the border was not meant to be a meeting place; it was a protective boundary for his country. And it was failing.

Craig had been living on a sailboat moored at the St. Augustine marina, which was cheaper than renting an apartment. He was getting by as a sidewalk musician, strumming the guitar and singing his bluesy, country ballads ("folk music for the talk radio set," he called it), when he first learned about the civilian border patrols, more than likely on the Internet. "I'm not sure exactly how I tumbled to it," he said, his voice rolling with the soft cadences of his native Georgia. "I wasn't actively looking for something."

A rangy, muscular man with a ruddy complexion and a shock of blond hair under his broad-brimmed canvas hat, Craig wore a black patch over his left eye, a constant reminder of the war's enduring scars. The other Minutemen called him "the pirate."

Craig shook some dry cat food into a cast-iron skillet and set it on the ground with a dish of water. Then he extracted an ammunition cartridge from the van and clicked a ten-round magazine into the 9-millimeter Beretta 92 semiautomatic pistol concealed in his waistband under a Libertarian party T-shirt. A bumper sticker on the van's front fender read, "Blaming guns for Columbine is like blaming spoons for Rosie O'Donnell being fat!"

"Now I'm here to seal the border," said Craig. "But when I first went to the Arizona showdown, I looked at it as more of a Second Amendment thing. They said, 'Arm yourselves. Call yourselves Minutemen.' I came out because it was a citizens' militia, which I believe in. Militia got a bad name, but it's a good process. They don't like you to say militia, but that's what it is. We are vigilantes."

Craig's two-way radio crackled to life. "Kingfish, this is Jefe. Come in." It was Jim Chase, the commander of this bare-bones endeavor he called the California Minutemen, reporting the positions of his other scouts. The evening's operation had begun with a strategy session at a makeshift sandbag bunker smack up against the steel-plate border fence behind the Jacumba library. The eight men and one woman led by Chase, himself a former marine wounded in Vietnam, strapped on binoculars and sidearms and fanned out to monitor a series of smuggling trails. Craig took the central posting on the hill to act as the group's communication hub because his was the only cell phone that would get a signal. Anyone who spotted migrants or drug smugglers was to radio him, and he would phone the Border Patrol. The stationary assignment suited him, he said, because he didn't want to leave the cats alone in the van for long stretches.

It was out of admiration for Chase that Craig had returned for this September border vigil. An energetic, gray-haired man with a Santa Claus belly and Teva sandals, Chase had emerged as a minor leader in the April 2005 Minuteman event. But he soon split off from that effort, in part because he favored carrying rifles and shotguns at the border, while the leaders, Chris Simcox and Jim Gilchrist, were adamant that volunteers stick with pistols so as not to project too militaristic an image in the press. "He's fearless, but he's stepping on some toes," said Craig, who also supported long guns. "He's a highly moral person who loves his country."

The weapons were not only for protection against smugglers, Chase asserted, but to resist intimidation by anti-Minuteman protesters, who had flocked to the border actions in the early weeks and months. "I don't like anybody to be out there if he doesn't have a gun," said Chase when, a little later, he stopped by Craig's camp to touch base. "The Che Guevara communists and the Aztlanders told me we're in a war." Then he backed off the aggressive rhetoric. "All we are is supporters of immigration law. Our enemy, if we have an enemy, is the Bush administration that's not enforcing the law."

Chase, fifty-eight, a retired postal worker from Oceanside, had gained a reputation as a hothead, using his Web site to encourage volunteers to come to the border with baseball bats, machetes, and stun guns.[1] He got into public spats with not only Simcox and Gilchrist but another would-be leader, Andy Ramirez, who tried unsuccessfully to start his own border operation in California, dubbed Friends of the Border Patrol. Ramirez renounced weapons altogether and raised a fuss to the press when he said Chase had suggested bringing "snipers" to the border, a charge Chase disputed.[2]

Chase liked to talk. And like many in the movement, he began conversations by focusing not on garden-variety illegal immigration but on the threat of criminals crossing the border and his desire to uphold the rule of law. "My main reason is: Al Qaeda, drug smugglers, felons," he said, squatting by Craig under the piñon tree. "We're trying to show the people of the United States that you can shut an area down." As he talked, though, Chase's tone shifted to one of frustration and discomfort with the social changes connected to immigration. "The press puts it out as 'Poor Juan and Maria coming across the border because they just want a job.' Yeah, there's Juan and Maria, but there's also a lot of scum who come across. You know, charity begins at home, and there's only so much pie to go around. These people don't assimilate. I know one guy up here, he's been in the country for twenty-five years and he doesn't speak any English." Chase's small crew of volunteers was outmatched by the smugglers, he went on, but at least it was taking a stand. "I feel like we are kind of peeing against the wind, but we have to do something."

The border militia movement arose at a time when the U.S. government was already putting unprecedented resources into border enforcement. The Border Patrol's budget in 2005 was triple that of a decade earlier. The federal buildup was initially spurred by a vehement reaction against illegal immigration in Southern California during the recession of the early 1990s, a political response that became central to the gubernatorial campaign of Pete Wilson and culminated in the passage in 1994 of Proposition 187—a measure that would have cut off education and health services to illegal immigrants had it not been struck down in the courts.

The resulting Border Patrol strategy, known as "prevention through deterrence," escalated a quasi-militarization of the border during the Clinton administration. It began with Operation Blockade (later renamed Operation Hold the Line) in El Paso in 1993, followed by Operation Gatekeeper in San Diego in 1994. An increased force of Border Patrol agents, combined with more fencing, lights, cameras, motion detectors, and night vision scopes, succeeded in choking off illegal crossings in those urban areas. In the process, it shifted unauthorized immigration to more remote stretches of the border, notably into Arizona.

Just as the highly visible crossings of undocumented immigrants into San Diego in the early 1990s became a rallying point for Wilson's campaign, so the arrival of migrants in southeastern Arizona in the early years of the next decade became a focal point for the emergence of the militias there. At the same time, cultural tensions and economic insecurity in other parts of the country where the unauthorized population was growing created a climate receptive to the message of the Minutemen.

The outrage about uncontrolled immigration expressed by the Minutemen and crystallized by elected officials such as Rep. Tom Tancredo of Colorado built political will for tougher measures at the border and beyond. Though a punitive House bill pushed by Rep. James Sensenbrenner of Wisconsin in 2005 did not pass the U.S. Senate, it set the terms of the immigration debate, and the following year Congress passed and the president signed a bill for seven hundred miles of fencing along the border. The Bush administration subsequently ratcheted up the pace of workplace raids and deportations, the so-called "interior enforcement" of immigration law, which had been ignored for years.

Spending on border enforcement continued to grow, and from 1992 to 2009 the Border Patrol's force had more than quadrupled, to almost nineteen thousand agents, and its annual budget had grown more than sevenfold to $3.5 billion.[3] Fencing of some kind had been built along more than six hundred miles of border.[4] By 2009, it had cost $2.4 billion.[5] The nonpartisan Congressional Research Service put the eventual tab as high as $49 billion, counting not just construction but maintenance over the expected twenty-five-year life span of the fence.[6] Even that price tag did not include the cost of land acquisition or the lawsuits that were likely to arise, however.

In response to the political call to seal the border, U.S. Customs and Border Protection also developed plans for a "virtual fence" of infrared cameras, ground sensors, radar, airborne drones, and other monitoring technology. The agency initially estimated that that entire project, dubbed the Secure Border Initiative Network, would cost $2.5 billion. In late 2006, the Department of Homeland Security's inspector general told Congress that the cost could actually reach $30 billion.[7] And the U.S. Government Accountability Office (GAO) repeatedly chastised the department for lacking a specific plan that spelled out costs, time frame, and measurable outcomes. The GAO said the program was at "considerable risk" of wasting taxpayer money.[8] The government contracted with the Boeing Corp. to develop an initial twenty-eight miles of virtual fence in a heavily trafficked stretch of the border around Sasabe, Arizona. By the end of 2008, Boeing had been paid almost $1 billion for the project.[9] But members of Congress complained that Boeing's rollout was not only months behind schedule but riddled with technical problems.[10] Nevertheless, President Obama's Homeland Security secretary, Janet Napolitano, reiterated support for the virtual fence at a border security conference in El Paso in the summer of 2009.[11]

Though the government's border enforcement strategy has continued to escalate, there has been debate among scholars and political leaders as to whether it has been effective. The number of arrests of would-be immigrants trying to enter the United States from Mexico, a very rough gauge of the number of crossings, has fluctuated over the years but dropped dramatically in 2008 and 2009.[12] But whether the decrease has been due to tougher border enforcement or increased interior enforcement (with word of immigration raids traveling back to Mexico and Central America and deterring people from migrating), or whether it has been primarily a consequence of the slowing U.S. economy is a matter for controversy.

Whatever the case, the growing issue of illegal immigration in the early 2000s spawned the Minutemen. The story of the movement is a jumbled tale of unlikely characters who were driven as much by their own fractured psyches as by a larger mission. They nevertheless struck a raw nerve with Americans concerned by illegal immigration and succeeded in influencing the debate. The Minuteman movement was the brainchild of Gilchrist and Simcox. Gilchrist, a retired Orange County accountant and also a Vietnam veteran, contacted Simcox after hearing him speak on the radio about how he was rounding up undocumented immigrants along the border in southeastern Arizona.[13] Together they devised the Minuteman Project and captured public attention with rhetoric and imagery evoking the small bands of rugged American patriots who took up arms to fight for nationhood during the Revolutionary War.

Simcox had been tracking illegal border crossers for a few years already, with a "committee of vigilantes" he first dubbed the Tombstone Militia in 2002 and later called Civil Homeland Defense.[14] He and a handful of armed compatriots would stake out commonly used routes at night, catch a group of migrants in the beams of their flashlights, then close in and detain them until the Border Patrol arrived, according to Bill Dore, a Douglas man who participated. Simcox, a former Los Angeles schoolteacher, had landed in the Arizona desert after a post-9/11 breakdown cost him his job, his marriage, and his relationship with his adolescent son. He went to Tombstone and found work in the daily reenactments for tourists of the Gunfight at the OK Corral. Then he bought the local paper, the *Tombstone Tumbleweed,* and turned it into a broadside for his "call to arms" to protect America from invasion.[15]

Simcox was not the only one drawn to Cochise County, in southeastern Arizona, to try out vigilantism. Some longtime residents there, chiefly Douglas rancher and towing company owner Roger Barnett and his brother Donald, had been rounding up unauthorized migrants for years and turning them over to the Border Patrol. The Barnetts' example drew others to the county who were keen to emulate them, donning camouflage fatigues, taking up guns, and tracking immigrants.[16] In 2002, another Californian, Glenn Spencer, moved to the town of Sierra Vista and established his own operation, American Border Patrol—which boasted an unmanned aerial drone and other high-tech tools—as well as maintaining his anti-immigrant Web site, American Patrol. The following year, a Texan named Jack Foote and a former Southern California bounty hunter named Casey Nethercott established a base in Douglas for their border militia, Ranch Rescue, the most paramilitary group of all.

In 2005 Simcox and Gilchrist launched the Minuteman Project, calling on volunteers to help stop the "invasion" of illegal immigrants. They broadcast their message through mainstream news outlets, which were captivated by the story of a grassroots militia. In the weeks leading up to the group's first and biggest gathering, the April 2005 muster, the pair trumpeted the news that thousands of people were heeding the call. But the actual number of participants fell far below those predictions. Journalists on the ground with the Minutemen in Arizona reported that roughly two hundred volunteers turned out during the first week of the event, which was the most heavily attended.[17] Over the next couple of years, periodic calls for border volunteers yielded no more than a few dozen participants.

The people who came out for patrols ranged from border landowners weary of illegal migrants trooping across their property to construction workers anxious about losing their jobs and nostalgic for a time when they didn't hear Spanish spoken in their neighborhoods. One who showed up was Britt Craig. He was among a cadre of regular volunteers, many of them retired or underemployed, and quite a number of them Vietnam veterans, who embraced the crusade.

Craig was drawn to the operation in part because a civilian militia appealed to his libertarian sensibilities and in part for the sheer outdoorsy exhilaration of it. "There isn't much that moves me like this," he said. "It's an extended hunting and fishing trip."

Craig grew up in Thomasville, Georgia, a small town sixty miles south of Albany, where his father was a public affairs officer for the U.S. civil defense agency and his mother kept house. He was named for an uncle, Britt Craig, an Atlanta newspaperman who figured in the Broadway musical *Parade*. Craig never knew his uncle, who died young, but was impressed with the fact that he had become a biplane pilot and taught aerial acrobatics.

As a kid, Craig was happiest out in the woods. He loved guns. He watched every cowboy movie he could find. At seventeen, he enlisted in the army and went to Vietnam as an infantryman with the First Brigade, 101st Airborne Division. He was sent into combat in the northern highlands and it thrilled him. "It forged a high tolerance for excitement," he said. "It's very difficult to find that same thing in civilian life."

In a place called Chu Lai, a grenade booby trap took out Craig's left eye, damaged nerves in his right leg, and left him with a "twinky" trigger finger. He was just nineteen and his dream of a life in the military was dead. "When I got injured I was lying around in Walter Reed Hospital and a colonel comes by," Craig remembered. "I asked him, 'Am I going to be able to stay on jump status?' He said, 'No combat arms for you.' I said,

'I want out.' That was the end of the world for me. That was my career plan, shot all to hell."

But it wasn't the worst. As a full moon rose in Jacumba's inky twilight, Craig sat cross-legged on a bed of pine needles and let his thoughts revisit the bitter slap he felt on returning to a country that was ambivalent, if not openly hostile to him. "I joined the army, volunteered for the paratroopers, volunteered for Vietnam, and I come back and I'm the anti-Christ," he said, his words catching in his throat. "We [veterans] were something apart. I remember going to a fair and there was a shooting-gallery thing, and this guy made a big fuss about me being a good shot. To him, I was the *other*. Even in trying to compliment me, it was the demonization of all of us."

After his injuries healed, Craig was frustrated and footloose. He worked as a roadie for bands and as a commercial fisherman. He wrote songs and self-produced a couple of CDs. "I never really did anything thoughtful and appropriate," said the soft-spoken vet. "I just bounced around. Did a lot of things, but nothing you'd really call a career." When it got too hard to deal with America, he moved to Puerto Rico and lived there for years, coming back eventually to sort out a dispute with the Veterans Administration. Lately he'd been collecting his military pension and finding work when he needed extra cash. "I float a genteel poverty," said Craig.

In his early twenties, Craig fathered a son. He tried to remain in the boy's life though he didn't stay with his son's mother. "It was not, 'Daddy's home, fetch the pipe and slippers,'" he observed. "But I had quite a bit of influence and time with him." Craig's kid pursued a much more traditional path than he ever had, growing up to be a stockbroker with an Atlanta brokerage house. "I'm bemused but proud of him," said the vet. Then, as Craig was cementing his commitment to the Minutemen, his son surprised him by enlisting in the army, prepared for deployment to Iraq or Afghanistan. "It's his expression of patriotism, of really not liking what's going on with the terrorism thing."

For Craig, volunteering for border duty was his own act of patriotism. But it also served a more personal need. "This gives me the opportunity to get the 1945 homecoming that I didn't get in 1968," he said. "In my hometown, people are very, very supportive. They tell me, 'Good job. Way to go!'"

Browsing through a box of food donated by Minuteman supporters, Craig found a bag of hamburger buns and ate a couple, washing them down with 7-Up. It would have to do for supper. He said he had met a lot of veterans among the Minutemen and he believed many were thinking about more than curbing uncontrolled immigration. "Gilchrist mentioned being a vet and it was kind of a distress call," he said. "It did influence me to go back him up. It resonated with a lot of other people too. . . . In Arizona there were an amazing number of Vietnam-era people trying to work something out. I suspect it's trying to rectify what had become a love-hate relationship with the United States. This has been a really good place for me to work that out. I'm glad I lived long enough."

A proliferation of new groups was inspired by the Minutemen. One was Chase's outfit (the name of which would change repeatedly, from the California Minutemen to the United States Border Patrol Auxiliary and later California Border Watch). In addition to the crews tracking illegal immigrants in communities that touch the Mexican border, there were numerous far-flung groups such as the Colorado Minuteman Project, Florida Minutemen Patriots, and Iowa Minuteman Civil Defense Corps calling for tough immigration enforcement. Even in the politically liberal San Francisco Bay Area a group called the Golden Gate Minutemen attracted a small following. The San Diego Minutemen made a practice of harassing migrant workers living in a makeshift encampment in a rough canyon north of town until a wildfire forced the migrants to flee, abandoning the campsite.[18]

Though the original Minuteman organization was riven repeatedly by factional infighting and none of the spin-off groups commanded more than a handful of supporters, the name that Simcox and Gilchrist had coined became a household word. The movement struck a chord with Americans anxious about an increasingly globalized society. And the Minutemen gained a voice in the national political debate over immigration control.

The fears and frustrations driving the restrictionist movement were expressed vividly by some of those who attended a workshop in San Diego in the autumn of 2005 for Ramirez's group, Friends of the Border Patrol, which planned to deploy its own border watch teams. Though the effort never got off the ground, a couple of dozen people turned out for the daylong training at a hotel beside a freeway.

Skip Coleman, a retired Las Vegas police lieutenant, said he was drawn to groups trying to restrict illegal immigration because in his city's booming economy he could see immigrants—presumably undocumented—rushing to fill jobs he felt should belong to Americans. "Bush said illegals came to take jobs Americans didn't want, but construction is being slowly taken over by illegal aliens," said Coleman, fifty-eight. "The service jobs, maids and so on, those jobs have been taken over and now they're branching out into middle-class jobs. Americans are being shut out." Not only that, he went on, "when they flood across the border, they're swamping our social services, and there's more crime." Coleman said that if Ramirez and his group were as professional as they sounded, he was willing to drive the 350 miles to Southern California a couple of times a month to offer a few days of service patrolling the border. "I want to do something for my country," he said. "I want to preserve my way of life that I like very much."

Beverly Crawford, a self-described "retired repo lady" and a grandmother of seven, said she had been shocked by the cultural change when she moved back to Southern California from Washington State three years earlier. "I thought, 'This is not right.' Everything was written in Spanish first and the American language second," she said. "Everywhere I go into a store, I don't find an American standing behind the counter. I'm hoping we can get back the way we were twenty years ago, when we were an American state." Crawford, fifty-four, said it was the first time she had ever really gotten involved with a cause, but she was moved to act on behalf of her grandchildren. "I hate to think that our country is going downhill," she said. "Our ancestors fought for it and we're letting it slip through our fingers. I feel like they've taken away a lot of our rights, because when I go into grocery stores, they don't want to hear English. I'd like to be able to put my footprint into helping."

Tim Whitney, fifty, who lived in Chula Vista, a growing city in San Diego County that nearly touches Mexico, said he wished that Mexican immigrants would go back home and build up their own economy, rather than seeking prosperity in the United States. "I'm tired of people coming here and then making me the enemy. I'm tired of the word *racist* being thrown out there to stop the argument," he said during a break in the training session, his body tense with agitation. "The truth is, we need to stop it, we need to put people on the border and keep people out." A construction worker, Whitney said he had become used to working in crews that were overwhelmingly made up of immigrants. But he had taken a fall and was sidelined with an injury, getting by on workers' compensation insurance. "I have trouble with the capitalists, too. They should pay their people better," he went on. "Time was, a carpenter could send his kids through school and his wife didn't have to work. Illegal aliens? Yeah, they're helping our economy . . . by the rich getting richer." As he talked, sweat beaded on his anguished face. "But what do I know? I'm just a dumbass who never got an education. Because we're rich Americans, is that a reason to hate me? I'm not rich, I'm poor." He had decided to get out on the border, he said bitterly, because "I want to feel like I have something to say. I want to feel like I have some power."

The anxiety Whitney and others voiced, over immigrants elbowing in on American jobs, reflects real concerns over changes in the U.S. economy, some scholars say. And while the influx of foreign-born workers into the U.S. construction industry is real, there are larger shifts under way that don't have much to do with immigrants. Restructuring and outsourcing in the American economy are causing insecurity, especially for older and less educated workers, said Frank Bean, a sociology professor who heads the Center for Research on Immigration, Population, and Public Policy at the University of California at Irvine. "It doesn't take as many workers to make steel as it used to. And jobs get moved to other countries," he said. "Of course new jobs are being created all the time, but if a fifty-five-year-old person's job is restructured, it's not as easy for that person to reinvent himself into a new job as it is for a twenty-five-year-old." The forces behind the outsourcing of manufacturing jobs are hard to see, said Bean, "but the immigrants are all around, in the restaurants and here and there."

The social cost of absorbing immigrants is also a real concern to people, especially at a time when important aspects of the American social safety net are in flux, said Bean, the author of *Immigration and Opportunity: Race, Ethnicity, and Employment in the United States.* When the U.S. economy hits a recession, jobs are scarcer and local and state tax revenues drop, but the costs of health care, education, and criminal justice for immigrants—the same as for the rest of the population—continue. "That can hit the ordinary citizen kind of hard," he said. "And there are lots of things going on in American society that are increasing insecurity: pensions are disappearing, the social security system gets attacked from the right and the left, health insurance is under threat. It's not a time, as compared to twenty years ago, when people can feel too secure."

On top of the economic insecurity that can trigger animus toward immigrants, there's often a sense of dislocation as American society expands to encompass unfamiliar cultures. "The price of immigration is a challenging one for any society because it means you have to confront newcomers," said Harvard University public policy professor Robert Putnam. "Old-timers have to confront issues of identity and connection. Our natural instinct is to want to be around other people who are like us. Therefore it takes time to develop a new 'we.' The most important challenge facing any society is to create a new, more encompassing 'we,' not in terms of skin color or religion, but in terms of Americanness."

Putnam is the author of *E Pluribus Unum: Diversity and Community in the Twenty-first Century*, a 2007 study that found that the more diverse a community, the less civic engagement exists among its members. The United States has successfully incorporated immigrants before, he said, notably in the wake of the last big immigration wave a century ago. "The pledge of allegiance was created in 1906 as part of a process of creating a sense of national identity," said Putnam. "You could be American without being a WASP as long as you pledged to support these principles. It's a doable task. It will take some time, but we have to all realize and learn to live with difference."

Most Americans have immigration stories in their own family history, but they share a visceral sense that it's unfair to sneak across the border into this country, Putnam added. "The public, for better or worse, makes a huge distinction between legal and illegal immigration," he said. "Insofar as the issue gets cast as illegal immigration, a substantial majority of Americans are opposed to it. It triggers issues about the rule of law and the fundamental notion that you don't cut in line in front of other people." Very few Americans want to be seen as opposing immigration itself, said Putnam, so discomfort with foreigners is often framed in terms of fair play and rejecting those who don't abide by immigration laws.

The arrival of new waves of immigrants, over the course of American history, has frequently triggered a violent response from more established groups, said Susan Olzak, a Stanford University sociologist. Such a backlash was in evidence after the massive street protests in the spring of 2006, when immigrants marched through American cities demanding respect and fair treatment. "Surges in the number of immigrants or migrants often produce certain kinds of political and collective actions, sometimes mob attacks," said Olzak. "This has happened against the Chinese, southern and eastern Europeans, and black migrants moving to the North. In many ways I don't think it's new. What's new is the political mobilization and activity and participation of Mexican Americans."

A number of politicians and other public figures have seized on and amplified the popular concern for the rule of law, the post-9/11 fear of terrorism, and the more inchoate economic and cultural anxieties that immigration—and the new visibility of immigrants—has triggered. Tancredo built his reputation on his uncompromising opposition to immigration. The former Colorado congressman, who made a bid for the 2008

Figure 18. Outside Sasabe, Sonora, a group of migrants, including a young girl, prepare to cross the border fence illegally and hike across the punishing Arizona desert. Photo by Carlos Avila González/San Francisco Chronicle.

Republican presidential nomination, called not only for tough enforcement to prevent and punish illegal immigration but for the nation's borders to be closed to all legal immigrants and for the American-born children of undocumented immigrants to be denied U.S. citizenship.[19] Rep. Sensenbrenner made headlines with his bill that sought to beef up border fencing and enforcement and, most punitively, to make "unlawful presence" in the country a felony rather than an administrative violation and to criminalize those who would aid illegal immigrants. San Diego representatives Duncan Hunter and Brian Bilbray, along with New York representative Pete King, former Colorado governor Roger Lamm, Maricopa County sheriff Joe Arpaio, and others, have all made political hay out of a tough stance on the border and illegal immigration.

Meanwhile, national media figures, including Lou Dobbs on CNN and Bill O'Reilly and Glenn Beck on Fox, made the real and perceived transgressions of illegal immigrants into regular fodder for their nationally broadcast television shows. And an assortment of blatantly nativist freelance pundits, including Patrick Buchanan and Peter Brimelow, have contributed to a climate of intolerance. These voices have celebrated the vigilante activism of the Minutemen and have given credence to the positions of those who espouse anti-immigrant and at times openly racist views. Dobbs featured Simcox repeatedly on his show, as well as the late Madeleine Cosman, who raised alarms about illegal aliens as sexual predators and carriers of leprosy and other diseases. Dobbs hosted Glenn Spencer, whose American Patrol Web site spewed anti-Mexican vitriol and warned of an impending "reconquest" of the Southwest by Mexico. Another guest was Barbara Coe, who helped write California's Proposition 187 and who has claimed membership in the white nationalist Council of Conservative Citizens. O'Reilly has frequently referred to Mexican immigrants as "wetbacks" and has played fast and loose with immigration statistics.

Lost in the cacophony has been any sense of historical or economic context to explain why Mexican and other migrant workers come to the United States without legal authorization. With undocumented immigrants spreading into new regions of the United States (and in the absence of comprehensive national immigration reform), the cultural and political debate has been waged in local communities across the country that are often ill prepared to integrate immigrants and especially susceptible to the nativist message of Minuteman groups and their supporters.

Meanwhile, an assortment of national immigration restrictionist organizations has engaged in advocacy that bolsters the anti-immigrant cause. Many of the groups—from the Center for Immigration Studies, a conservative Washington, D.C., think tank, to the Federation for American Immigration Reform, US English, Numbers USA, and other pressure groups—were founded and funded by Michigan ophthalmologist John Tanton, known as the godfather of the anti-immigration movement, who came to his restrictionist stance by way of environmentalism.[20]

These anti-immigrant views (which go beyond the debate over the causes and solutions to undocumented immigration) have gained legitimacy and visibility through such think tanks, elected officials, and national television hosts. Meanwhile, on-air "shock jocks" have taken the message a step further with racist and violent humor targeting immigrants and Latinos. When undocumented immigrant students waged a weeklong fast in favor of the DREAM Act, a bill that would give them legal residence, radio personality Michael Savage quipped in July 2007, "Let them fast until they starve to death, then that solves the problem." A year earlier,

Phoenix radio talk show host Brian James suggested on the air, "What we'll do is randomly pick one night—every week—when we will kill whoever crosses the border. Step over there and you die." James lost his job over the comment, though he later told the *Arizona Republic* his remarks had been taken out of context.

Anti-immigrant sentiment bled over into racist messages, especially in the spring of 2006 when Latino activism culminated in a surge of pro-immigrant marches and rallies across the country. Strategic Forecasting Inc., a consulting firm that monitors foreign and domestic terrorism, noted an uptick in recruiting by white supremacists "whose chat rooms are abuzz with anti-immigration sentiment directed especially against illegal Mexican and other Latin American immigrants. White supremacist groups such as the National Vanguard and the National Socialist Movement hope to use the immigration issue as a public relations and recruiting tool."[21] Several Latino elected officials in California reported death threats and hate mail at about the same time. And a computer game called Border Patrol appeared on a white supremacist group's Web site among its "Racist Games." In it, players would watch crudely animated illegal immigrants, including a pregnant woman with two children in tow, run across the desert, then shoot the figures to win points, splattering blood across the screen.

Simcox and Gilchrist worked to distance themselves from the neo-Nazis who were drawn to the Minuteman cause. They featured "the granny brigade" and emphasized the presence of retirees in lawn chairs with binoculars to help project a sanitized version of a border militia.

Other vigilante groups were not so media savvy. Ranch Rescue leader Casey Nethercott was blunt, if unconvincing, in his denial of violence and bigotry when interviewed in February 2004 about felony charges he faced in South Texas for allegedly detaining and beating two illegal Salvadoran immigrants the year before. "They made it up," Nethercott said of the charges, as he patted his Rottweiler. "If I had pistol-whipped these people, they'd have been dead. . . . They're making me out to be a racist and a liar, and they're lying."

At a compound of neglected ranch buildings on his property in Douglas, Arizona, dubbed Camp Thunderbird, Nethercott grabbed a walkie-talkie, barked an order to his hulking, gun-toting sentry, "Tiny," and sped off to join a pair of volunteers who were patrolling along the Mexican border of the ranch. Out among the dry, spiny mesquite bushes that covered the land, Nethercott's deputies had stumbled upon a Ford Bronco, abandoned, they believed, by drug smugglers. The men hammered at the steer-

Figure 19. Vigilante Kalen Riddle stands sentry on the Ranch Rescue compound in Douglas, Arizona. Photo by Carlos Avila González/San Francisco Chronicle.

ing column with a pick and a crowbar, trying to release the wheels so they could tow the vehicle back to their compound.

"We've got about five more years and this country is ruined," Nethercott said. "Illegals are destroying our fabric of life." He and Foote had advertised on the Internet for recruits to come down with firearms and camping gear to join Ranch Rescue's border protection efforts. Their Web site featured photographs of men in camouflage posing with bales of marijuana they said they had intercepted in the Arizona desert. One of those who showed up was twenty-one-year-old Tiny, whose real name was Kalen Riddle. He had arrived a few days earlier from his home in Aberdeen, Washington, after a friend showed him the Ranch Rescue Web site. "Someone needs to be doing the government's job," said the towering, heavyset Riddle as he scanned the perimeter of the base. "I was unemployed."

Another volunteer, sixty-four-year-old Bill Dore, said he had retired to Douglas five years earlier when his job as a television technician went overseas. He said that he understood the attraction the United States poses for migrants from Mexico and other developing countries but that he devoted his time to patrolling the border to keep illegal immigrants out. "Our country is going down the tubes," he said, hanging around Nethercott's ramshackle ranch house. "The people coming across here, they don't want to be assimilated. They don't want to use our language."

Cochise County law enforcement officials largely left Ranch Rescue and the other groups alone, and a spokeswoman for the Cochise County sheriff said that "as long as they remain within the limits of Arizona law, they're treated like everybody else. If they're firing their weapons to create an endangerment situation . . . or if they physically hold [the immigrants] or point a gun at them, [that's illegal]." A spokesman for the U.S. Border Patrol said that he welcomed the watchful presence of ranchers and civilian patrol groups. "Every law enforcement agency appreciates a neighborhood watch," he said, then added, "I would caution them to be very careful not to violate someone's civil liberties."

Eventually, though, the group's erratic, inflammatory behavior couldn't be ignored. In 2004 Nethercott and Riddle ended up in a tense standoff at the ranch with Border Patrol agents who drew their guns after Nethercott allegedly failed to comply with a traffic stop and threatened agents with a shootout.[22] Two weeks later, FBI agents acted to arrest Nethercott outside the Douglas Safeway supermarket on assault charges. They ended up shooting and seriously wounding Riddle after agents thought he was reaching for a gun.[23] A subsequent search of the ranch turned up fifteen assault rifles, several handguns, thousands of rounds of ammunition, and M-80-type explosives, according to news reports.[24]

Nethercott, who had previously served time in California for assault, was acquitted in the Arizona case but stood trial on the Texas charges of beating the Salvadoran migrants. Though the jury deadlocked on the pistol-whipping, he was sentenced to five years in prison in Texas for gun possession, which is illegal for a felon.[25] The Salvadorans (aided by the Mexican American Legal Defense and Education Fund and the Southern Poverty Law Center) subsequently sued Foote and Nethercott. They won a $1 million judgment against them and took title to Nethercott's seventy-acre property in Douglas. Foote was also charged in Arizona that year with illegal possession of a firearm.[26] The men's combined legal troubles led to the collapse of Ranch Rescue.

Foote and Nethercott were not the only Cochise County militia leaders who had run-ins with the law. Glenn Spencer was sentenced to a year's probation and a $2,500 fine in 2004 for recklessly firing a gun and hitting a neighbor's garage. Chris Simcox was convicted in 2004 of carrying a concealed weapon on federal land while tracking migrants, then lying to a federal officer about it. He was sentenced to a year's probation. Roger Barnett never faced criminal charges but lost a civil suit in 2006 brought by two Mexican American families he had detained at gunpoint on his land, mistaking them for migrants. A jury ordered Barnett to pay the families almost $99,000 in damages. He and his wife and brother also faced a suit in federal court that accused them of threatening sixteen illegal immigrants with dogs and guns and kicking one woman in the group.[27]

In a 2005 petition to the Inter-American Commission on Human Rights, a Tucson immigrant rights organization, Border Action Network, detailed sixty-five incidents compiled by the Mexican consulate in Douglas and a number of other incidents drawn from reports to the Cochise County sheriff and the U.S. Border Patrol in which immigrants were forcibly detained or otherwise abused by vigilantes between 1999 and 2005. Though many of the cases included physical violence or threats made at gunpoint, prosecutors consistently failed to bring charges, the petition said.[28] Many more cases likely went unreported, the group maintained, because undocumented immigrants either feared coming forward or were removed from the country.

Bats whirled over the quiet hill where Craig sat by his van. Musing about his experiences on the border, he chuckled at the memory of one particularly ironic moment in Willcox, Arizona, just after the first Minuteman showdown had ended. "These four kids came along and they were obviously illegals, they didn't speak a word of English," he said. "They were looking for a ride, wanted to get out of Arizona. I lived in Puerto Rico so I can get by in Spanish. I said, 'You made it over. You're here. God bless you. Have a good life. But I just spent three weeks trying to seal the border, so I can't give you a ride. My friends would kill me.'"

The radio was quiet. So far none of his crew had spotted any suspicious incursions. Then, with the crunch of shoes on gravel, a local property owner appeared on the dirt road. He had come out to investigate the Minutemen. "I heard you guys were coming," he told Craig, with guarded tolerance. "I do my own patrols when there's a full moon." He looked up at the great orange orb suspended above the horizon. He was vexed, he said, by the problem of illegal immigration from Mexico. "The only thing you can do is hope some of the money trickles down to the peasants over there, because they're desperate." Then he sauntered back down the road toward the border.

After a bit, another local sputtered up on a rickety motorbike. The small volatile man, who gave his name as Walt, worked as a caretaker for the landowner who had permitted Chase's crew to use his property. Walt railed against the threat posed to the American way of life by "wetbacks," "faggots" and other deviants. Craig responded with southern good manners, courteous but reserved.

The conversation was interrupted by the hum of an automobile. A Honda CRV pulled up and parked, and out sprang Judy, a cheerful middle-aged nurse from San Diego. "I came up here because I need a piece of this piñon tree," she said. "I'm doing a talk at the natural history museum on pine trees. I have a Coulter pine, which has the biggest cone, and I need a piñon cone, which is the smallest. I knew I would find it here." Judy was torn about the Minutemen. They were interlopers on this familiar land, and some looked a bit threatening. On the other hand, the drug smugglers from Mexico were getting terribly brazen, and if the Minutemen could put a stop to it, good. "Oh look! The bats are out! Goodie!" she interjected. As she chattered to Craig about meteor showers, Walt revved up his bike and departed. Soon she too, took her pine branches and bade Craig good night.

Quiet descended, and darkness. A coyote howled. Homegirl, who, like her owner, was missing an eye, sidled close to get her head scratched. Craig sank down again on the pine needle duff. "I'm a happy man," he said. "I've got a mission. I've got compatriots. And I've got my cats."

Shortly after they first burst onto the scene, Simcox and Gilchrist parted ways in acrimony. Simcox continued to head up a border-monitoring operation he called the Minuteman Civil Defense Corps. The group enlisted help from Washington, D.C., consultants and maintained an active Internet presence and a busy e-mail fundraising campaign. Simcox and his new cohorts threw their energy into an effort to build a border fence on private lands, an action designed to highlight the government's lack of progress in securing the country. The original plan was for two layers of "Israeli-style" steel fencing, twelve to fifteen feet high, separated by a roadway and fortified with lights, motion sensors, ditching, and coils of barbed wire. The reality was a bit scaled back. The group erected ten miles of barbed wire fencing on a ranch in Palominas, Arizona, and then went to work on a one-mile steel-mesh fence on a ranch near Bisbee, Arizona.[29]

Gilchrist returned to California in possession of the name of the original Minuteman Project, which he said would monitor businesses that hired illegal immigrants. Most of the group's efforts, including those of a small group of Southern California women, calling themselves Gilchrist

Angels, focused on picketing day labor pickup sites and hassling employers who hired casual workers, on the assumption that the majority of those workers were undocumented. Gilchrist also ran for Congress in 2005 on the American Independent Party ticket and won 25 percent of the vote, coming in third.[30]

But both Simcox and Gilchrist were accused of financial malfeasance by fellow members of their new organizations, and their groups fractured further as a result. In 2006 Simcox came under scrutiny by the conservative *Washington Times* after Minuteman supporters began questioning what had happened to hundreds of thousands of dollars in donations. The dispute led to the departure of several leaders of the group and a lawsuit charging fraud and breach of contract filed by a Phoenix-area man who had mortgaged his home in order to donate $100,000 to the fence project.[31] In 2007, several of the ousted members of the Minuteman Civil Defense Corps formed a new splinter group, the Patriots' Border Alliance, and announced on their Web site a competing border deployment called Operation: Allied Minutemen.[32]

Gilchrist, meanwhile, was embroiled in his own battle with three of the seven board members of his Minuteman Project. The board members accused Gilchrist of failing to account for hundreds of thousands of dollars, and they voted to oust him as president. Gilchrist responded with a lawsuit in early 2007, saying the three had no voting power.[33] He withdrew the suit a little while later, abandoned the group, and incorporated a new organization, the Jim Gilchrist Minuteman Project.[34]

While the Minuteman organizations fractured and their leaders became mired in internecine bickering, violence, and legal trouble, the movement nonetheless projected an image—of citizens taking action to secure their country—that continued to resonate with many Americans. For Craig, the movement gave him a mission that organized his life and offered a long-sought sense of peace.

Through it he also found love. "A Minute-lady activist wandered up to my hill," said Craig by cell phone one day. "I got married." Debbie Sattler, an insurance claims adjuster, had taken her twelve-year-old son to the Arizona muster, had helped start Gilchrist Angels in Orange County, and had thrown herself into illegal-immigration protests. Guests at their wedding, in July 2006, were asked to dress in red, white, and blue and to join a "patriotic rally" in Hollywood after the ceremony.

"One thing that got Debbie and me together was her deep, deep commitment with the Minuteman phenomenon," Craig said. "It really is nice to have somebody that you share the larger thing with. It adds flavor and meaning to everything." Craig took to dividing his time between Sattler's condo in Mission Viejo and the hill in Campo, California, that had become his regular border outpost. "I do about four days on the border and then wave signs with her three days a week," he said. The National Guard patrols, vaunted by the Bush administration, had come and gone. Chase had receded from the border watch scene, and the scouts like Craig who patrolled eastern San Diego County had dwindled to a small handful of lone wolves. For Craig, the border started as a symbol. It still was that, but in the course of his spending time there, the borderlands had become a real and important place for him—not a place of cross-cultural connection but a compelling piece of land.

Craig made another trip back east, trading the old van for a one-ton box truck he had inherited from his brother-in-law in South Carolina, and returned to California with his guitars and some old family photographs. "I'm not as optimistic as I was," said Craig, thinking of the hopes he had once had that a citizen's militia could close the border. But still he kept his vigil under the brilliant stars, pistol at the ready, staying true to the movement that had given his life meaning again.

EIGHT

Tijuana

"A constant drumbeat of killings"

ON A TIJUANA SIDE STREET, just steps from the rusting steel border fence, two dozen preschoolers ate a lunch of spaghetti and milk one December day at the Mother Antonia Child Care Center for the families of police officers. After their teachers cleared the little tables and wiped the small hands clean, the children erupted in squeals of excitement: the Christmas *posada* was about to begin.

A clown twisted long balloons into the shapes of butterflies and dachshunds. His wife painted tiger stripes and whiskers on the children's faces. And a teacher passed a basket of colorful *cascarones,* blown eggs filled with confetti. Soon the kids were chasing each other around the playroom, smashing the eggshells on each others' heads and raining bits of pastel paper over everything.

The nursery school, named for an aging nun who sat in the midst of the cheerful chaos, formed a cocoon of safety around these children. On the streets outside, thirty-three of their parents' colleagues had been murdered over the course of that year—gunned down in a vicious war over drug smuggling turf. "We haven't lost any parents, but sometimes there's this sadness because their co-workers have been killed," said Palmira Flores, the center's director. "I tell them, 'Don't fight with your husband in the morning, because you don't know if he's coming home at night.'"

Smuggling has a long history in the borderlands. It is one more way—subterranean and insidious—that the United States and Mexico are intertwined: through exchanges driven by greed, and sometimes need, and enforced by ferocious violence whose consequences have flowed both north and south from the border. The booming drug trade has dealt Tijuana and other border cities a crippling one-two punch. Mexican drug cartels have been competing to control trafficking routes to the vast U.S. market of drug consumers. Tijuana saw more than 843 murders in 2008, many of them drug related, more than twice the annual number in recent years.[1] In addition, the city suffered hundreds of kidnappings for ransom and corruption so widespread that citizens lost faith in law enforcement and the judicial system. The numbers—and tragedies—have multiplied as the same story has played out in other border cities, including Nuevo Laredo and Ciudad Juárez, and spread deep into the country and all the way to Mexico City. Mexico experienced an unprecedented 5,200 drug-related killings in 2008, more than double the number just a year earlier.[2] And the number of narco-killings in 2009 reached 6,000. One particularly bloody weekend in Tijuana claimed the lives of thirty-seven people, including four children caught in shootouts.[3]

In Tijuana and along the border, drug abuse has also been rising among Mexicans, and with it a proliferation of neighborhood methamphetamine kitchens, street-level dealing, and robberies by addicts desperate for a fix. Many Tijuanans with the means to do so have moved across the line to San Diego to escape the insecurity. Others have just tried to keep their heads down and insulate their children from the violence.

When it comes to drugs, the United States has been a consumer nation and Mexico has been a supplier nation for a long time, and drug trafficking syndicates have grown strong along the border feeding the American market, said David Eisenberg, a police sergeant in the growing California border city of Chula Vista who served as a liaison to the Tijuana police. "One of the consequences of tightening up control at the border is that excess supply of drugs gets backed up and bartered in Mexico," said Eisenberg, fifty-nine, who holds a doctorate in social work and researched transnational crime at the University of San Diego. "So we've got murders, extortion and kidnapping, and skyrocketing addiction rates in Mexico that are starting to match addiction rates in the United States."

The anxiety almost spilled into the preschool playroom a few weeks before the Christmas party when Nancy Gómez Terán, a secretary in her twenties who had worked in the police station at the end of the block, was shot to death along with two officers who were giving her a ride home. The trio died in a hail of bullets after their patrol car was ambushed, according to news reports. "Nancy was a good friend," said Flores, who, with the other teachers, had wept in the center's kitchen as they watched television coverage the day after the shooting. "She was a really lovely woman."

Flores and Mother Antonia, the eighty-year-old American nun whose ruddy face was framed by a white veil, talked of the secretary while several other nuns distributed Christmas presents to the children. "We always go to the funerals of the officers who have died," said Mother Antonia, who had seen more than her share of violence—and at very close range. For thirty years the former white-gloved socialite from Beverly Hills had lived inside Tijuana's hulking La Mesa state prison, ministering to the needs of the inmates. She had extended her compassion equally to the guards and police officers and had founded a charity for police widows and orphans.

More than 450 police, soldiers, and prosecutors lost their lives in Mexico's drug war in 2008 alone.[4] Some of the policemen who died were honest crime fighters, but many were corrupt. Those officers were killed by one cartel because they were working for its rival, or by a cartel unsatisfied with the protection from official scrutiny the cops were paid to provide, say scholars, journalists, and law enforcement officials who study crime at the border.

Police killings have also wracked other Mexican border cities. In Nuevo Laredo, the police chief was gunned down in June 2005 on his first day on the job. The hit was apparently carried out by a squad known as the Zetas, former federal antidrug troops who defected to work for the Gulf cartel, which was vying with the Sinaloa cartel and its enforcers, the Negros, for control of Nuevo Laredo. The prize: the largest trucking corridor into the United States, where 40 percent of Mexican cargo crosses the border, and, mixed in with it, much of the contraband as well. In Juárez, the city's No. 2 police officer was murdered in May 2008, prompting the police chief to quit after he, too, received death threats over the police force's own radio frequency.[5]

The attacks have reached the highest levels of Mexican law enforcement. In September 2007, Omar Ramírez, a high-ranking commander with the Federal Investigative Agency, known by its Spanish acronym AFI, was gunned down as he drove through busy downtown Mexico City. Prosecutors believe his assassins were tied to the Gulf cartel, which he had been investigating. The following spring, the acting chief of the federal police force, or PFP, Commissioner Edgar Millán Gómez, was murdered inside the garage of his Mexico City apartment by a gunman who may have been a federal police officer with ties to the Sinaloa cartel.[6]

In Tijuana, the bodies of three dead cops were found decapitated, with their badges stuffed in their mouths.[7] The index finger of a murdered state investigator was severed and hung from a wire around his neck, tagging him as a *dedo,* or "finger," slang for a snitch.[8] Previous surges in violence have been just as deadly, say longtime observers of organized crime here, but the level of brutality is mounting. During the mid-1990s, the Arellano Félix brothers were consolidating their control of the *plaza,* the concession from authorities to run drugs through the city.[9] Numerous police officers were killed in those years, including crusading Tijuana police chief Federico Benítez, as the cartel aimed to silence reform-minded officers. The Arellano brothers also murdered Catholic cardinal Juan Jesús Posadas Ocampo at the Guadalajara airport in 1993. Another spasm of violence occurred in late 1999 and early 2000 when the Arellanos were under attack by rival trafficker Ismael Zambada García of Mexicali.[10] The brutality spiked up again more recently as the Tijuana cartel, weakened by the arrests of many of its leaders, faced infighting among internal factions as well as attacks by the rival Sinaloa cartel.

One Tijuana patrol officer acquainted with Mother Antonia said corruption had reached the police department's highest level and was worse than he had seen it in his twenty-six years on the force. "I can't do my job right because if I do, they'll kill me," said the officer, who, like many others in Tijuana, did not want his name used because he feared for his life. "Half the police are on the take. I drive this old truck and they drive the latest model. I've got five dollars in my pocket and they've got five thousand. We can't fix this problem alone. We need federal help."

Mexican president Felipe Calderón did send federal help. In his second month in office, he deployed more than three thousand soldiers and federal police officers to Tijuana in a high-profile campaign to quell drug-related violence. The federal troops stripped municipal police of their firearms and tested the weapons to see if any could be linked to homicides or other crimes. That operation was the start of a federal campaign that has deployed forty-thousand soldiers and five thousand federal police officers to drug trafficking hot spots around the country.[11] In 2008 federal officials performed background checks and security tests on more than fifty-six thousand state and local police officers and deemed almost half of them—nine out of ten in Baja California, where Tijuana is located—unfit for police work. Calderón reported the results to Mexico's Congress but did not make clear whether the failing officers would be retrained, dismissed, or criminally investigated.[12]

Though the Mexican military is more respected than the police, some analysts say a show of force by itself is not sufficient. To effectively combat the power of the drug cartels, Mexico needs to make deeper reforms to its law enforcement and judicial systems, they say. In the meantime, the current strategy appears to be contributing to the carnage. "Moving the military in has not necessarily been a deterrent," said David Shirk, director of the University of San Diego's Trans-Border Institute. "What's really causing the violence are the successes against high-level members of these groups. Every time we take down a *capo*, there are three or four guys who are vying for his spot or taking revenge. . . . The problem with that, in my view, is the hydra effect: wherever you cut off a head, a new one springs up. You're cutting them down to size, but you're making them more volatile and less easy to control."[13]

Though the violence spawned by the drug trade has exacted a terrible toll, militarizing Mexican society is not a long-term solution, according to Howard Campbell, a professor of anthropology at the University of Texas at El Paso. In the spring of 2009, he told members of a U.S. Senate committee about the ways that the drug war had disrupted law and order in his town's sister city, Ciudad Juárez, which had suffered more than 1,350 drug-related murders in 2008:[14] "These homicides—the result of a power struggle between the Juárez and Sinaloa Cartels—have occurred in broad daylight. They include acts of horrific torture, decapitation, and mutilation. Policemen, laborers, lawyers, college students, journalists, housewives and children are among the victims. Massacres have taken place on main streets, in bars and restaurants, and close to the international bridges between El Paso and Juárez. . . . The damage to Mexican society is profound. . . . The impact on the psychology of border people witnessing daily violence, threats and terror is a kind of collective post-traumatic stress disorder." Although the deployment of nine thousand troops to the city had lessened the violence, it had also led to human rights violations and other abuses against the population, allegedly committed by Mexican troops, he said, adding: "The growing power of the military in Mexican society, though reducing drug homicides, is harmful to Mexican democracy."[15]

Tijuana is a city of hills and mesas cut by canyons, with the Tijuana River meandering through the middle of it and emptying into the ocean just north of the border. The gritty nightclub strip around Avenida Revolución hangs on, but in recent years the city's center of gravity has shifted to its new downtown, the Zona Río, with its steel-and-glass office build-ings, swanky hotels, and high-end restaurants. Tijuana's population has swelled, from a mere thirty thousand residents sixty years ago to about 1.5 million today. Over the decades, neighborhoods that began as dirt-poor shantytowns have grown into solid middle-class communities, as squatters gained title to their parcels and improved their homes little by little and the city consented to run water and power lines in.

But the constant flow of new migrants from further south in Mexico—seventy thousand a year by one estimate—has multiplied those struggling *barrios* many times over.[16] Four in ten people in Baja California come from another state, according to the Mexican census bureau. Maquiladora industrial parks have sprawled away to the city's south and east, with workers' shacks crowding nearby. New settlers have laid claim to even the steepest parcels and have erected homes of scrap wood, tin, even card-board. City services have not kept pace and sewage problems have been legendary. At the same time, new shopping centers have also been spring-ing up, full of Gymboree indoor playgrounds, digital gadgets, and "Happy Meals" for those with some money to spend.

María de Socorro Zendejas de García was a child of six when her family moved up to the border from Mexico City in 1948. In those days there was so little crime that her parents always left the doors open. "Tijuana was a little *rancho* when we came here. It was *pura tierra,* just dirt," she recalled, sipping a cup of tea in a brightly lit downtown coffee shop. "All our shop-ping, trips to the park, everything, was over on the other side [in San Diego]. I didn't know what Mexican coins looked like because we always used dollars. We called it *oro y plata,* gold and silver. We never used silver unless we had to go to the post office or send a telegram or something." After a peso devaluation in the 1960s, though, their bank accounts lost value and residents were obliged to shop in Mexico, said Zendejas. Over time, that injection of cash allowed Tijuana to develop better shops, restaurants, even hospitals, and the local economy grew. "Now the city is much better," she said. "But we have other problems, like drug trafficking and kidnappings."

Shortly before the federal troops arrived in 2006, Tijuana police stepped up raids aimed at *narcomenudeo,* the domestic petty drug trade—whether to keep a lid on street dealing or merely as a show of force. In one joint op-eration by local and federal police, a convoy of five pickup trucks surged up the narrow, unpaved streets of Colonia Chula Vista, a struggling Tijuana neighborhood. Fingering the triggers of their submachine guns,

Figure 20. Tijuana police officers with an antidrug squad surge through a struggling shantytown in pursuit of *narcomenudeo,* the domestic petty drug trade.
Photo by Sandy Huffaker Jr.

the black-clad agents scanned the shanties clinging to the steep hillsides
and the faces of the people they passed. Abruptly the trucks stopped. The
agents swarmed down a rocky slope and surrounded a plywood shack.
The middle-aged man they dragged out clutched a hunk of bread in one
of his upraised hands as the officers frisked him for drugs. They found
nothing. The man was let go and they continued on, cruising the narrow
streets and searching residents at random.

The police commander had selected the neighborhood on the basis of a
newspaper clipping about rampant drug dealing there. But the police
agencies did not appear to be investing time in even the most basic intelligence gathering to focus the raids. "If someone sees us and they take off
running, they're suspect," remarked one cop. "We're after the little guys,
but they're all part of a chain run by the bigger operations," said another.
The agents admitted that anyone actually dealing drugs in the neighborhood probably would have seen the convoy from afar and slipped out of
sight before it arrived. Still, the police presence served as a deterrent, the
officers maintained.

They also knew that their commander's strategy made them sitting ducks. The very visible convoy could have easily been trapped by assailants in the narrow canyons of the city's poorest *colonias*. A few months earlier, three trucks on a similar operation had been surrounded and strafed with bullets, they said, leaving one officer dead and five wounded. "It hurts a lot when a fellow officer is killed," said Ernesto González Valencia, a nine-year veteran of the Tijuana force who had spent four years on the tactical squad. "The most painful thing is to hear a colleague calling for backup on the radio and not to be able to help him." Perched in one truck bed, González, thirty-one, showed off a cell phone photograph of his three-year-old daughter. He said he worried for her sake about putting his life at risk, but not so much so that he'd find a new line of work. "I like this job," he said. "It's dangerous but it's exciting. You can grab the action and get the bad guys." On that day, however, no bad guys were found, though by recent estimates the city had as many as twenty thousand *tienditas* and *picaderos,* shooting galleries and houses where methamphetamine was sold.[17]

Laurie Freeman, a Mexico expert at the Washington Office on Latin America, a liberal think tank with a focus on human rights, warned that federal involvement was unlikely to resolve the problem. The AFI, which led the Tijuana patrol, was created during the administration of President Vicente Fox to replace the discredited Federal Judicial Police, which in its turn had supplanted a previous federal police agency that had been found to be collaborating with drug traffickers. Soon the AFI too was facing corruption allegations.[18] Though the Mexican army had a reputation for being less corrupt than the police, the more that troops were called on to engage in drug interdiction, the more they fell prey to the same corrupting pressures, said Freeman.

Bribes by narco-traffickers were not always easy to turn down. Not only were policemen poorly paid, but such offers were often presented as *plata o plomo,* silver or lead: take the money or take the bullet. "There's a lot more Mexico could do to try to create institutions that are more effective and less easily corrupted, but it's difficult under all this pressure from drug traffickers to corrupt and intimidate," said Freeman, who studied the dynamics of drug cartel violence in Nuevo Laredo. "[The United States has] stronger, more transparent institutions, but we have cases of corruption all the time. As long as there is this huge black market, there will be corruption." And as long as drugs were both illegal and in high demand in the United States, said Freeman, Mexico would continue to pay a steep price.

A 2009 investigation by the Associated Press found that scores of U.S. officials at the federal, state, and local levels were indeed susceptible to border-related corruption.[19]

Beginning in the late nineteenth and early twentieth centuries, local farmers and Chinese settlers cultivated opium poppies in northwestern Mexico, particularly the state of Sinaloa. The drug was outlawed in the United States in 1923 and in Mexico in 1926, but by then Sinaloa's *gomeros,* or opium producers, had established routes for shipping heroin through Baja California to the western United States. During World War II the United States actually encouraged Mexican opium production for medical morphine to treat wounded soldiers.[20] After the war, the U.S. government again pushed for a crackdown. Still the smuggling continued, and when marijuana became popular in the United States in the 1960s, the same drug-growing families commercialized that crop as well.

Even today, many of Mexico's drug lords are from Sinaloa, including the Arellano Félix family, which has controlled Tijuana's drug trade since 1989; Rafael Caro Quintero, a founder of the Guadalajara cartel, who is in prison for the murder of a U.S. DEA agent; Amado Carrillo Fuentes, the onetime kingpin of the Juárez cartel, who died in 1997; and Joaquin "El Chapo" Guzmán, the current *capo* of the Sinaloa cartel, who escaped from prison in 2001 and has been one of the border's most entrepreneurial and brutal players in recent years.[21]

Smuggling across the U.S.-Mexico border dates back at least to Prohibition in the 1920s, when Americans were willing to pay a high price for liquor brought in from Mexico. Customs agents learned to rock a car and listen for the slosh of whiskey from bottles stashed in secret compartments. But other agents took kickbacks and the liquor went on through. In those years casinos, nightclubs, and speakeasies thrived in Tijuana and other dusty border towns, attracting Americans who wanted to party and providing an early economic stimulus on the frontier.

Contraband hasn't moved only from south to north. Everything from cars and appliances to potatoes and fruit was smuggled into Mexico in the past to avoid the country's high import duties. And these days traffickers do a brisk business in firearms, which are tightly restricted in Mexico. High-powered guns and ammunition smuggled into Mexico have provided the cartels with the firepower critical to maintaining their primacy. Nine out of every ten seized weapons have been traced by the U.S. Bureau of Alcohol, Tobacco and Firearms back to gun dealers in the United States, especially to the border states of Texas and Arizona, both of which have lax gun laws.[22] Meanwhile, the highest value is in narcotics smuggled north. The cash—anywhere from $8 billion to $25 billion a year, according to a Department of Justice estimate—is smuggled back to Mexico.[23]

After decades of moving home-grown heroin and marijuana across the border, the Mexican drug trade exploded in the 1990s in the wake of U.S. enforcement that sealed off Florida from cocaine smuggling. Colombian drug lords seeking new routes made deals with Mexican traffickers to move their cocaine as well. Soon the Mexican cartels were taking half the loads as payment and forging their own distribution networks in the United States. The Department of Justice has estimated that 90 percent of the cocaine in the United States now comes through Mexico.[24] The money and power of the cartels have grown exponentially.

The volume of drugs and money in Mexico expanded again as Mexican syndicates got into the methamphetamine business. U.S. law enforcement has come down hard on domestic meth labs, especially in California, and enacted strict controls on precursor chemicals like pseudoephedrine. But the supply of meth on the U.S. market has diminished only slightly. Instead, Mexican producers have moved aggressively to fill the breach, and the majority of meth in the United States now comes from south of the border. One of the largest meth labs ever found was busted in a Guadalajara industrial park in 2006, and small-scale kitchens are rife in Tijuana.[25]

Marijuana production in Mexico has declined a bit but remains high. Plenty of it was still smuggled over the line, in backpacks or on horseback across the desert, as well as in cars and trucks driving through ports of entry. But pot is bulky, smelly, and perishable. And Mexican organizations have increasingly found ways to grow it in California and the Pacific Northwest, either hydroponically under grow lights indoors or on large plantations hidden on public lands.[26]

The flow of illegal drugs to the United States has continued unabated, according to the U.S. Department of Justice's annual National Drug Threat Assessment, despite stepped-up enforcement at the border and international eradication efforts. And Mexican drug traffickers have been consolidating their dominance of U.S. distribution networks so that they have come to call the shots in what the United Nations estimates is a $142 billion business in the United States.[27] Several federal agencies that monitor drug trafficking in the United States have found that Mexican smuggling operations are involved in controlling the drug trade in almost every U.S. state. Meanwhile cartel-related violence has spilled over the border into the United States on several occasions. In 2002 a rival faction of the

Arellano Félix operation known as Los Palillos moved into San Diego, where it carried out killings, kidnappings, extortion, and methamphetamine trafficking until the FBI shut it down in 2007.[28]

In the summer of 2008, the U.S. Congress approved and funded a joint United States-Mexico antinarcotics operation known as the Mérida Initiative. The bilateral initiative was aimed at combating drug, human, and weapons trafficking. It included funding for training in areas such as courts management, police professionalization, and witness protection programs, as well as for hardware, including helicopters, x-ray scanners, and armored vehicles, and for computer database upgrades and forensic analysis tools.[29] Analysts and diplomats have called the collaborative approach an important step forward because it has implicated both countries in the drug trafficking problem and engaged both in seeking a solution. Critics fear the initiative is creating a police state, but other analysts say it goes beyond a militarized crime-fighting approach to include joint efforts to develop intelligence to combat money laundering and arms smuggling. Importantly, the Mérida Initiative includes long-term efforts to strengthen Mexico's legal and judicial systems. And it provides some funding for similar efforts in Central American countries, which have become trans-shipment routes for South American cocaine moving north.

U.S. President Barack Obama has repeatedly expressed his support for Mexican President Felipe Calderón's aggressive prosecution of the war on Mexico's drug cartels and has reiterated the U.S. commitment to help fund the effort.[30] Under Obama, the U.S. Department of Homeland Security began to vigorously interdict firearms and cash being trafficked from the United States into Mexico, an effort Mexican officials had long sought.[31] On the Mexican side, Calderón replaced all 700 of his country's customs agents in August 2009 with a new, college-educated force of 1,400 agents, trained to detect contraband and root out tax evasion. Observers called it a good start. But some human rights groups voiced concern that the Mexican military and police were themselves perpetrating human and civil rights violations as they combated drug traffickers.[32] And U.S. Senator Patrick Leahy, chairman of the Senate Appropriations Foreign Operations Subcommittee, moved to hold back a portion of the Mérida funding in 2009 on human rights grounds.[33] That move won applause from Mexican political commentator Denise Dresser, who wrote in the *Los Angeles Times* that the war on drugs was becoming a war on the civilian population. "Unless the Obama administration insists that those requirements be met, the Merida Initiative will simply be financing impunity," she wrote. "It will heighten the climate of fear that deeper binational collaboration sought to eradicate. It will allow the Mexican military and police forces to do what they do now: arbitrarily detain people, kill innocent bystanders at army checkpoints, threaten and abuse alleged suspects, ignore due process while carrying out arrests and get away with it because Calderon believes they can and should."[34]

Other Mexican observers have expressed concern that the Mérida Initiative doesn't go far enough in addressing the root causes of the drug trafficking problem. Respect for the rule of law in Mexico is fundamentally compromised, according to Mexican law professor Miguel Sarre, and crime cannot be combated effectively until basic reforms are in place. Injecting large amounts of money and technology into the Mexican military and police forces before corrupt elements are rooted out may be counterproductive, he said. And, he added, any effort to reduce drug trafficking and associated criminality must involve a much stronger effort by the United States to reduce the demand for illegal drugs.[35]

Talk of legalization—or at least decriminalization—of narcotics, particularly marijuana, appears to be gaining traction in some quarters in the United States. Voters in Massachusetts approved a measure in 2008 to decriminalize possession of marijuana for personal use, joining a dozen other states that consider possession a misdemeanor offense or less. Several states allow marijuana use for medical purposes with a doctor's recommendation. Harvard University economics professor Jeffrey A. Miron and former Princeton University professor Ethan Nadelmann are among the scholarly voices calling for an end to drug prohibition in the United States as a strategy to reduce the savage cartel violence and lawlessness wracking Mexico.[36] The British news magazine the *Economist* called in a 2009 editorial for the legalization of drugs by consumer countries. "Indeed, far from reducing crime, prohibition has fostered gangsterism on a scale the world has never seen before," the article read. "Even a relatively developed democracy such as Mexico now finds itself in a life-or-death struggle against gangsters. American officials, including a former drug tsar, have publicly worried about having a 'narco state' as their neighbor."[37] But such a policy change, which could defang organized crime in drug-producing countries, is likely to be a hard sell with voters and elected officials in drug-consuming nations such as the United States.

Though the volume of drugs and the profits involved have remained as high as ever, in spite of binational counternarcotics efforts, the balance of power among smuggling organizations has shifted, along with Mexico's changing political landscape. After Fox's election in 2000 ended seventy-one years of one-party rule by the Institutional Revolutionary Party, the new president made good on a promise to come down hard on Mexico's drug trade. High-profile raids early in the decade led to the arrest of a number of cartel bosses, including leaders of the Arellano Félix family.

In August 2006 the U.S. Coast Guard picked up the then-*capo* Francisco Javier Arellano Félix on a yacht in international waters off Baja. He was sentenced in 2007 to life in U.S. federal prison after pleading guilty to operating a criminal enterprise and conspiring to launder money.[38] Another cartel-running brother, Eduardo Arellano Félix, was arrested by Mexican authorities in Tijuana in October 2008. U.S. and Mexican officials were negotiating his extradition to the United States. That case involved one of an increasing number of criminal suspects arrested in Mexico and turned over to the United States for prosecution—an estimated 150 were extradited in 2007 and 2008—a reflection of a closer collaboration between U.S. and Mexican authorities in battling organized crime and an effort to remove drug kingpins from Mexican prisons, where they have often continued to run their operations from behind bars.[39]

But the weakening of once-dominant criminal organizations like the Tijuana and Juárez cartels has left the field open for cutthroat competitors, such as the Sinaloa and Gulf cartels, to push their way in. "It has been a constant drumbeat of killings and more radical measures by these groups. . . . As the Sinaloa cartel has come to move in on the turf of the Tijuana cartel, that's where you've seen the violence—the buying off of law enforcement, the assassination attempts against people on the take from the Arellano Félix cartel," said USD's Shirk. "The violence is picking up. The problem is: When was it lower? It's just a sustained, ongoing war between drug trafficking organizations." Individual cartels have also been riven by infighting, including warring among the remnants of the Arellano Félix group and a brutal contest between the Beltrán Leyva brothers and "El Chapo" Guzman for control of the Sinaloa organization.

The battle contributed to between 350 and 450 homicides in Tijuana each year between 2003 and 2007, according to the Baja California Attorney General's Office. The following year, the violence exploded and the death toll doubled. The pace of killings in Ciudad Juárez surpassed even Tijuana's, with more than 1,350 murders in 2008.[40] The nation's homicide rate was roughly eleven homicides per one hundred thousand in the 1990s, but it doubled over the succeeding decade to levels that the World Health Organization has categorized as epidemic.[41]

The police murders in particular were a potent symbol of the insidious way corruption has undermined the public trust and public safety. Meanwhile law enforcement has had little success addressing the petty crime and addiction that have plagued poor neighborhoods or the growing threat of kidnapping—organized crime's latest money-making venture—that has hung over more affluent residents.

For residents all across Tijuana, the double pressures of cartel violence and street crime were taking their toll. A professional truck driver steering through the city's congested streets remarked that he was careful to avoid tangling with late-model SUVs because they probably belonged to either narco-traffickers or corrupt cops, either of which meant trouble. A public-interest lawyer with a modest Japanese sedan said she wouldn't buy a fancy car even if she could afford one because it would only make her a target of kidnappers. Taxi driver Juan Contreras described feeling exposed in his job. "I'm on the street ten hours a day," said the cabbie, a grandfather of eight. "My fear is that the gunmen don't care who they hit with their bullets." A Presbyterian minister, whose impoverished congregation was made up of migrants from southern Mexico, said drug addiction was unraveling the fragile fabric of his neighborhood. "There are assaults, robberies, prostitution," said the pastor, Enrique Romero. "It's producing all kinds of misery. They'll steal anything they can sell: phone cables, gas lines, whatever."

Socorro Zendejas, a physician's wife, stirring her tea, recited a litany of fear and suspicion as she described how her city has been overtaken by a pervasive sense of disorder. When her daughters had been students at an elite Catholic high school in the 1980s, many of their classmates had found the criminal life alluring and had become "narco juniors" doing the bidding of the Arellano Félix family. The ones who got too ambitious were killed. More recently, her doctor's son had been murdered when he got romantically involved with the ex-girlfriend of a drug dealer. The dealer, though jailed, issued the order that he be killed, said Zendejas. When the doctor's daughter became frustrated with the unresponsive justice system and began talking publicly about the crime, she too paid with her life. The year before, a friend's adult daughter had been abducted from a supermarket parking lot and held for nine days until the family paid a ransom. Another friend had been beaten almost to death in front of his wife and children when the family couldn't come up with money to pay the kidnappers. Zendejas had seen these traumas scar people she loved, and that had affected her in turn. "Tijuana is turning into a *maquila de raptos*," she said, "A kidnapping factory."

Some kidnappings have been linked to criminal organizations already engaged in drug smuggling that have expanded into a new line of business. Others have been attributed to unaffiliated gangs. Operations have ranged from carefully targeted, months-long abductions with ransoms of millions of dollars to "express" kidnappings that last a few hours and yield a few thousand bucks. In still other cases of extortion by fakery, callers say, "We've got your daughter. You'd better pay," and play a recording of a crying child. Many of those calls originate on cell phones from prisons, according to some law enforcement officials.

Faced with such a climate, an increasing number of prosperous Tijuanans have moved across the border, gaining work visas as skilled professionals or investing their savings in the San Diego area to obtain an entrepreneur's visa. Tijuana newspapers have called the exodus a "brain drain." Eisenberg, the Chula Vista police sergeant, called his city a "bedroom community" for Tijuana.

Moises, forty-four, a Mexican businessman who was scared to use his last name, moved his family to Chula Vista after he was held hostage at his Tijuana office supply company by gunmen looking for cash on payday. The assailants kicked and pistol-whipped him, then put a gun to his head and began to count down, he said. But when they realized there was no cash in the building because he hadn't gone to the bank, they made off with his Volkswagen Jetta and he escaped with his life. "We know dozens of people who have moved here for security reasons," said Sara, his wife, as they sat at a Starbucks cafe in their new town, six miles north of the border. "We don't go to Tijuana much any more—just to visit the doctor or take the plane to Mexico City. All our friends have moved here."

After the Mexican Revolution, the state and the party evolved into a centralized, pyramidal power structure, and the business of drug trafficking—which wasn't addicting Mexicans—was tolerated and controlled, especially by governors in northern states, who profited from it, according to Luis Astorga, a sociologist at the National Autonomous University of Mexico. In the late 1940s, though, political leaders sought distance from the illegal trade, and the military and police agencies assumed the role of mediating drug trafficking, the very thing they were supposedly combating, while passing along a share of the profits to their political superiors, Astorga wrote in an analysis for the United Nations. "Since the beginning of prohibition . . . cultivators and wholesalers were not autonomous players; their success depended on political protection. They did not buy politicians; rather, politicians obliged them to pay a sort of 'tax.' If they didn't pay, their business was over. The power was on the political side."[42]

The outlines of this relationship could be glimpsed in the late 1990s, when dead bodies and Swiss bank accounts linked the family of former President Carlos Salinas de Gortari, particularly his brother Raúl, and the narco-traffickers. Former Tijuana mayor Jorge Hank Rhon, the son of a big wheel in the Institutional Revolutionary Party, has also been suspected of ties to the drug world—and of masterminding the murder of a journalist, Hector Félix Miranda, at Tijuana's crusading weekly newspaper *Zeta*. Two security guards at Hank's racetrack were convicted of the 1988 killing, but Hank was never charged. *Zeta*'s late editor Jesús Blancornelas made a name for himself by investigating the drug trade and pointing a finger squarely at government complicity. He survived an attempt on his life in 1997 (though he died of cancer some years later). A crime reporter in Ciudad Juárez was not so lucky. Armando Rodríguez, forty, a reporter for *El Diario* newspaper who had reported on alleged ties between the government and the drug trade, was gunned down in November 2008 in front of his eight-year-old daughter as he was warming up the car to drive her to school.[43]

The system by which public officials regulated the illegal market—accepting bribes to allow one cartel to dominate one region and another to control a different route—served to contain the violence as long as political power was centralized in the hands of the PRI, the ruling party, said Mónica Serrano, a professor of international studies at the Colegio de México in Mexico City. But as the country became more politically pluralistic and the cartels came to wield more wealth and power, the state no longer had the upper hand, she said. "The magnitude of the challenge is such that it would require a totally authoritarian government in order to really control this," said Serrano. "Drug organizations are for the first time declaring a direct war against the security apparatus of the state."

Freeman, at the Washington Office on Latin America, believed the United States could play a role in helping Mexico restore order. While the primary focus of the U.S.-funded Mérida Initiative has been counternarcotics equipment and training, Freeman and others have questioned the effectiveness of Mexico's militarized response. Instead, she said, the United States could do more to encourage fundamental police and prosecutorial reforms, among other things, ensuring officers a decent salary and creating systematic oversight and accountability, so that crooked cops were not only detected but punished.[44]

Reducing the American appetite for drugs could provide a more lasting solution than interdiction. "That's part of the problem of drug policy: if you make it harder to cross through one area it just shifts it somewhere else," said Freeman. "As long as there's this market in the United States, you're ignoring a huge part of the picture: this crazy demand that's out of control that we're not doing enough to bring down in the U.S."

America's demand for illicit drugs has not abated, however, the annual National Survey on Drug Use and Health shows. The study estimated that in 2007 about 8 percent of Americans age twelve and older were current drug users (three out of four of them smoked marijuana), a figure that barely changed from 2002. That was ten times the Mexican national average.[45]

The U.S. drug control budget was close to $13 billion, but just one out of every three dollars went to prevention and treatment efforts, according to the Council on Foreign Relations, and that percentage was dropping.[46] Combating the illegal drug trade requires working on five different fronts: drug treatment, prevention campaigns, domestic law enforcement, border interdiction, and source-country eradication, said John Carnevale, who had worked in the "drug czar's" office under presidents Reagan, George H. W. Bush, and Clinton and became a Washington, D.C.–based consultant. "The debate is always about the mix of the ingredients. [Under the George W. Bush administration] the prevention budget has been cut back and treatment has hardly grown. There has been a very dramatic policy shift targeting the border and source countries. I think there's a substantial body of research that focusing on those areas alone is not going to do it, as long as there's a demand up here."

Part of the key to penetrating the U.S. drug market is an effective distribution system, and for that Mexican cartels have relied on U.S. gangs. It's one of several ways that criminal organizations have straddled the international boundary. And the border region's bilingual, bicultural residents are especially valuable, said Veronica Baeza, director of the San Diego–Tijuana Border Initiative, a public health advocacy group focused on substance abuse. "What we're seeing for the first time is how much San Diego and Tijuana are actually linked at the level of crime," said Baeza. "When they do a bust, say for some sort of [meth] lab activity, of those arrested maybe 50 percent have residence in Chula Vista or Imperial Beach. They're U.S. citizens but because they speak the language and can move seamlessly back and forth, they went to work for the cartels."

One such worker was Salvador, a twenty-two-year-old Mexican American who was born in Los Angeles and raised on both sides of the border.

When his stepfather was imprisoned in San Diego for smuggling marijuana, his mother moved the family to Tijuana, where it was easier to make ends meet, he said. Salvador, who wouldn't give his last name because of his illegal line of work, moved out of his mother's house at sixteen and started rooming with a friend, who soon recruited him as a mule. He would walk into the United States through the San Ysidro border crossing—one of almost thirty thousand pedestrians a day at the world's busiest port of entry—with packages of marijuana or methamphetamine taped to his arms and legs beneath his clothes. Before long, he had forged off on his own.

"I'd buy a kilo of top notch Del Valle weed for $500," he explained in an interview in Tijuana. "I'd split it in half and seal it with my vacuum sealer. Over there I'd sell it for $500 a pound to a dealer. I'd double my money and get three ounces to smoke." In five years of almost daily crossings, Salvador said he was caught twice. The first time, he spent eleven months in juvenile detention. An adult the second time, he was fined $5,000, though a judge cut it down to $500.

Intercepting two-bit drug smugglers like Salvador, let alone large-scale shippers, posed a daunting challenge for law enforcement on one of the world's busiest borders. "It's like catching a needle in a haystack," said San Ysidro port director Bruce Ward. "But we're pretty good at it." The haystack has grown tremendously in the years since NAFTA went into effect. The volume of trade and traffic with Mexico has almost tripled since then.

At 7:30 on a foggy winter morning, columns of cars were backed up on Tijuana's streets, creeping toward the on-ramps to the highway that would take them to the border crossing. Newspaper vendors hawked Tijuana's dailies, *Frontera* and *El Mexicano,* and the weekly *Zeta.* A few also offered the *San Diego Union-Tribune.* Drivers scanned the headlines as they waited out the rush-hour commute that routinely took an hour or two. The cars bore a mixture of California and Baja California license plates. Food vendors bundled in heavy sweatshirts and aprons, their breath fogging in the chilly air, wheeled pushcarts up those same freeway ramps and parked themselves between lanes of traffic. *"Avena. Chocolate."* A hand-lettered sign advertised hot cocoa and milky oatmeal for breakfast. One salesman sold a Styrofoam cup of hot chocolate to a red Toyota, ladled up two more from his cart, then sprinted after his customer as the traffic crawled past him. Just before the yellow line on the pavement that marked the international boundary, a small-boned Indian woman with a long black braid, a migrant from the south of Mexico, begged for change with her three young children. The children darted among the slow-moving cars and gazed appealingly at the drivers, proffering paper cups to collect the alms.

At the border checkpoint, Customs and Border Protection had a staff of seven hundred agents to inspect the nearly thirty thousand pedestrians and fifty thousand vehicles that pass through the port each day. One officer roved among the twenty-four lanes of idling traffic as his trained Belgian Malenois sniffed the cars. Other agents in their booths glanced at computer screens that gave a readout based on an electronic scan of each license plate, showing the vehicle's registered owner and its recent history of crossing the border. The agents had less than a minute to size up most crossers.

"The first thing I look at—always, always, always—is the license plate," said a blond officer with eighteen months on the force, a recent graduate of the University of Maryland. "If a person crosses often, they're usually okay. But 99 percent of the time if they're smuggling, they're more sporadic."

Another agent, an Ohio native two years out of college, took the keys from a Mexican driver with a "laser visa," or U.S. border crossing card, issued to Mexican citizens who live in border communities to allow them to enter the United States for short visits. The officer walked around the pickup truck, tapping the truck's compartments with a screwdriver to check if any sounded like they were packed with contraband.

"I don't ask a lot of questions," the agent said, after returning the keys and waving the driver on. "I look to see if the person and the car make sense together."

In the port's secondary inspection area, agent Ian Bow tore out the paneling inside a green Dodge van with California plates. The booth officer had spotted mismatched screws on the quarter panels in the back of the van and sent it to secondary for a closer look. A dog picked up the scent of the dope, and an x-ray of the vehicle helped locate it. Bow hauled 220 pounds of marijuana out of the walls and gas tank.

In 2006, agents at San Ysidro snagged more than 140,000 pounds of drugs, most of it marijuana, some coke and heroin, and almost twice the methamphetamine seized the year before. That amounted to almost a third of all the narcotics seized at ports of entry on the Mexican border that year. Another 1.4 million pounds was apprehended along the border in between the ports, according to Homeland Security officials.

Across the United States in 2006, the government seized 2.5 million pounds of marijuana, 332,000 pounds of cocaine, 9,000 pounds of

Figure 21. U.S. Customs and Border Protection agent Ian Bow discovers more than two hundred pounds of marijuana stashed inside the quarter panels of a Dodge van that attempted to drive through the San Ysidro port of entry. Photo by Sandy Huffaker Jr.

methamphetamine, and 4,000 pounds of heroin, according to the National Drug Threat Assessment.[47] But that amounts to just 10 to 15 percent of the drugs that make it into the country, estimated Bruce Bagley, a political science professor from the University of Miami and an expert on the drug trade. "The interdiction of drugs is the same as with people: they reroute it, they don't stop it. They're constantly innovating," he said.

Tijuana has continued to be one of the most significant smuggling centers for drugs coming from South America, said Peter Núñez, a former U.S. Attorney in San Diego, who has studied transnational crime for decades. "[Border inspectors] are effective because they catch lots of people. They're ineffective because lots of people get by. How do you measure it?" Núñez asked.

"There are forty-five million people who cross that port of entry every year, seventeen million cars, and each entry takes an average of forty-five seconds to clear," he said. "So smugglers for three decades have said: 'If we put three hundred pounds in ten different cars, nine of them are going to make it.' That's the strategy: flood the port of entry. They know that with the law of averages, most will make it through."

Drug use in Mexico is still far lower than in the United States. But Mexico's National Anti-Addiction Council reported in 1998 that Tijuana had a drug use rate more than four times the national average. Four years later, the agency found drug consumption in Mexican border states had climbed 24 percent, while dropping slightly in the rest of the country.[48] In Tijuana, the new drug of choice was highly addictive crystal meth, a cheap but toxic brew of chemicals that produces a euphoric high but can cause brain damage over time. Directors at Tijuana drug treatment centers said 85 percent of their patients are addicted to meth.

Dr. Raúl Palacios, clinical director at the state-funded inpatient Centro de Integración Juvenil, said drug addiction was an especially high risk in his city because so many drugs passed through and sometimes got bottled up here, and because so many people from other parts of Mexico and Latin America landed here with no roots and few prospects, hoping for a factory job or a route to the United States. "Tijuana is a pass-through city, but it has become a city where drugs stay," he said. "Mexico is becoming a consumer nation. That's the problem."

One former addict said his meth habit had led him to join the hundreds of mules who carried thousands of pounds of marijuana, cocaine, heroin, and methamphetamine into the United States from Mexico every day. Agustín Bravo, twenty-eight, the son of a furniture upholsterer, started in the drug trade while still a teenager. His girlfriend's father recruited him to work as a lookout and to drive drugs around inside the city. Soon his bosses had him moving pot—half a ton to a load—hundreds of miles from southern Sonora and Nayarit up to Tijuana. He liked the money, getting high, and that invincible feeling he had strutting around with a pistol in his waistband. When he and his buddies would saunter into a nightclub, other patrons would make way.

"At first I didn't cross it to the other side," Bravo said, sitting on a bench at Tesoros Escondidos (or Hidden Treasures), a Christian rehabilitation center on a rutted dirt road overlooking the Pacific Ocean. "That was riskier and I didn't need to. I would find people to drive it across: guys, girls, whole families. But I got so addicted: I needed more and more *cristal*. I was feeling really low and I decided to cross."

On his fifth run he was caught. He had already driven one load to San Diego that morning, crossed back to Tijuana and gotten high. Then his bosses called him again: they needed him to take another car over. Not thinking straight, he agreed. He was busted with 128 pounds of marijuana hidden in the dashboard of the car. He wouldn't have been caught, he says, if not for his own drug addiction. The agent's trained dog didn't sniff out the vacuum-sealed bricks of marijuana. But it did pick up the scent of a little bag of crystal meth Bravo had stuffed in the pocket of his pants. And that led to a further inspection and the seizure of the pot. Bravo ended up doing eight months in San Diego County Jail. In jail he was clean for the first time in years, but his old habits overtook him after he returned to Tijuana. Bravo said he got too strung out to smuggle, and with no other source of income he took to stealing. "I was sleeping under bridges and eating out of trash cans when my family found me and brought me here," he said.

These days Bravo spent most of his time at Tesoros Escondidos, where he lived as a resident counselor. At the center, the word of God was the principal form of therapy. And Bravo feared that if he left, temptation would overcome him again. He counted his blessings that he hadn't ended up a statistic of Tijuana's drug trade, prey to either the ravages of meth or a vengeful cartel. "Some of the guys I worked with are in prison now. Or they're dead," he said. "I never knew the *capos,* just the workers. And thank God. Because they say if you know the bosses, you can never leave."

The causes and consequences of the drug trade—and the brutal violence it has spawned—link the United States and Mexico in a knotty web of interdependence. The appetite for these outlawed substances originates north of the border, along with the cash to pay for them and the weapons the traffickers use to enforce their power. But as the drugs move north through Mexico, the money and firepower that have come from the United States are threatening the foundations of Mexican civil society. The drugs are increasingly leaving a trail of addiction in the Mexican borderlands, just as they are spreading corruption through the border region of both countries.

"The thing the United States needs to do—we've started with the Mérida Initiative—is take a shared responsibility for the problem of drug trafficking, in the same way that Mexico has to take responsibility for illegal immigration," said Shirk. The border hasn't worked very well as a filter to interdict cross-border flows of drugs or people or other contraband, he added, but if the two governments could get over the hurdle of mistrust, the sharing of intelligence information would prove a smarter approach.

Until something changes, Mexicans will continue to suffer a horrifying price for the U.S. demand for drugs. Shirk and other scholars of the border believe the United States must address its own contribution to the problem. "If you want a game-changing policy shift, you have to think about how you deal with demand. Are we ready to move to a serious campaign to either reduce or accommodate demand? . . . I think the verdict is out," said Shirk. "Right now Mexico is bearing the cost . . . and I don't think we've tried very hard to think outside the box."

Mother Antonia maintained that the drug trade exacted a crushing toll not only from the lives of the innocent victims it touched but equally from those who got caught up in the criminal world itself. At every streetlight on the drive from the preschool through the labyrinthine streets of Tijuana back to the prison, she offered up a handful of pesos for each window washer and beggar. Each man in turn called her *madre* and asked her blessing as she patted his cheek and squeezed his hand. *"Dios te bendiga, m'ijo,"* she called in her American-accented Spanish, as the light turned green and the car drove on.

Crime is an outgrowth of hunger and humiliation, she said, heading back to her office in the house of her religious order, where she worked the phones each day to arrange bail for indigent inmates and supportive housing for those about to be released from prison. "The root of almost all drug dealing is poverty," said Mother Antonia. "I believe poverty breeds violence. . . . The *capos* came from *ranchos* in the interior of Mexico. I've known two hundred of them and they all came from poverty."

She had seen women take jobs transporting heroin or other drugs from the countryside to Tijuana to earn money to support their children. Others did it as a favor to a boyfriend, she said, and sometimes they didn't know that the package they were carrying contained drugs, or they didn't realize the danger it posed until they got sentenced to years in prison.

"They're very humble, very good women," said Mother Antonia. "At mass the night before last—the *visperas* for Our Lady—the prison church was full. They sang. They hugged each other. Their eyes sparkled. You couldn't go anywhere in the world and meet a nicer group of women. And I thought, 'They really don't belong in here.'"

Conclusion

THE STORIES OF PEOPLE WHO live in the borderlands reveal the complexity of the place and the myriad connections that link families, friends, coworkers, and counterparts across the international frontier. Those linkages are not always individual relationships. Sometimes they are reflections of the way that lives on either side are shaped by larger, binational forces, whether the quantity of water released across the border in an ancient riverbed, the transmission of infectious diseases in adjacent urban centers, or the border's ceaseless commerce in manufactured goods, agricultural products, labor, and intellectual capital.

From the everyday experiences of people who call the borderlands home—doctors, police officers, environmentalists, ranchers, factory workers, teachers, and students—it becomes viscerally clear that the border is not a line, as it appears from afar, but a region, and that it should be treated as such. While the border is the site of intractable binational problems that are unlikely to be resolved without national policies, it is a place with a long history of coexistence between the people of the United States and Mexico. For those who have migrated to the region because of the presence of the border, life there can feel rootless, transitory. For others, with generations-long ties to the place, the borderlands embody the deepest imaginable roots. Some border people live lives confined to one side of the line or the other, but many cross frequently between Mexico and the United States.

Most know people from both sides. Many are bilingual in English and Spanish. "Code switching," that distinctive blending of English words and phrases into Spanish speech, and vice versa, and the coining of border-isms are common and constant.

Life in the borderlands often isn't easy. For some it includes a perennial sense of being an outsider, of living in the interstices between cultures. The late Gloria Anzaldúa, a Chicana feminist poet and onetime migrant farmworker from the Rio Grande Valley, described herself as a "border woman" and wrote: "I have been straddling that *tejas*-Mexican border, and others, all my life. It's not a comfortable territory to live in, this place of contradictions. Hatred, anger and exploitation are the prominent features of this landscape."[1] But she and others—including Maribel Saenz, the Texas student; Enrique Contreras, the Sonoran physician; Harriet Toro, the Tohono O'odham tribal leader; and David Eisenberg, the California cop—have also found the blended culture of their border world profoundly satisfying. "There have been compensations for this *mestiza,* and certain joys," wrote Anzaldúa. "Living on borders and in margins, keeping intact one's shifting and multiple identity and integrity, is like trying to swim in a new element, an 'alien' element. There is an exhilaration in being a participant in the further evolution of humankind."[2]

Just about everyone living in the borderlands—the Hurt brothers in New Mexico and their ranch hands, the Chavezes from Chihuahua; Char Taylor, the maquiladora manager's wife, and María de la Luz Modesto, the wife of the factory worker; the Mexican ornithologist Osvel Hinojosa Huerta and San Diego engineer Bill Powers—shares a keen awareness of proximity to another country and to people from the other side. But the current American political thinking, rather than viewing the border as the place where the societies, cultures, and economies of two countries meet, has cast the border as a breach or a barrier that divides them.

In a frenzied push at the end of President George W. Bush's second term and before Barack Obama took office, Homeland Security officials completed almost six hundred miles of fortified fencing along the border line, shy of the 670 miles spelled out by the Bush administration but a massive expansion from the 78 miles of pedestrian fence and 57 miles of vehicle fence that had stood previously.[3] Across the Tohono O'odham nation, waist-high vehicle barriers replaced the old barbed-wire fence. In the Lower Rio Grande Valley, eighteen-foot-high posts were incorporated into reinforced riverside levees. And in Friendship Park, above the Pacific Ocean, where Mexican American families divided between San Diego and Tijuana

Figure 22. Vanessa Robles and her son Jonathan, who live in California, meet at Friendship Park, where the border fence runs between San Diego and Tijuana, for a visit with her son Junior, who lives in Mexico. Photo by Sandy Huffaker Jr.

have long passed picnic food and held hands through gaps in the fence, a new impermeable mesh wall was to be erected.

In a United States fraught by national security concerns, the fence became a physical display that the government was protecting its citizens from foreign dangers and unauthorized interlopers. That's one way of conceptualizing the border: strengthening its capacity to divide. But the fence construction ran into opposition from border dwellers, including lawsuits by Texas Apaches, whose rights to the land had been formalized since the Spanish land grants in the 1700s. The University of Texas at Brownsville, which has a binational educational mission, resisted the federal government's plan to bisect the campus near the mouth of the Rio Grande and persuaded a judge to order a compromise involving the strengthening of an existing university fence. Many residents of South Texas slapped "No Border Wall" bumper stickers on their cars.[4] Though they were well aware of the problem of illegal crossings, for them the border was primarily a point of contact with people and places in Mexico that were part of their heritage and their community.

Border landowners in South Texas, including University of Texas–Brownsville nursing professor Eloisa Tamez, had hoped that the Obama administration would take a new approach and halt the building of the fence. But in Obama's first months, construction continued to complete the 670 miles spelled out by President Bush, including an eighteen-foot-high steel wall in Tamez's backyard.[5]

At Los Ebanos—where men with calloused palms pulled the rope that propelled the barge across the Rio Grande, ferrying their neighbors across and back, across and back, as men have for generations—the Department of Homeland Security planned to build two miles of fence. There was talk of closing down the anachronistic river crossing, as the government has done with other informal ferryboats and border gates. But the final plan called for a movable fence flanking the old ford site, where the Los Ebanos ferry plied the murky water. That was the plan, until concerns about flooding on the river stalled it.

The border predates the fence, of course. As a place, it predates even the creation of the United States and Mexico and, indeed, the arrival of Europeans. And as a place, it will endure: meandering river, arid grasslands, saguaro-studded desert, boulder-strewn hills. The borderland, with all its history, is an essential part of both countries, as well as being a place unto itself. The presence of the international dividing line there has served to define the region, but so has the country across the way and all the connections between the people who inhabit the two parts of the region. An attempt to partition the borderlands, to wall ourselves off, is unlikely to succeed. And it diminishes the fluidity of the linkages, the back-and-forth interactions that give the region its particular value.

The fence was built primarily as a way to deter illegal immigration, which is the most prominent issue that Americans associate with the border. But immigration is only one of several thorny problems that play out in the borderlands and affect the people who live there. Equally pressing are the environmental concerns the United States and Mexico share, the economic issues of trade and development—in industry and agriculture—and the urgent need for human services and infrastructure. Most alarming is the drug trade, with its cruel toll of violence and corruption. Border dwellers, in both Mexico and the United States, navigate these issues as well as they can, often devising creative and collaborative responses across the international line. But none of these problems can effectively be solved at the border because they are not simply border problems; they are problems for all of us. Until the two nations tackle them seriously and jointly, however, the brunt of these problems will continue to be borne by border people.

Obama's Homeland Security secretary, Janet Napolitano, speaking at a border security conference at University of Texas–El Paso in August 2009, continued to use tough rhetoric, but her words also revealed a subtle shift in tone. Napolitano, a former governor of Arizona, emphasized her own border ties and the notion that border issues cannot be divorced from the concerns of the country as a whole, or from a relationship with Mexico.

> For the past eight years or so, the federal government's approach to the Southwest border was to treat it as a problem set and to treat it as something to be dealt with separately from our nation's broader challenges with immigration, security, counternarcotics enforcement and international relations. . . . [Today] the overall approach is very, very different. It's more strategic, it's more cooperative, more multilateral and in the long run, it will be more effective. And it begins with the paradigm that you cannot segregate the Southwest border from the rest of our nation, nor can we segregate our efforts on the Southwest border from the efforts and the partnership we must have with Mexico.[6]

In terms of the rancorous issue of illegal immigration, the U.S.-Mexico border has become the symbolic location on which American policy makers and activists have focused their attention. Plenty of unauthorized immigration does take place at the border, and it has real consequences for border communities in both countries. Yet everything we know about the border suggests that we can't solve the immigration problem there. And to turn the border into a dividing line is to ignore and undercut the ways in which it is a meeting place.

Vast increases in fencing and policing at the border have not succeeded in reducing the number of unauthorized migrants in the United States from Mexico. Stepped-up border enforcement has caused a tragic surge in border deaths, however, and it has encouraged Mexicans who enter the United States illegally to stay put and send for their families rather than returning home at the end of each season of work. The fence has calmed the disorder locally in certain border communities affected by illegal crossings, but it has moved the problem to other areas. And in many cases, the increased fencing and policing have led to a sense of division between previously integrated cross-border communities.

In fact, crossing the U.S.-Mexico border is not the only way that undocumented immigrants enter the United States. At least a third of the people in this country without authorization entered legally on temporary visas and overstayed them.[7] So sealing the border, were such a thing possible, would not eliminate illegal immigration.

It is legitimate for a country to exercise control of its borders, to want to regulate immigration and trade and limit contraband. The United States will continue to do that, as do most countries in the world. But given the geography and history of North America—the United States' very long borders with Canada and Mexico, its interest in neighborliness with those countries, and its tradition of openness in an increasingly global world—turning the United States into a fortress is neither feasible nor desirable, and it would be prohibitively costly to attempt.

If illegal immigration could be reduced in other ways, either by granting migrants a legal way to enter the United States or by reducing their need to migrate, border enforcement could be focused on preventing serious crime, whether drug smuggling or unauthorized entry by people who intend to do harm in the United States. That was the conclusion of the chief patrol agent for the Border Patrol's San Diego sector, who told a congressional committee in 2006 that if his agents didn't have to worry about catching would-be tomato pickers they would be sufficiently staffed to handle the small number of incursions of people from so-called "special interest" countries.[8] The stresses inflicted on border communities and the environment by illegal immigration would also be much alleviated if the United States and Mexico could create legal channels for Mexican migration or reduce it altogether.

Mexico is not the only country from which undocumented immigrants come to the United States. But it is the source of almost six in ten of them—for reasons of history and geography as well as economics. Mexicans have long-standing ties to the United States, especially in the border region. But the current wave of immigration consists primarily of Mexicans from further south, displaced by economic upheaval and a lack of opportunity, who are heading for employers deep inside the United States that seek their labor. If Mexico's economy were able to provide meaningful jobs and living wages to a greater share of the population, and if the country's physical infrastructure, social safety net, and civic institutions offered citizens more stability and opportunity, fewer Mexicans would feel the need to upend their families and risk their lives to migrate north.

The principal solutions to illegal immigration put forward by American policy makers are stronger immigration enforcement—both at the border and inside the United States—and so-called "comprehensive immigration reform," which would combine increased policing with legalization for undocumented immigrants already in the country and, for future immigrants, either expanded temporary worker programs or a greater number of green cards or both. The United States is already on the enforcement path. Annual outlays for border enforcement quadrupled between 1993 and 2008. Construction of physical fencing and development of a high-tech "virtual fence" have already cost the country billions of dollars. Maintaining and expanding those barriers in coming years could run to tens of billions. An overhaul of immigration laws that includes legal ways to enter the country for the low-skilled workers who are already coming from Mexico and Central America without papers could certainly help reduce unauthorized border crossings. It might be especially effective if it were combined with tough penalties for employers who flout immigration laws and a universal work authorization document by which all workers in the United States could verify their eligibility to be employed here. But those approaches constitute a unilateral American response that doesn't fundamentally fix the problem. U.S. policy makers would do well to look at the deeper causes of illegal immigration, including the profound economic disparities between the United States and Mexico and the long history of links between the two countries.

During Obama's campaign for the presidency, his position on immigration reform was distinct in its mention of wanting to help Mexico develop and strengthen its economy and civil society. In his first months in office, President Obama and several members of his cabinet held high-level meetings with Mexican leaders, signaling a serious commitment to work collaboratively on issues that affect both countries and their shared borderlands. But how deeply Obama understood Mexico, how urgently he ranked it on his priority list, and how much political support he would be able to muster for a new approach to Mexico were not immediately clear. Arguably, the future well-being of the United States, and certainly its border regions, is inextricably linked to Mexico's welfare—as border residents already understand. The most lasting and effective solution to unauthorized immigration is likely to be a joint response crafted by both the United States and Mexico. Investments in improving Mexico's economy, infrastructure, educational system, and the democratic and judicial institutions of civil society are more likely to deter migration than the billions of dollars spent on fences, border patrol agents, and technology for intercepting migrants, argues former Mexican foreign minister Jorge Castañeda, a professor of politics and Latin American studies at New York University. Those investments could also help Mexico more effectively curb the devastating drug trade.

"Today, each country is extraordinarily sensitive to what goes on in the other. And so whether Mexico develops or doesn't develop, and whether the United States adopts certain policies, which can be conducive to Mexico's development or not, is something that is truly a joint effort. Without U.S. support for Mexican development, Mexico will not develop as quickly as it can and as it should," Castañeda said in a 2006 speech he gave at a Trans-Border Migration and Development Conference at the University of San Diego.[9] "Why in the world should the United States, and particularly American taxpayers who have so many problems of their own, worry about Mexican highways, or Mexican education, or Mexican ports, or Mexican rule of law, or Mexican law enforcement and security? Why should the U.S. pay for this? Why should it care either way? Well, because the countries are so intertwined that everything spills over and if you don't have jobs, and you don't have law enforcement, and you don't have cooperation on these issues between the two countries, you have consequences; you have drug trafficking, you have immigration, you have less trade, you have real dangers and problems for American citizens in Mexico."

With time, the demographic basis for Mexican emigration will subside. At present, the population of Mexico is younger than that of the United States, and many more Mexicans reach workforce age every year than the country has jobs available. But the Mexican baby boom of the 1970s and 1980s has slowed, and those people are going to age. Demographers predict that in another generation Mexicans won't be migrating out of their country because the number of working-age adults will reach an equilibrium with the number of positions in the Mexican workforce. At the same time, the U.S. population is also aging and the impending retirement of America's baby boomers may make the influx of younger foreign workers more politically palatable.

On a grassroots level, private foundations, social entrepreneurs, and Mexican immigrants in the United States are already making modest efforts to strengthen the ability of poor Mexicans to provide a decent livelihood for themselves and their families without having to leave their home communities. Nonprofit organizations are funding rural job-creating enterprises in Mexico. Organic and fair-trade certifying organizations in the United States and Europe are helping small-scale agricultural producers in Mexico and other developing countries capture a premium price for their products. And hometown associations of Mexican immigrants in the

United States are channeling funds to local improvement projects in their communities of origin, $20 million in 2006.[10]

But a number of political and economic analysts believe a much larger institutional commitment is needed on the part of the United States to encourage and enable Mexico to invest in its own development. The responsibility lies ultimately on Mexican leaders themselves, but as a neighbor and a partner in the North American Free Trade Agreement the United States can play an important role. The United States stands to benefit on a variety of levels from a stronger Mexican economy and democracy. Two leading voices—American University political scientist Robert Pastor, formerly national security adviser for Latin America to President Jimmy Carter, and Jeff Faux, founder of the Economic Policy Institute, a liberal Washington, D.C., think tank—have both persuasively made the point that the solution to illegal immigration is in helping Mexico develop and that the special relationship created by NAFTA provides the framework to do so. Both men look to the European Union as a rough model of how more developed countries have invested in reducing the development gap with their poorer neighbors.

As U.S. senators debated an immigration reform bill in early 2006 (the measure passed the Senate but was never taken up in the House of Representatives), Pastor wrote in an opinion piece in the *Miami Herald* that neither tighter border security nor a temporary worker program, nor even the combination of the two, would solve the United States' problem with illegal immigration. "The only solution is to reduce the gap in incomes between Mexico and the United States," he wrote. "If we don't start now with a bold program, illegal immigration will only get worse. . . . The European Union figured out this problem, invested great sums of money in their poorest countries and significantly reduced the income gap. Migration almost stopped. We would be foolish not to learn lessons from their experience. They succeeded because of free trade, foreign investment and a transfer of almost $500 billion in 20 years. About half of those funds were used badly, but the investment in infrastructure had a huge multiplier effect."[11]

According to Pastor, NAFTA succeeded at what it was designed to do—dismantle trade and investment barriers to facilitate commerce between the three countries—but it was not sufficient to reduce the development gap between Mexico and its wealthier North American neighbors. The gross domestic product per capita of the United States remains six times that of Mexico, while hourly wages in manufacturing are eight times higher in the United States, he showed. Pastor advocates further integration between the three countries, including greater economic integration and shared continental border security. Central to his vision is a North American investment fund to reduce the economic gap by improving Mexico's infrastructure, especially in regions further from the border.

"The fund should target $20 billion a year to connect central and southern Mexico to the United States with roads, ports, and communications," he wrote in a 2008 article in *Foreign Affairs* magazine. "With the goal of building a North American Community, all three governments should commit to narrowing the income gap, with each deciding how it could best contribute. Since it will benefit the most, Mexico should consider contributing half the money for the fund, and also undertake reforms—fiscal, energy, and labor—to ensure that the resources would be effectively used. The United States should contribute each year 40 percent of the fund's resources—less than half the cost each week of the war in Iraq—and Canada, 10 percent. Since NAFTA was put into place, the northern part of Mexico has grown ten times as fast as the southern part because it is connected to the Canadian and U.S. markets. North America can wait a hundred years for southern Mexico to catch up, or it can help accelerate its development—which would have positive consequences in terms of reducing emigration, expanding trade, and investing in infrastructure to help Mexico enter the developed world."[12]

Pastor proposes that Mexico generate its share of the fund through increased tax collection. He has suggested that 80 to 90 percent of the fund be spent on infrastructure and the remainder on improving education, particularly through developing rural community colleges. (In Spain and Portugal, he noted, such community colleges proved to be magnets that drew college-educated people back from the cities to teach and in the process catalyzed improvement in elementary and secondary schools that the instructors' children attended.) Under Pastor's proposal, the U.S. and Canadian contributions would not be committed unless Mexico implemented reforms in the areas of energy, taxes, labor, and the rule of law. Specifically, he says, Mexico must stop relying on its oil monopoly, Pemex, as a cash cow to fund social services and must instead start assessing income taxes in earnest and allow Pemex to reinvest its earnings in energy exploration. Under Pastor's plan, the development fund would be administered by the World Bank and the Inter-American Development Bank and supervised by a board appointed by the three North American governments. Investing in Mexico's development "will not affect undocumented immigration in the short term, but it is the only solution in the long term," he says.[13]

Faux also endorses the creation of a development fund for Mexico, but he proposes that it be part of a renegotiation of NAFTA geared toward ensuring that the benefits of economic growth in all three countries be distributed more equitably. Faux takes a more critical view of NAFTA than Pastor does, and a less conciliatory tone toward Mexico's leaders. "Mexico's problem is that it is ruled by an oligarchy of rich families in a system of hyper-crony capitalism," he wrote in a 2008 article in the *American Prospect* magazine. "By facilitating business partnerships between the rich and powerful in all three countries, NAFTA reinforced that system, putting off the need for the Mexican elite to share the benefits of growth with their country's people."[14]

Faux's proposed fund is similar to Pastor's but with a greater focus on social spending rather than infrastructure investment, and an emphasis on protecting labor rights. "The aim of a renegotiated NAFTA would be to provide for a similar fund for investment in Mexico in exchange for changes in Mexican law and institutions that would allow the income of Mexican workers to rise as their economy grows. These would include guarantees for free trade unions, enforceable minimum wages, and an increase in education, and other social spending. The cost would be about $100 billion, although much of it would be in the form of loan guarantees rather than cash. Not an insignificant sum, but certainly affordable." Sooner or later, he writes, the United States will have to include Mexico in any serious effort to control illegal immigration, and this is the most effective approach.[15]

Such proposals to aid the development of Mexico's economy, infrastructure, and civic institutions would arguably go a long way toward addressing not just unauthorized immigration but other border issues, including crime and economic disparities. They are likely to be a hard sell in the United States in a period of recession and record deficits, but they can be viewed as long-term investments in a relationship that is, after all, permanent. There are other binational approaches the two countries can take to shared problems. Effectively tackling drug trafficking is likely to require economic development in Mexico and concerted efforts to strengthen the integrity and capacity of Mexican law enforcement and judicial institutions, as well as measures to reduce demand for drugs (or even decriminalize them) in the United States and to control the flow of weapons and drug profits from the United States back to Mexico. Binational commissions already exist to address issues of border health care and environmental hazards, but a greater commitment from the two countries would make those efforts more effective. The economic health of border communities in the United States is highly dependent on the economic vitality in their Mexican counterparts and vice versa. Manufacturing, retail commerce, and the cross-border movement of goods are tightly interwoven in the borderlands. Improvements in the standard of living, the protection of labor rights, and the provision of basic services in Mexican border cities would contribute, directly or indirectly, to the prosperity and well-being in U.S. border communities as well.

In his borderlands novel, *The Crystal Frontier,* Mexican novelist Carlos Fuentes asked, "Will there be time for us to see each other and accept each other as we really are, gringos and Mexicans, destined to live together at the border of the river . . . ?"[16] Even as they wait for the federal policies of their governments to catch up, Mexican and American border dwellers are showing the way—caring for each others' ill and injured, exchanging scientific knowledge and environmental protection strategies, and sharing food and music and religious rituals, as they have done for long generations.

In many cases, faced with overwhelming challenges, border residents have had to improvise their own solutions, and they often reach across the international line to do it. People in the borderlands tend to view themselves as neighbors with shared interests and concerns, just as people do in nearby communities all over the world. It may be a little more of a stretch for those who do not live in the borderlands—coping directly with drug cartel gun battles or toxic emissions from power plants—to recognize that border problems are ultimately national problems. But national they are, and if they are to be resolved in an enduring way, they will have to be addressed by the federal governments on each side. In tackling these issues, in turn, the governments would do well to heed the approaches of the people who live at the border and, rather than adopt an us-versus-them attitude, take note of the spirit of pragmatic neighborliness with which border dwellers engage solutions.

Meanwhile, each day, Mexicans and Americans interact as they cross from one country to the other, whether commuting to work in a twenty-four-lane traffic jam or running errands on a hand-pulled ferry boat. They know from experience that the solutions to be found at the border are less about hardening the boundary between the two countries and more about increasing understanding and cooperation between them. And they reveal the many ways that both countries are richer for the shared culture, history, and kinship that is the heritage of the borderlands.

The future of the ferry crossing at Los Ebanos is so far unclear. The fence has been halted by engineering difficulties presented by the Rio Grande floodplain, but the federal government has not stepped back from plans to build it. Yet as the government spends billions of dollars to construct an impassible barrier, it has nonetheless agreed to leave a gap for the human-powered barge to continue—with rope and pulleys and the hand-over-hand labor of local people—carrying passengers across the river to conduct their daily business, as they always have.

ACKNOWLEDGMENTS

I WANT TO EXTEND MY foremost appreciation to the many residents of the borderlands, in both Mexico and the United States, whose stories are told in these pages. They opened their homes and their workplaces to me, sharing their experiences, viewpoints, hospitality, and, above all, trust. This is their book.

The stories began at the *San Francisco Chronicle*, where several current and former editors gave me the opportunity to pursue the work and helped me to craft it. I am grateful to metro editor Ken Conner, who launched me on the reporting by sending me to the border to see what I would find there. My very first border story was assigned by Carl Hall, who dispatched me to Tijuana on awfully short notice. Pati Poblete oversaw my next border foray. Laura Impellizzeri steered me through the intensive reporting and editing of the *Chronicle*'s "On the Border" series. Steve Proctor, Robert Rosenthal, and Phil Bronstein granted me the time to begin turning the series into a book.

The photographers with whom I shared my journeys through the borderlands, Julie Plasencia, Carlos Avila González, Chris Stewart, and Sandy Huffaker Jr., are all talented professionals who were steadfast colleagues and good company, even in tight quarters and under sometimes trying circumstances.

A number of sources, friends, and fellow journalists proffered introductions and suggestions that helped guide my reporting in the border region, among them Frank Martín del Campo, Bernardo Méndez, David Maung, Gabriela Quiros, Macarena Hernández, Harley Shaiken, Susan Carroll, Garrett Brown, Elvia Díaz, and Leslie Berestein.

I would like to thank my editors at the University of California Press: Randy Heyman for his initial interest, which launched this project and helped shape it along the way; Naomi Schneider for her keen vision, which transformed it from a collection of stories into a full-fledged book, and Francisco Reinking, who shepherded the manuscript into production.

Three exceptional mentors at the University of California at Berkeley Graduate School of Journalism, Lydia Chávez, Neil Henry, and Cynthia Gorney, not only encouraged and counseled me as I approached this book but have played pivotal roles in my development as a journalist.

Several friends, colleagues, and family members very generously made the time to read part or all of the manuscript and to share their insights and impressions. My husband, Paul Muñiz, read and reread chapters, listened to my thoughts, doubts, and questions, and talked through countless revisions. Peter Schrag offered his perceptive editor's eye, collegial brainstorming, and unstinting support. Cynthia Gorney gave a well-timed and incisive critique. And Judith Hill-Weld, Ellen Elias-Bursać, Joe Garofoli, and my mother, Nye Ffarrabas, all shared valuable feedback on the work and essential moral support.

Numerous current and former *Chronicle* colleagues offered wisdom, humor, and encouragement throughout the writing of the book. They include Lesley Guth, Vanessa Hua, Katy Raddatz, Matthai Kuruvila, Jonathan Curiel, Louis Freedberg, Pat Yollin, Joe Garofoli, Jack Epstein, Rob Collier, Susan Sward, Dick Rogers, Jane Kay, Kathleen Rhodes, Erin McCormick, Tanya Schevitz, Leslie Fulbright, Kim Komenich, Don Lattin, Kevin Fagan, Matt Stannard, and Jill Tucker. I also tip my hat to my fellows at the Newspaper Guild who have worked tirelessly for the well-being of professional journalists; Linda Frediani was an especially stalwart ally at a critical juncture.

Profound gratitude goes to my parents, Nye Ffarrabas and Geoffrey Hendricks, for imparting their curiosity, creativity, and courage, a moral compass, and a quest for excellence. The echo of my father's query, "So, how's the book coming?" became an internal goad to get back at it. And my mother's unswerving confidence in me was a source of solace. I'm grateful to my brother, Bracken Hendricks, for fraternal camaraderie and commiseration as we wrote our first books simultaneously.

I thank my stepsons, Ian, Toby, Jonah, and Jonathan, for their interest in and enthusiasm for my work. And I'm deeply thankful to my daughter, Amelia, not only for her long-suffering patience with Mama's book over too many sacrificed weekends and evenings, but for the joy and love that enliven my every day.

First, last, and always, I am grateful to my husband, Paul. This book is the product of his labor as much as mine. He shouldered the daily work that kept our domestic life on an even keel, ensuring food in the fridge and ink in the printer. And he shared his curiosity about issues and ideas, empathy for people and stories, patience, equanimity, contagious humor, and faith in my abilities, all of which made this project possible.

NOTES

INTRODUCTION

1. Oscar J. Martínez, *Border People: Life and Society in the U.S.-Mexico Borderlands* (Tucson: University of Arizona Press, 1994), 54–55.

2. Michael Dear and Jacqueline Holzer, "Altered States: The U.S.-Mexico Borderlands as a Third Nation," in *Contested Spaces: Sites, Representations and Histories of Conflict,* ed. Louise Purbrick, Jim Aulich, and Graham Dawson (New York: Palgrave, 2007), 74–93.

3. Oscar J. Martínez, "A Binational Region: The Borderlands," in *Regional Studies: The Interplay of Land and People,* ed. Glen E. Lich (College Station: Texas A&M University Press, 1992), 137.

4. Ibid., 147.

5. Tyche Hendricks, "Dangerous Border: Crossing into U.S. Has Increasingly Become a Matter of Life and Death," *San Francisco Chronicle,* May 30, 2004.

6. Megan Davy and Deborah Meyers, "United States-Canada-Mexico Fact Sheet on Trade and Migration," Fact Sheet #11, Migration Policy Institute, October 2005, www.migrationpolicy.org/pubs/fact_sheets.php.

7. U.S. Census Bureau, "Foreign Trade Statistics: Top Trading Partners—Total Trade, Exports, Imports, Year-to-Date December 2007," www.census.gov/foreign-trade/statistics/highlights/top/top0712.html.

8. U.S. Bureau of Transportation Statistics, "Surface Trade with Canada and Mexico Reached a Monthly Record High in October 2007," press release,

January 7, 2008, www.bts.gov/press_releases/2008/bts001_08/html/bts001_08
.html.

9. U.S. Department of Homeland Security, "Securing America's Borders: CBP 2008 Fiscal Year in Review," Customs and Border Protection Factsheet, November 5, 2008, www.cbp.gov/xp/cgov/newsroom/highlights/08year_review .xml.

10. Data provided by U.S. Customs and Border Protection officials, telephone interviews by author, 2008.

11. The available terminology to describe people who are in the United States without government authorization—and who in many cases "entered without inspection" by Customs and Border Protection officials—is cumbersome and difficult. The U.S. government considers foreign nationals "aliens" and does not use the term *immigrant* until a person has become a "lawful permanent resident" or "green card" holder. Even if a foreign-born person becomes a naturalized U.S. citizen, he or she continues to be an immigrant. In common parlance, however, Americans often refer to foreign-born people as immigrants, regardless of their immigration status, a practice I continue. I dislike the dehumanizing implications of the word *alien*. A foreign national who entered the country without being cleared at a port of entry, or who entered legally and overstayed or otherwise violated the terms of a temporary visa, is to some an "illegal immigrant," to others an "undocumented immigrant." Both terms are politically loaded, and some social scientists have tried to get around the problem by using the term *unauthorized immigrant*. I find *undocumented* and *unauthorized* to be more precise terms than *illegal,* a word that risks branding the person who has committed an illegal act (generally an administrative violation of immigration law, not criminal law) as an illegal person. But because the terms are so politically fraught, in my work as a newspaper reporter and throughout this book I have chosen to use *illegal* and *undocumented* interchangeably.

12. Tyche Hendricks, "On the Border: Civilian Border Patrols across the Country Have Helped Polarize Political Debate over Immigration Reform," *San Francisco Chronicle,* December 5, 2005.

13. Carrie Kahn, "Bush Renews Call for Changes on Immigration," *Morning Edition,* National Public Radio, April 10, 2007.

14. U.S. Department of Homeland Security, "Remarks by Secretary Napolitano at the Border Security Conference," University of Texas at El Paso, August 11, 2009, www.dhs.gov/ynews/speeches/sp_1250028863008.shtm.

15. David Shirk, director, Trans-Border Institute, University of San Diego, telephone interview by author, September 4, 2008.

16. Tyche Hendricks, "Danger at the Border: From North to South, People Flock to Tijuana—along with HIV, Which Flourishes in an Area with Little Prevention or Treatment," *San Francisco Chronicle,* April 7, 2002.

CHAPTER I. ELSA

Some of the material in this chapter first appeared in different form in my article "On the Border: Elsa, Texas," *San Francisco Chronicle*, November 28, 2005.

1. U.S. Census Bureau, "Hidalgo County, Texas, ACS Demographic and Housing Estimates," 2007 American Community Survey 1-Year Estimates, http://factfinder.census.gov/.

2. John S. D. Eisenhower, *So Far from God: The U.S. War with Mexico, 1846–1848* (New York: Random House, 1989), 12. See also *The Handbook of Texas Online*, s.v. "Mexican Texas" (by Arnoldo de León), Texas State Historical Association, www.tshaonline.org, accessed March 23, 2009.

3. Michael Dear, "Monuments, Manifest Destiny, and Mexico," *Prologue* 37 (Summer 2005), U.S. National Archives and Records Administration, www.archives.gov/publications/prologue/2005/summer/mexico-1.html.

4. David G. Gutiérrez, *Walls and Mirrors: Mexican Americans, Mexican Immigrants, and the Politics of Ethnicity* (Berkeley: University of California Press, 1995), 13.

5. Michael Dear and Jacqueline Holzer, "Altered States: The U.S.-Mexico Borderlands as a Third Nation," in *Contested Spaces: Sites, Representations and Histories of Conflict*, ed. Louise Purbrick, Jim Aulich, and Graham Dawson (New York: Palgrave, 2007), 74–93.

6. Joseph Nevins, *Operation Gatekeeper: The Rise of the "Illegal Alien" and the Making of the U.S.-Mexico Boundary* (New York: Routledge, 2002), 55.

7. Jorge Bustamante, interview by author, August 2005.

8. Nevins, *Operation Gatekeeper*, 45.

9. Benjamin Heber Johnson, *Revolution in Texas: How a Forgotten Rebellion and Its Bloody Suppression Turned Mexicans into Americans* (New Haven: Yale University Press, 2003), 13–27.

10. Ibid., 27–34.

11. Ibid., 34–37.

12. Ibid., 71–124.

13. Ibid., 178.

14. Powerpoint presentation by Adan Alfonso Perales, history teacher at Carlos F. Truan Jr. High School, entitled "History of Elsa, Texas: The Planned Valley Town," 2006, www.aaperales.com/school/files/local/elsa.pdf, as well as his reproductions of historical documents and photographs, "City of Elsa History" resource page, 2006, www.aaperales.com/school/elsa.html. See also the City of Elsa's Web site, www.cityofelsa.com/history/index.html.

15. U.S. Census Bureau, "Hidalgo County, Texas, Table S1903: Median Income in the Past 12 Months," and "Hidalgo County, Texas, Table S1702: Poverty

Status in the Past 12 Months of Families," 2007 American Community Survey 1-Year Estimates, www.factfinder.census.gov.

16. Texas Education Agency: Region One Education Service Center, Public Education Information Management System, "Disaggregation of PEIMS Data—Student, Oct. 26, 2007, All Region One Districts," www.esc1.net/peims.

17. Senate Judiciary Committee, Subcommittee on the Constitution, Civil Rights, and Property Rights, "Renewing the Temporary Provisions of the Voting Rights Act: Legislative Options after LULAC v. Perry," testimony of Nina Perales, Southwest Regional Counsel, Mexican American Legal Defense and Education Fund, July 13, 2006, http://judiciarysenate.gov/pdf/7–13–06ninaperales.pdf.

18. Kathy Reeves Bracco, "State Structures for the Governance of Higher Education: Texas Case Study Summary," technical paper prepared for State Structures for the Governance of Higher Education and the California Higher Education Policy Center, Spring 1997, www.capolicycenter.org/texas/texas .html.

CHAPTER 2. MCALLEN/REYNOSA

Some of the material in this chapter was first published in different form in my article "On the Border: Reynosa, Mexico," *San Francisco Chronicle,* November 25, 2005.

1. Instituto Nacional de Estadística Geografía e Informática, "Industria Maquiladora de Exportación, Indicadores Mensuales," December 2006, http:// dgcnesyp.inegi.gob.mx/cgi-win/bdieintsi.exe.

2. Kathryn Kopinak, "Accounts Payable: An Introduction," in *The Social Costs of Industrial Growth in Northern Mexico,* ed. Kathryn Kopinak (La Jolla: Center for U.S.-Mexican Studies, University of California, San Diego, 2004), 1.

3. Julia Preston and Samuel Dillon, *Opening Mexico: The Making of a Democracy* (New York: Farrar, Straus and Giroux, 2004), 185–86.

4. Kathryn Kopinak, *Desert Capitalism: Maquiladoras in North America's Western Industrial Corridor* (Tucson: University of Arizona Press, 1996), 16.

5. James M. Cypher, "Development Diverted: Socioeconomic Characteristics and Impacts of Mature Maquilization," in Kopinak, *Social Costs,* 343–47.

6. M. Angeles Villarreal, "U.S.-Mexico Economic Relations: Trends, Issues and Implications," Congressional Research Service report, July 11, 2005, 9.

7. Daniel Lederman, William F. Maloney, and Luis Servén, "Lessons from NAFTA for Latin American and Caribbean Countries: A Summary of Research Findings," report, World Bank, December 2003, v–viii.

8. Jesus Cañas, Roberto Coronado, and Robert W. Gilmer, "Texas Border Employment and Maquiladora Growth," Federal Reserve Bank of Dallas, October 2005, http://ideas.repec.org/b/fip/feddmo/2005tbeam.html, 31.

31. Mary E. Kelly, "Free Trade: The Politics of Toxic Waste," in Kamel and Hoffman, *Maquiladora Reader,* 47.

32. Mike Lee, "Crossing Over: Toxic Waste; U.S. Lacks Good Data on Hazardous Materials Trucked from Mexico," *San Diego Union-Tribune,* June 12, 2006.

33. Cyrus Reed, "Hazardous Waste Management on the Border: Problems with Practices and Oversight Continue," in Kamel and Hoffman, *Maquiladora Reader,* 57–59.

34. Lee, "Crossing Over."

35. Frank Clifford, "Executive Gets Prison Term in Pollution Case," *Los Angeles Times,* December 16, 1993.

36. NAFTA Commission on Environmental Cooperation, "Metales y Derivados, Submission #SEM-98–007," Citizen Submissions on Enforcement Matters, summary of the matter addressed in the submission, November 2, 2002, www.cec.org/citizen/submissions/details/index.cfm?varlan=english& ID=67.

37. Reed, "Hazardous Waste Management," 58.

38. Bacon, *Children of NAFTA,* 62–68.

39. Cirila Quintero Ramírez, "Unions and Social Benefits in the Maquiladoras," in Kopinak, *Social Costs,* 285–88.

40. Lederman, Maloney, and Servén, "Lessons from NAFTA," vii.

41. Ibid., vi.

42. Quintero Ramírez, "Unions and Social Benefits," 289–97.

43. Preston and Dillon, *Opening Mexico,* 461–74.

44. Susan Fleck, "A Gender Perspective on Maquila Employment and Wages in Mexico," in *The Economics of Gender in Mexico: Work, Family, State, and Market,* ed. Elizabeth G. Katz and Maria C. Correia (Washington, DC: World Bank, 2001), 166.

45. Bill Mongelluzzo, "Maquiladoras Rebound: Plants along Mexico's Northern Border Are Emphasizing Efficient Production and Proximity to the U.S. Market," *Journal of Commerce,* Commonwealth Business Media, February 20, 2006, 28.

46. Geri Smith and Cristina Lindblad, "Mexico: Was NAFTA Worth It?" *Business Week,* December 22, 2003, 66–72.

47. Cypher, "Development Diverted," 356.

48. Ibid., 353–60.

49. Ibid., 346, 361–64.

CHAPTER 3. HACHITA

Some of the material in this chapter was first published in different form in my articles "On the Border: Deming, NM," *San Francisco Chronicle,* December 26,

9. Ibid.

10. Charles Lewis and Margaret Ebrahim, "Can Mexico and Big Business USA Buy NAFTA?" *Nation,* June 14, 1993, 826.

11. William K. Meyers, "NAFTA South of the Border: High Stakes, Big Hopes, Real Fears," *Commonweal,* September 24, 1993, 5.

12. Paul Krugman, "The Uncomfortable Truth about NAFTA: It's Foreign Policy, Stupid," *Foreign Affairs* 72 (November–December 1993): 13.

13. Sandra Polaski, "The Employment Consequences of NAFTA," testimony submitted to the Senate Subcommittee on International Trade of the Committee on Finance, September 11, 2006, 8, www.carnegieendowment.org/publications index.cfm?fa=view&id=18703&prog=zgp&proj=zted.

14. Ibid., 10–11.

15. John J. Audley et al., "NAFTA's Promise and Reality: Lessons from Mexico for the Hemisphere," Carnegie Endowment for International Peace 2004, 7, www.carnegieendowment.org/files/nafta1.pdf.

16. Ibid., 7–8.

17. Polaski, "Employment Consequences of NAFTA," 10.

18. Ibid., 3.

19. Ibid., 14.

20. David Bacon, *The Children of NAFTA: Labor Wars on the U.S./Mexic Border* (Berkeley: University of California Press, 2004), 27.

21. J. F. Hornbeck, "NAFTA at Ten: Lessons from Recent Studies," Congressional Research Service report, February 13, 2004, 4.

22. U.S. General Accounting Office [now Government Accountability Office] "International Trade: Mexico's Decline Affects U.S.-Mexico Border Communities and Trade; Recovery Depends in Part on Mexico's Actions," report congressional requesters #03–891, July 2003, 7–10 and 46–47, www.gao.gov cgi-bin/getrpt?GAO-03–891.

23. Kopinak, *Desert Capitalism,* 109.

24. Ibid., 192.

25. Cypher, "Development Diverted," 369.

26. Ibid., 376.

27. U.S. National Administrative Office, "Public Report of Review NAO Submission #2000–01," U.S. Department of Labor, April 6, 2001, 56–5

28. Ibid., 58.

29. Rachael Kamel and Anya Hoffman, eds., *The Maquiladora Reader Cross-Border Organizing since NAFTA* (Philadelphia: American Friends Service Committee, 1999), 41–46.

30. Siobán Harlow, Catalina Denman, and Leonor Cedillo, "Occupation and Population Health Profiles: A Public Health Perspective on the Social Costs and Benefits of Export-Led Development," in Kopinak, *Social Cos* 149–57.

2006, and "On the Border: Agua Prieta, Mexico," *San Francisco Chronicle*, March 12, 2007.

1. Nathan F. Sayre, *Working Wilderness: The Malpai Borderlands Group and the Future of the Western Range* (Tucson, AZ: Rio Nuevo, 2005), 32–66.

2. Michael Dear, "Monuments, Manifest Destiny, and Mexico," *Prologue* 37 (Summer 2005), U.S. National Archives and Records Administration, www.archives.gov/publications/prologue/2005/summer/mexico-1.html.

3. David G. Gutiérrez, *Walls and Mirrors: Mexican Americans, Mexican Immigrants, and the Politics of Ethnicity* (Berkeley: University of California Press, 1995), 72.

4. Douglas S. Massey, Jorge Durand, and Nolan J. Malone, *Beyond Smoke and Mirrors: Mexican Immigration in an Era of Economic Integration* (New York: Russell Sage Foundation, 2002), 128–29.

5. Jeffrey S. Passel and D'Vera Cohn, "Trends in Unauthorized Immigration: Undocumented Inflow Now Trails Legal Inflow," report, Pew Hispanic Center, Washington, DC, October 2, 2008, 1, www.pewhispanic.org.

6. Jeffrey S. Passel, "The Size and Characteristics of the Unauthorized Migrant Population in the U.S.: Estimates Based on the March 2005 Current Population Survey," report, Pew Hispanic Center, Washington, DC, March 7, 2006, www.pewhispanic.org.

7. Mexican migrant death data collected by Mexican consular officials and obtained by the author from the Mexican Foreign Ministry.

8. David Shirk, telephone interview by author, September 4, 2008.

9. U.S. Department of Homeland Security, "Remarks by Secretary Napolitano at the Border Security Conference," University of Texas at El Paso, August 11, 2009, www.dhs.gov/ynews/speeches/sp_1250028863008.shtm.

10. U.S. Census Bureau, International Data Base, "Table 028: Age-Specific Fertility Rates and Selected Derived Measures," www.census.gov.

11. John J. Audley et al., "NAFTA's Promise and Reality: Lessons from Mexico for the Hemisphere," report, Carnegie Endowment for International Peace, 2004, 6–7, www.carnegieendowment.org/files/nafta1.pdf.

12. Joseph Nevins, *Operation Gatekeeper: The Rise of the "Illegal Alien" and the Making of the U.S.-Mexico Boundary* (New York: Routledge, 2002), 31.

13. Massey, Durand, and Malone, *Beyond Smoke and Mirrors*, 27–33.

14. Ibid., 34; see also Gutiérrez, *Walls and Mirrors*, 72.

15. Gutiérrez, *Walls and Mirrors*, 42–45.

16. Nevins, *Operation Gatekeeper*, 34.

17. Ibid., 53.

18. Deborah Waller Meyers, "Temporary Worker Programs: A Patchwork Policy Response," report, Migration Policy Institute, Washington, DC, January 2006, www.migrationpolicy.org.

19. Jeffrey S. Passell and Roberto Suro, "Rise, Peak and Decline: Trends in U.S. Immigration, 1990–2004," report, Pew Hispanic Center, Washington, DC, September 27, 2005, www.pewhispanic.org.

20. Passell, "Trends in Unauthorized Immigration," 4.

21. Nevins, *Operation Gatekeeper,* 35.

22. Ibid., 36.

23. Peter Andreas, *Border Games: Policing the U.S.-Mexico Divide* (Ithaca: Cornell University Press, 2000), 86.

24. Massey, Durand, and Malone, *Beyond Smoke and Mirrors,* 13.

25. Douglas Massey, "Mexico, Markets and Migrants," lecture at a panel presented by the Carnegie Endowment for International Peace, March 20, 1998.

26. Kurt J. Bauman and Nikki L. Graf, "Educational Attainment: 2000," Census 2000 Brief, U.S. Census Bureau, August 2003, www.census.gov/prod/2003pubs/c2kbr-24.pdf. See also U.S. Census Bureau, "Census 2000 PHC-T-9. Population by Age, Sex, Race, and Hispanic or Latino Origin for the United States: 2000, Table 7. Median Age of Population: 1820–2000," www.census.gov/population/www/cen2000/briefs/phc-t9/tables/tab07.pdf.

27. Elliot Spagat, "Border Crackdown Fuels Smugglers' Boom," Associated Press, December 30, 2006, www.associatedpress.com/.

28. Wayne Cornelius, telephone interview by author, December 2006.

CHAPTER 4. NOGALES/NOGALES

Some of the material in this chapter was first published in different form in my articles "On The Border: Nogales, Arizona," *San Francisco Chronicle,* December 1, 2005, and "Danger at the Border: From North and South, People Flock to Tijuana—Along with HIV, Which Flourishes in an Area with Little Prevention or Treatment," *San Francisco Chronicle,* April 7, 2002.

1. Roman Catholic Diocese of Tucson, "Monday Memo from Bishop Gerald F. Kicanas," April 2, 2007, www.diocesetucson.org/April07memo.html. See also Carrie Kilman, "Escuela de la Frontera," *Teaching Tolerance,* no. 29, Spring 2006, www.tolerance.org/teach/magazine.

2. Miriam Davidson, *Lives on the Line: Dispatches from the U.S.-Mexico Border* (Tucson: University of Arizona Press, 2000), 14.

3. Susan Carroll, "Hospitals in Arizona Fund Clinics in Mexico," *Arizona Republic,* February 17, 2005.

4. Kevin J. Burns, "How Does Illegal Immigration Impact American Taxpayers and Will the Reid-Kennedy Amnesty Worsen the Blow?" testimony before the Committee on the Judiciary of the U.S. House of Representatives, 109th Cong., 2nd sess., August 2, 2006, Serial No. 1091–35.

5. U.S./Mexico Border Counties Coalition, "Medical Emergency: Who Pays the Price for Uncompensated Emergency Medical Care along the Southwest Border?" September 2002, www.bordercounties.org.

6. Tyche Hendricks, "Mexico's Health Czar Seeks Better Care for Mexicans in California," *San Francisco Chronicle,* April 24, 2007.

7. Jason Felch, "County Feels Symptoms of Health Crisis Relapse; A Familiar Scenario, the Fear of System Collapse Is Part of a Long-Standing Problem with Uninsured," *Los Angeles Times,* August 29, 2004.

8. Anne T. Denogean, "Traumatic Decisions," and Oscar Abeyta, "Tobacco Money Will Be Sought for Centers," both in *Tucson Citizen,* October 10, 2001.

9. Donald L. Bartlett and James B. Steele, "Who Left the Door Open?" *Time,* September 20, 2004, 51.

10. National Advisory Committee on Rural Health and Human Services, Tucson, AZ, summary of meeting, June 9–11, 2002, http://ruralcommittee.hrsa .gov/June2002/June2002minutes.htm.

11. Michael Janofsky, "Burden Grows for Southwest Hospitals," *New York Times,* April 14, 2003.

12. Pan American Health Organization, "Mexico Country Profile, 2001," www.paho.org/english/sha/prflmex.htm.

13. Debra Kain, "HIV/AIDS Rates in Tijuana, Mexico, Increasing at Alarming Rate: Interventions to Reduce On-going Spread of HIV Urgently Needed, According to Researchers at the UCSD School of Medicine," press release, University of California San Diego, February 27, 2006, http://ucsdnews .ucsd.edu/newsrel/health/hiv_aids.asp.

14. David Perlman, "HIV Infection Cases Surging among Latinos: Gays in Border Towns Most at Risk," *San Francisco Chronicle,* March 17, 2002.

15. Steffanie A. Strathdee et al., "Characteristics of Female Sex Workers with U.S. Clients in Two Mexico-U.S. Border Cities," *Sexually Transmitted Diseases* 35 (December 2007): 263–68.

16. Lisa Richardson, "Patients without Borders; Amid Rising Health Costs, Illegal Immigrants in San Diego-Area Hospitals Are Being Transferred Back to Mexico for Treatment," *Los Angeles Times,* November 5, 2003.

17. Richard Marosi, "Health Care Is Migrating South of the Border; California Employers Are Steering Latinos to Mexico, Where Care Is Less Costly but Uneven," *Los Angeles Times,* August 21, 2005.

CHAPTER 5. SELLS

Some of the material in this chapter was first published in different form in my article "On the Border: San Miguel, Arizona," *San Francisco Chronicle,* December 3, 2005.

1. Tohono O'odham Nation police chief Joseph Delgado, telephone interview by author, January 12, 2009.

2. Henry F. Dobyns, *The Papago People* (Phoenix, AZ: Indian Tribal Series, 1972), 50–51.

3. Vivian Juan-Saunders, then tribal chairwoman, Tohono O'odham Nation, interview by author, June 23, 2005, Sells, AZ.

4. Gary Paul Nabhan, *The Desert Smells Like Rain: A Naturalist in Papago Indian Country* (San Francisco: North Point Press, 1982), 72.

5. Ruth Underhill, *The Papago Indians of Arizona and Their Relatives the Pima* (Washington, DC: U.S. Department of the Interior, Bureau of Indian Affairs, 1941), 31.

6. Peter MacMillan Booth, "Tohono O'odham (Papago)," in *Encyclopedia of North American Indians,* ed. Frederick E. Hoxie (Boston: Houghton Mifflin, 1996), 636.

7. Nabhan, *Desert Smells Like Rain,* 69.

8. Ruth M. Underhill et al., *Rainhouse and Ocean: Speeches for the Papago Year* (Flagstaff: Museum of Northern Arizona Press, 1979), 24.

9. Ibid., 19.

10. Nabhan, *Desert Smells Like Rain,* 17.

11. Underhill, *Papago Indians of Arizona,* 9.

12. Nabhan, *Desert Smells Like Rain,* 105.

13. Ibid., 107.

14. Dobyns, *Papago People,* 51–52.

15. Ibid., 1.

16. Nabhan, *Desert Smells Like Rain,* 47.

17. Tohono O'odham Community Action and Tohono O'odham Community College, "Community Attitudes toward Traditional Tohono O'odham Foods," report prepared for 2002 annual conference of the U.S. Department of Agriculture's Economic Research Service, 2002, www.nptao.arizona.edu/pdf/CommunityAttitudesTowardsTraditional5.pdf.

18. Vicki Mabrey, "Why Is America So Fat?" CBS News, July 14, 2004, www.cbsnews.com/stories/2004/07/12/60II/printable628877.shml.

19. Underhill, *Papago Indians of Arizona,* 15.

20. Nabhan, *Desert Smells Like Rain,* 102.

21. Ibid., 107.

22. Mabrey, "Why Is America So Fat?"

23. Underhill, *Rainhouse and Ocean,* 37–54.

24. Underhill, *Papago Indians of Arizona,* 60.

25. Dobyns, *Papago People,* 20–32.

26. Ibid., 45.

27. Nabhan, *Desert Smells Like Rain,* 68.

28. James S. Griffith, "The Arizona-Sonora Border: Line, Region Magnet, and Filter," Migrations in History, Smithsonian Center for Education and Museum Studies, http://smithsonianeducation.org/migrations/bord/azsb.html. See also James S. Griffith, *Beliefs and Holy Places: A Spiritual Geography of the Pimeria Alta* (Tucson: University of Arizona Press, 1992).

29. Underhill, *Papago Indians of Arizona,* 63–64.

30. Underhill, *Rainhouse and Ocean,* 2.

31. Dobyns, *The Papago People,* 36.

32. Nabhan, *Desert Smells Like Rain,* 114–16.

33. Barbara Ferry, "For Migrants, a Brutal Toll," *Santa Fe New Mexican,* July 24, 2005.

34. Claudine LoMonaco, "Son Wants Chance to Find Mom's Body: Migrant Awaits Nod to Join Desert Search," *Tucson Citizen,* July 14, 2005.

35. John Annerino, *Dead in Their Tracks: Crossing America's Desert Borderlands* (New York: Four Walls Eight Windows Press, 1999), 116.

36. Testimony of Chairman Ned Norris Jr., Tohono O'odham Nation, before U.S. Senate Committee on Homeland Security and Governmental Affairs, at the hearing "Southern Border Violence: State and Local Perspectives," April 20, 2009, http://hsgac.senate.gov/public/_files/042009Norris.pdf.

37. Fred Leonard, "The Logbook: Counting the Casualties of a Relentless Flood," *Los Angeles Times Magazine,* April 24, 2005, 46.

38. U.S. Customs and Border Protection, "Border Patrol Seizes a Ton of Pot Stashed inside Abandoned Building," press release, November 21, 2007, www.cbp.gov/xp/cgov/newsroom/news_releases/archives/2007_news_releases.

39. Data provided to author by U.S. Customs and Border Protection public information officers.

40. Cathalena E. Burch and Becky Pallack, "Casino Millions Don't Fix Tribal Social Woes: Despite Gaming Revenue, O'odham, Yaquis Remain Dependent on U.S. Taxpayer Money," *Arizona Daily Star,* October 14, 2007, and "O'odham Aiding Elderly, but Youth Needs Unmet: Casino Cash Does Little about Gangs, Dropouts, Need for Jobs, Homes," *Arizona Daily Star,* October 16, 2007.

41. Underhill, *Papago Indians of Arizona,* 44.

42. Subcommittee on Criminal Justice, Drug Policy, and Human Resources of the House Committee on Government Reform, "The Impact of the Drug Trade on Border Security and National Parks," hearing before the House of Representatives, 108th Cong., 1st sess., March 10, 2003, http://purl.access.gpo.gov/GPO/LPS35669.

43. Ibid.

44. Delgado, interview, January 12, 2009.

45. Sean Holstege, "Cartels Outrun, Outgun the Law at Arizona Border: Fed Report Details Thriving Business behind Violent International Industry," *Arizona Republic,* October 3, 2007.

46. Russell Morse, "Fence in the Sky: Border Wall Cuts through Native Land," New America Media, YO! Youth Outlook Multimedia, December 24, 2006, http://news.newamericamedia.org/news/view_article.html?article _id=4ab13dbeafea01c7a2e94c60ea38cb9e.

47. Tim Gaynor, "Indians Complain Graves Dug Up for Border Fence," Reuters, June 24, 2007, www.reuters.com/.

48. Tohono O'odham tribal chairman Ned Norris Jr., telephone interview by author, November 19, 2008.

49. Norris, testimony before U.S. Senate Committee on Homeland Security and Government Affairs, April 20, 2009.

CHAPTER 6. MEXICALI

Some of the material in this chapter was first published in different form in my article "On the Border: Mexicali, Mexico," *San Francisco Chronicle,* December 10, 2005.

1. For the populations of California, Arizona, and Nevada in 1990, see the Web site of the U.S. Census Bureau's American Factfinder, http://factfinder .census.gov, under Population Finder (figures from 1990 Census of Population and Housing, 1990 Summary Tape File 1, 100-Percent data, Table P001); for the populations of those three states in 2007, see that Web site under Data Sets, Annual Population Estimates, 2007 Population Estimates, Table T1. For the population of Sonora and Baja California in 1990, see the Web site of Instituto Nacional de Estadística Geographía e Informática (INEGI), www.inegi.org .mx, under Estadísticas, Fuente/Proyecto, Censos y Conteos, Censo general de población y vivienda 1990, Consulta interactiva de datos, Población total (con información hasta localidad). For the population of Sonora and Baja California in 2005, see that same Web site under Estadística, Temas, Sociodemografía y género, Población, Volumen, estructura, crecimiento y distribución, Habitantes— género, 2000 y 2005, entidad federativa.

2. Robert Kunzig, "Drying of the West: The American West Was Won by Water Management. What Happens When There's No Water Left to Manage?" *National Geographic,* February 2008, 96.

3. Anthony Harrup, "Mexican Government Seeks Political Support for Electricity Sector Reform," Associated Press Worldstream, Financial News, September 25, 2003.

4. Central Intelligence Agency, "The World Factbook," Mexico and United States country profiles, 2008, www.cia.gov/library/publications/the-world-factbook.

5. Associated Press, "San Diego Judge Finds Permits for U.S.-Mexico Power Lines Were Improper," May 5, 2003. See also Diane Lindquist, "U.S. to Review

Mexicali Power Plants, Lines," Copley News Service, November 12, 2003; Diane Lindquist, "InterGen Gives In, Unplugs Turbine," *San Diego Union-Tribune,* January 17, 2004; States News Service, "InterGen Agrees to Speed Up Installation of Pollution-Control Technology on Turbines," January 28, 2004; Diane Lindquist, "Permits on 2 Power Plants in Mexico OK; Environmental Issues Satisfied, Judge Rules," *San Diego Union-Tribune,* December 1, 2006.

6. U.S. Government Accountability Office, "Air Pollution: Estimated Emissions from Two New Mexicali Power Plants Are Low, but Health Impacts Are Unknown," report to congressional requesters, GAO-05–823, Table 4, 15, August 2005.

7. Christopher Helman, "Gas Guzzler: Sempra Energy Is Doing the Unthinkable: Building LNG Plants in North America," *Forbes,* September 17, 2007, www.forbes.com.

8. Chris Hawley, "U.S. Natural Gas Companies Pick International Sites for Terminals," *Arizona Republic,* October 22, 2007.

9. Sempra LNG, "Energía Costa Azul Project Overview," fact sheet, www.sempralng.com/Pages/Terminals/Energia/default.htm, accessed March 28, 2009.

10. California Energy Commission, "State Energy Policy on Liquefied Natural Gas," www.energy.ca.gov/lng/policy.html, accessed March 28, 2009.

11. Helman, "Gas Guzzler."

12. Ethan Howland, "Sempra Plans Cross-Border Transmission Line to Access Wind Energy in Mexico," *Electric Utility Week,* March 3, 2008, 15, www.platts.com.

13. Helman, "Gas Guzzler."

14. Hawley, "Gas Companies Pick Sites."

15. Ocean Oasis Conservation, "The Northern Gulf: The Preservation of the Alto Golfo," 2000, www.oceanoasis.org/conservation/study1.html.

16. Frank Clifford, "A Trickle of Water Might Save Estuary," *Los Angeles Times,* September 17, 2007.

17. Marc Reisner, *Cadillac Desert: The American West and Its Disappearing Water* (New York: Viking Penguin, 1986), 120–21.

18. Mark Lellouch, Karen Hyun, and Sylvia Tognetti, "Ecosystem Changes and Water Policy Choices: Four Scenarios for the Lower Colorado River Basin to 2050," Sonoran Institute report, September 2007, 29, www.sonoraninstitute.org/index.php?option=com_docman&Itemid=181.

19. Reisner, *Cadillac Desert,* 121–22.

20. Ibid., 125.

21. Lellouch, Hyun, and Tognetti, "Ecosystem Changes," 4.

22. Kunzig, "Drying of the West," 97.

23. Celia Rosario Rivas and Luis Carlos Romero-Davis, "The Colorado River Story: A Tribe without a River," *Tucson Citizen,* June 20, 2006.

24. Chris Elphick, John B. Dunning Jr., and David Allen Sibley, eds., *The Sibley Guide to Bird Life and Behavior* (New York: Alfred A. Knopf, 2001), 246–50.

25. U.S. Department of the Interior, Fish and Wildlife Service, "Memorandum Regarding Endangered Species Act Considerations in Mexico for the All-American Canal Lining Project," FWS-IMP-4265.4, January 11, 2006.

26. Lesley Fitzpatrick, "5-Year Review: Yuma Clapper Rail," U.S. Fish and Wildlife Service, 70 FR 5460–5463, May 30, 2006.

27. Aldo Leopold, *A Sand County Almanac and Sketches Here and There* (New York: Oxford University Press, 1949), 141–48.

28. Brent Langellier, "The Colorado River Story: Accidental Oasis," *Tucson Citizen*, June 20, 2006.

29. Francisco Zamora-Arroyo et al., "Conservation Priorities in the Colorado River Delta: Mexico and the United States," report prepared by the Sonoran Institute, Environmental Defense, University of Arizona, Pronatura Noroeste Dirección de Conservación Sonora, Centro de Investigación en Alimentación y Desarrollo, and World Wildlife Fund—Gulf of California Program, 2005, 42.

30. Michelle Nijhuis, "The Accidental Wetland: A Plumbing Mistake Fills a Mexican Desert with Water, Wildlife and Irony," *Orion,* March–April 2005, 25–35.

31. Mari N. Jensen, "Hidden Cost of Colorado River Diversions: $2.4 Billion Annually," press release, University of Arizona, June 10, 2004, www.uanews.org.

32. Reisner, *Cadillac Desert,* 125.

33. *Consejo de Desarollo v. USA,* Case No. 06–16345, 17 (9th Cir. 2007), www.ca9.uscourts.gov/ca9/newopinions.nsf/.

34. Nicole Ries, "The (Almost) All-American Canal: *Consejo de Desarrollo Economico de Mexicali v. United States* and the Pursuit of Environmental Justice in Transboundary Resource Management," *Ecology Law Quarterly* 35 (2008): 515. www.boalt.org/elq/documents/elq35-3-08-ries-2008-1030.pdf.

CHAPTER 7. JACUMBA

Some of the material in this chapter was first published in different form in my articles "On the Border: Jacumba, CA," *San Francisco Chronicle,* December 5, 2005, and "Dangerous Border: Militias Round Up Illegal Immigrants in Desert; Migrant Advocates Say Deceptive Patrols Increase Peril, Seldom Face Legal Scrutiny," *San Francisco Chronicle,* May 31, 2004.

1. Leslie Berestein, "Border Watch and Protest Peaceful; Gathering Also Draws Lawmen and Journalists," *San Diego Union Tribune,* July 17, 2005.

See also Susy Buchanan and David Holthouse, "Playing Rough: The Anti-immigration Minuteman Project Set Off an Avalanche of Imitators. Some of Them Are Downright Frightening," Intelligence Report, Southern Poverty Law Center, Fall 2005.

2. Ben Ehrenreich, "Minuteman Divisions: Internal Squabbles Tear at Anti-immigrant Movement," *LA Weekly,* July 28, 2005.

3. Richard M. Stana, "CBP Could Improve Its Estimation of Funding Needed for New Border Patrol Agents," June 15, 2009, U.S. Government Accountability Office Report 09–542R, 6, www.gao.gov/new.items/d09542r.pdf; Tyche Hendricks, "On the Border: More Patrols, Stronger Fences," *San Francisco Chronicle,* March 12, 2007, A1, www.sfgate.com/cgi-bin/article.cgi?f=/c/a/2007/03/12/MNGEUOJLNF1.DTL.

4. Per U.S. Customs and Border Protection's public information office.

5. Richard M. Stana, "Secure Border Initiative Fence Construction Costs," January 29, 2009, U.S. Government Accountability Office Report 09–244R, 4, www.gao.gov/new.items/d09244r.pdf.

6. Blas Nuñez Soto and Stephen Viña, "Border Security: Barriers along the U.S. International Border," report for Congress, Congressional Research Service, December 12, 2006, Order Code RL33659.

7. Spencer S. Hsu and Griff Witte, "DHS Watchdog Warns 'Fence' Cost Will Grow," *Washington Post,* November 16, 2006.

8. Richard M. Stana and Randolph C. Hite, "Secure Border Initiative: SBInet Planning and Management Improvements Needed to Control Risks," U.S. Government Accountability Office, testimony before the Subcommittee on Homeland Security, Committee on Appropriations, U.S. House of Representatives, February 27, 2007, GAO-07–504T, www.gao.gov/news.items/d07504t.pdf.

9. Richard M. Stana, "Briefing on U.S. Customs and Border Protection's Secure Border Initiative Fiscal Year 2009 Expenditure Plan," April 30, 2009, U.S. Government Accountability Office Report 09–274R, 13, www.gao.gov/new.items/d09274r.pdf.

10. Daniel B. Wood, "Arizona's 'Virtual' Border Wall Gets a Reality Check," *Christian Science Monitor,* April 2, 2008.

11. U.S. Department of Homeland Security, "Remarks by Secretary Napolitano at the Border Security Conference," University of Texas at El Paso, August 11, 2009, www.dhs.gov/ynews/speeches/sp_1250028863008.shtm.

12. Jeffrey S. Passel and D'Vera Cohn, "Trends in Unauthorized Immigration: Undocumented Inflow Now Trails Legal Inflow," report, Pew Hispanic Center, October 2, 2008, www.pewhispanic.org.

13. Ben Ehrenreich, "The Minuteman's Tale, a Political Obituary: Jim Gilchrist, 2005–2007," *LA Weekly,* April 18, 2007.

14. Susy Buchanan and David Holthouse, "Locked and Loaded: Chris Simcox Mainstreamed the Minutemen. Now He'd Better Watch His Back," *Nation*, August 28, 2006, 29.

15. Christopher Ketcham, "The Angry Patriot," *Salon*, May 11, 2005, www.salon.com.

16. Randal C. Archibold, "A Border Watcher Finds Himself under Scrutiny," *New York Times*, November 24, 2006.

17. American Civil Liberties Union, "Creating the Minutemen: A Misinformation Campaign Fueled by a Small Group of Extremists," report, American Civil Liberties Unions of Arizona, New Mexico, and Texas, 2006.

18. Casey Sanchez, "Blunt Force: San Diego Nativist Group Faces Trouble," intelligence report, Southern Poverty Law Center, Summer 2007.

19. Grace D'arcy, "Tancredo Calls for Closed U.S. Borders during Dartmouth Meeting," *Dartmouth*, October 16, 2007, www.thedartmouth.com.

20. Christopher Hayes, "Keeping America Empty: How One Small-Town Conservationist Launched Today's Anti-immigration Movement," *In These Times*, April 24, 2006, www.inthesetimes.com. See also Max Blumenthal, "Vigilante Injustice: Arizona Militia Members, a Colorado Republican and a National Group with White Supremacist Ties Have Made a Remote Stretch of the Mexico Border a Flash Point for Anti-immigrant Hostility," *Salon*, May 22, 2003, www.salon.com.

21. Stratfor Daily Terrorism Brief, April 12, 2006.

22. Susan Carroll, "Border Group Member to Stay in U.S. Custody; Accused of Vowing Shootout with Agents," *Arizona Republic*, September 23, 2004.

23. Luke Turf, "FBI Shooting Leaves Vigilante's Cohort Critical," *Tucson Citizen*, September 17, 2004.

24. Ignacio Ibarra, "2nd Border-Militia Leader Held," *Arizona Daily Star*, September 23, 2004.

25. Andrew Pollack, "Two Illegal Immigrants Win Arizona Ranch in Court," *New York Times*, August 19, 2005.

26. Ibarra, "2nd Border-Militia Leader Held."

27. Archibold, "Border Watcher under Scrutiny."

28. Border Action Network, "Petition to the Inter-American Commission on Human Rights in Relation to Victims of Anti-immigrant Activities and Vigilante Violence in Southern Arizona," April 28, 2005, www.borderaction.org/PDFs/IACHR_petition.pdf.

29. Dan Glaister, "U.S. Border Control: America's Minutemen Build Their Own Fence against Mexican Migrants: Activists Spend $1 Million on Symbolic Wall to Demand Sealing of the Border," *Guardian* (London), January 2, 2007.

30. Ehrenreich, "Minuteman's Tale."

31. Jonathan Clark, "Man Sues Minutemen over Fence," *Sierra Vista Herald*, May 30, 2007.

32. Associated Press, "Watchers Prepare to Return to Border," *Monterey County Herald,* September 27, 2007.

33. Jennifer Delson, "A Minuteman Meets His Hour of Crisis," *Los Angeles Times,* March 11, 2007.

34. Jennifer Delson, "Minuteman Leader Founds New Group, Drops Lawsuit," *Los Angeles Times,* April 25, 2007.

CHAPTER 8. TIJUANA

Some of the material in this chapter was first published in different form in my article "On the Border: Tijuana," *San Francisco Chronicle,* January 28, 2007.

1. Sandra Dibble, "Tijuana's Bloodiest Year: Drug Feud Fuels Brutality That Has Ripped the Region," *San Diego Union-Tribune,* January, 4, 2009.

2. Justice in Mexico Project News Report, no. 39, January 2009, Trans-Border Institute, University of San Diego, 1, www.justiceinmexico.org.

3. Alexandra Olson and Elliot Spagat, "Tijuana Police Chief Fired after Weekend Violence," Associated Press, December 2, 2008.

4. Duncan Kennedy, "Mexico Extends Army's Drugs Fight," BBC News, May 28, 2008.

5. Ken Ellingwood, "Mexico vs. Drug Gangs: A Deadly Clash for Control," *Los Angeles Times,* June 3, 2008.

6. James C. McKinley Jr., "Mexico's War against Drugs Kills Its Police," *New York Times,* May 26, 2008.

7. Olson and Spagat, "Tijuana Police Chief Fired."

8. Anna Cearley, "Police Caught in Crosshairs of Tijuana Violence," *San Diego Union-Tribune,* December 4, 2006.

9. Laurie Freeman, "State of Siege: Drug-Related Violence and Corruption in Mexico: Unintended Consequences of the War on Drugs," Special Report, Washington Office on Latin America, June 2006, 9.

10. Cearley, "Police Caught in Crosshairs."

11. Ellingwood, "Mexico vs. Drug Gangs."

12. Mark Stevenson, "Nearly Half of Mexican Cops Fail Police Tests," Associated Press, November 27, 2008.

13. David Shirk, director, Trans-Border Institute, University of San Diego, telephone interview by author, September 4, 2008.

14. Ken Ellingwood, "Extreme Drug Violence Grips Mexico Border City," *Los Angeles Times,* December, 19, 2008, www.latimes.com/news/nationworld/world/latinamerica/la-fg-juarezkillings20-2008dec20,0,1725609,full.story.

15. Howard Campbell, "The Impact of Drug Violence on Mexican Border Communities," testimony before U.S. Senate Foreign Relations Committee

field hearing, El Paso, Texas, March 30, 2009, http://foreign.senate.gov/testimony/2009/CampbellTestimony090330a.pdf.

16. The estimate is from Victor Clark Alfaro, director, Binational Human Rights Center, interview by author, December 14, 2006.

17. Daniel Salinas, "Estiman que operan 20 mil 'tienditas,' " *Frontera,* November 1, 2007, www.frontera.info/edicionenlinea/pienota/Imprimirnota.asp?numnota=216057.

18. Tim Gaynor and Monica Medel, "Drug Gangs Corrupt Mexico's Elite 'FBI,' " Reuters, December 6, 2005, www.reuters.com.

19. Martha Mendoza and Christopher Sherman, "Associated Press Investigation: Border Police Being Busted More," August 9, 2009, www3.signonsandiego.com/stories/2009/aug/09/us-drug-war-border-corruption-080909/.

20. Edward Heath, former DEA attaché in Mexico, interview, PBS *Frontline* series, "Drug Wars," October 2000, www.pbs.org/wgbh/pages/frontline/shows/interviews/heath.html.

21. Luis Astorga, "Drug Trafficking in Mexico: A First General Assessment," United Nations Educational, Scientific and Cultural Organization, Management of Social Transformations Programme Discussion Paper #36, 1999.

22. James Verini, "Arming the Drug Wars," *Condé Nast Portfolio,* July 2008, www.portfolio.com.

23. U.S. Department of Justice, National Drug Intelligence Center, "National Drug Threat Assessment: 2007," October 2006, Product no. 2006-Q0317–003.

24. Ibid.

25. Richard Marosi, "U.S. Crackdown Sends Meth Labs South of Border," *Los Angeles Times,* November 26, 2006.

26. U.S. Department of Justice, "National Drug Threat Assessment: 2007."

27. Danna Harman, "Mexicans Take Over Drug Trade to U.S.," *Christian Science Monitor,* August 16, 2005.

28. Richard A. Serrano and Sam Quiñones, "Mexico under Siege: Borderless Drug Wars," *Los Angeles Times,* November 16, 2008.

29. Colleen W. Cook and Clare Ribando Seelke, "Mérida Initiative: Proposed U.S. Anticrime and Counterdrug Assistance for Mexico and Central America," report for Congress, Congressional Research Service, Library of Congress, July 7, 2008, Order code RS22837, http://assetsopencrs.com/rpts/RS22837_20080707.pdf.

30. "Press Conference by Obama, Calderón, and Harper, Guadalajara, Mexico, August 2009," August 10, 2009, www.cfr.org/publication/20006/press_conference_by_obama_calderon_and_harper_august_2009.html.

31. U.S. Department of Homeland Security, "Remarks by Secretary Napolitano Following the Signing of a Bilateral Agreement with Mexican Finance

Minister Agustín Carstens," June 15, 2009, Washington, DC, www.dhs.gov/ynews/releases/pr_1245155435074.shtm.

32. Bryna Subherwal, "Mexico: Merida Funds Must Be Withheld until Human Rights Conditions Are Met," Amnesty International USA, August 5, 2009, http://blog.amnestyusa.org/iar/mexico-merida-funds-must-be-witheld-until-human-rights-conditions-are-met/.

33. William Booth and Steve Fainaru, "Leahy Blocks Positive Report on Mexico's Rights Record," *Washington Post,* August 5, 2009, www.washingtonpost.com/wp-dyn/content/article/2009/08/04/AR2009080403334.html.

34. Denise Dresser, "Mexico's War on Civil Rights," *Los Angeles Times,* August 7, 2009, www.latimes.com/news/opinion/commentary/la-oe-dresser7–2009aug07,0,5621357.story.

35. Miguel Sarre, "Mexico's Judicial Reform and Long-Term Challenges," paper presented at a binational working group meeting, Woodrow Wilson International Center for Scholars, October 17, 2008, 4–6, www.wilsoncenter.org/news/docs/Sarre%20report.pdf.

36. Jeffrey A. Miron, "Commentary: Legalize Drugs to Stop Violence," CNN Politics.com, March 24, 2009, www.cnn.com/2009/POLITICS/03/24/miron.legalization.drugs; Ethan Nadelmann, "Fund Drug Treatment Rather Than Mexican Anti-drug Operations," *San Francisco Chronicle,* October 29, 2007, www.sfgate.com/cgi-bin/article.cgi?file=/c/a/2007/10/29/EDCFT0957.DTL.

37. "How to Stop the Drug Wars: Prohibition Has Failed; Legalisation Is the Least Bad Solution," *Economist,* March 7, 2009, 15.

38. Allison Hoffman, "Mexican Drug Lord Arellano Felix Sentenced to Life in Prison," Associated Press, November 5, 2007, www.sfgate.com/cgi-bin/article.cgi?f=/n/a/2007/11/05/state/n104507S63.DTL&type=printable.

39. Ken Ellingwood, "Mexico Now Extraditing Drug Suspects to U.S.," *Los Angeles Times,* December 1, 2008.

40. Ken Ellingwood, " Extreme Drug Violence Grips Mexico Border City," *Los Angeles Times,* December 19, 2008.

41. David Shirk, telephone interview by author, September 4, 2008.

42. Astorga, "Drug Trafficking in Mexico."

43. William Booth, "Violence against Journalists Grows in Mexico's Drug War," *Washington Post,* November 25, 2008.

44. Freeman, "State of Siege," 20–23.

45. U.S. Department of Health and Human Services, Substance Abuse and Mental Health Services, Office of Applied Studies, "2007 National Survey on Drug Use and Health," www.oas.samhsa.gov/nsduhLatest.htm. See also Mexican Secretary of Health, Consejo Nacional Contra las Adicciones, "Encuesta Nacional de Adicciones 2002," www.salud.gob.mx/unidades/conadic.

46. Lee Hudson Teslik, "The Forgotten Drug War," Council on Foreign Relations Backgrounder, April 6, 2006, www.cfr.org/publication/10373/forgotten_drug_war.html.

47. U.S. Department of Justice, National Drug Intelligence Center, "National Drug Threat Assessment: 2008," Appendix C, table 3, "Federal-Wide Drug Seizures," October 2007.

48. Mexican Secretary of Health, Consejo Nacional Contra las Adicciones, "Encuesta Nacional de Adicciones 1998" and "Encuesta Nacional de Adicciones 2002," www.salud.gob.mx/unidades/conadic.

CONCLUSION

1. Gloria Anzaldúa, *Borderlands/La Frontera: The New Mestiza,* 2nd ed. (San Francisco: Aunt Lute Books, 1999), 19.

2. Ibid.

3. Richard M. Stana, "Secure Border Initiative Fence Construction Costs," January 29, 2009, U.S. Government Accountability Office Report 09–244R, 5, www.gao.gov/new.items/d09244r.pdf.

4. Lynn Brezosky, "Valley Still Barrier to Border Fence," *San Antonio Express-News,* December 29, 2008.

5. María Hinojosa, "Obama's Border Fence," *NOW* on PBS, July 2, 2009, http://video.pbs.org/video/1171001273/program/1120797048.

6. U.S. Department of Homeland Security, "Remarks by Secretary Napolitano at the Border Security Conference," University of Texas at El Paso, August 11, 2009, www.dhs.gov/ynews/speeches/sp_1250028863008.shtm.

7. Jeff Passel, "Modes of Entry for the Unauthorized Population," fact sheet, Pew Hispanic Center, May 22, 2006, www.pewhispanic.org/files/factsheets/19.pdf.

8. Tyche Hendricks, "Little Common Ground on Border: Just Outside Mexico, GOP Tries to Rally Public to Tougher Approach," *San Francisco Chronicle,* July 6, 2006.

9. Jorge Castaneda, "The Challenge of Development in the U.S.-Mexican Context," University of San Diego, Trans-Border Institute, keynote address, October 5, 2006.

10. Tyche Hendricks, "Economic Aid to Give Mexicans, Central Americans Work at Home," *San Francisco Chronicle,* January 7, 2008.

11. Robert Pastor, "Help Mexico, Lift All Boats," *Miami Herald,* March 8, 2006.

12. Robert Pastor, "The Future of North America: Replacing a Bad Neighbor Policy," *Foreign Affairs* 87 (July–August 2008): 95.

13. Robert Pastor, ed., "The Paramount Challenge for North America: Closing the Development Gap," final report of the North American Develop-

ment Bank, March 14, 2005, 56, www1.american.edu/ia/cnas/pdfs/NADBank.pdf.

14. Jeff Faux, "What to Really Do about Immigration," *American Prospect,* January 17, 2008, www.prospect.org.

15. Ibid.

16. Carlos Fuentes, *The Crystal Frontier* (New York: Farrar, Straus and Giroux, 1997), 261.

SELECTED BIBLIOGRAPHY

A note on sources: This book draws on background material—including studies, data, and public testimony—and the scholarship and reportage of other writers, but it is fundamentally a work of journalism. Most of the material in the book was gathered through my own interviews and observations. Everyone I quoted or depicted in the book knew that I was writing for publication, and I followed the conventions and ethics of newspaper reporting in documenting what I saw and heard. Any errors are mine alone.

Anderson, Joan B., and James Gerber. *Fifty Years of Change on the U.S.-Mexico Border: Growth, Development, and Quality of Life.* Austin: University of Texas Press, 2008.

Andreas, Peter. *Border Games: Policing the U.S.-Mexico Divide.* Ithaca: Cornell University Press, 2000.

Annerino, John. *Dead in Their Tracks: Crossing America's Desert Borderlands.* New York: Four Walls Eight Windows Press, 1999.

Anzaldúa, Gloria. *Borderlands/La Frontera: The New Mestiza.* 2nd ed. San Francisco: Aunt Lute Books, 1999.

Arreola, Daniel D. *Tejano South Texas: A Mexican American Cultural Province.* Austin: University of Texas Press, 2002.

Astorga, Luis. "Drug Trafficking in Mexico: A First General Assessment." United Nations Educational, Scientific and Cultural Organization, Management of Social Transformations Programme, Discussion Paper #36, 1999.

Bacon, David. *The Children of NAFTA: Labor Wars on the U.S./Mexico Border.* Berkeley: University of California Press, 2004.

Bartlett, Donald L., and James B. Steele. "Who Left the Door Open?" *Time,* September 20, 2004, 51.

Blancornelas, Jesús. *Horas extra: Los nuevos tiempos del narcotrafico.* Mexico, DF: Plaza Janés, 2003.

Booth, Peter MacMillan. "Tohono O'odham (Papago)." In *Encyclopedia of North American Indians,* ed. Frederick E. Hoxie, 636. Boston: Houghton Mifflin, 1996.

Bowden, Charles. *Down by the River: Drugs, Money, Murder, and Family.* New York: Simon and Schuster, 2002.

Buchanan, Susy, and David Holthouse. "Locked and Loaded: Chris Simcox Mainstreamed the Minutemen. Now He'd Better Watch His Back." *Nation,* August 28, 2006, 29.

Clough-Riquelme, Jane, and Nora Bringas Rábago, eds. *Equity and Sustainable Development: Reflections from the U.S.-Mexico Border.* La Jolla: Center for U.S.-Mexican Studies, University of California, San Diego, 2006.

Conover, Ted. *Coyotes: A Journey through the Secret World of America's Illegal Aliens.* New York: Vintage Books, 1987.

Courtwright, David T. *Forces of Habit: Drugs and the Making of the Modern World.* Cambridge, MA: Harvard University Press, 2001.

Crosthwaite, Luis Humberto, John William Byrd, and Bobby Byrd. *Puro Border: Dispatches, Snapshots and Graffiti from La Frontera.* El Paso, TX: Cinco Puntos Press, 2003.

Cypher, James M. "Development Diverted: Socioeconomic Characteristics and Impacts of Mature Maquilization." In *The Social Costs of Industrial Growth in Northern Mexico,* ed. Kathryn Kopinak, 343–47. La Jolla: Center for U.S.-Mexican Studies, University of California, San Diego, 2004.

Davidson, Miriam. *Lives on the Line: Dispatches from the U.S.-Mexico Border.* Tucson: University of Arizona Press, 2000.

Dear, Michael. "Monuments, Manifest Destiny, and Mexico." *Prologue* 37 (Summer 2005). U.S. National Archives and Records Administration, www.archives.gov/publications/prologue/2005/summer/mexico-1.html.

Dear, Michael, and Jacqueline Holzer. "Altered States: The U.S.-Mexico Borderlands as a Third Nation." In *Contested Spaces: Sites, Representations and Histories of Conflict,* ed. Louise Purbrick, Jim Aulich, and Graham Dawson, 74–93. New York: Palgrave, 2007.

Demaris, Ovid. *Poso del Mundo: Inside the Mexican-American Border from Tijuana to Matamoros.* Boston: Little, Brown, 1970.

Dobyns, Henry F. *The Papago People.* Phoenix, AZ: Indian Tribal Series, 1972.

Eisenhower, John S. D. *So Far from God: The U.S. War with Mexico, 1846–1848.* New York: Random House, 1989.

Ellingwood, Ken. *Hard Line: Life and Death on the U.S.-Mexico Border.* New York: Vintage Books, 2004.

Faux, Jeff. "What to Really Do about Immigration." *American Prospect,* January 17, 2008, 41–42, www.prospect.org.

Fleck, Susan. "A Gender Perspective on Maquila Employment and Wages in Mexico." In *The Economics of Gender in Mexico: Work, Family, State, and Market,* ed. Elizabeth G. Katz and Maria C. Correia, 133–73. Washington, DC: World Bank, 2001.

Fradkin, Philip L. *A River No More: The Colorado River and the West.* New York: Alfred A. Knopf, 1981.

Fuentes, Carlos. *The Crystal Frontier.* New York: Farrar, Straus and Giroux, 1997.

Ganster, Paul, and David E. Lorey. *The U.S.-Mexican Border into the Twenty-First Century.* Lanham, MD: Rowman and Littlefield, 2008.

Gaynor, Tim. *Midnight on the Line: The Secret Life of the U.S.-Mexico Border.* New York: St. Martin's Press, 2009.

Griffith, James S. "The Arizona-Sonora Border: Line, Region Magnet, and Filter." Migrations in History, Smithsonian Center for Education and Museum Studies, http://smithsonianeducation.org/migrations/bord/azsb.html.

———. *Beliefs and Holy Places: A Spiritual Geography of the Pimeria Alta.* Tucson: University of Arizona Press, 1992.

Gutiérrez, David G. *Walls and Mirrors: Mexican Americans, Mexican Immigrants, and the Politics of Ethnicity.* Berkeley: University of California Press, 1995.

Harlow, Siobán, Catalina Denman, and Leonor Cedillo. "Occupational and Population Health Profiles: A Public Health Perspective on the Social Costs and Benefits of Export-Led Development." In *The Social Costs of Industrial Growth in Northern Mexico,* ed. Kathryn Kopinak, 149–57. La Jolla: Center for U.S.-Mexican Studies, University of California, San Diego, 2004.

Hayes, Christopher. "Keeping America Empty: How One Small-Town Conservationist Launched Today's Anti-immigration Movement." *In These Times,* April 24, 2006, www.inthesetimes.com.

Helman, Christopher. "Gas Guzzler: Sempra Energy Is Doing the Unthinkable: Building LNG Plants in North America." *Forbes,* September 17, 2007, www.forbes.com.

Herzog, Lawrence A. *Where North Meets South: Cities, Space, and Politics on the U.S.-Mexico Border.* Austin: Center for Mexican American Studies, University of Texas, 1990.

Howland, Ethan. "Sempra Plans Cross-Border Transmission Line to Access Wind Energy in Mexico." *Electric Utility Week,* March 3, 2008, 15, www.platts.com.

Johnson, Benjamin Heber. *Revolution in Texas: How a Forgotten Rebellion and*

Its Bloody Suppression Turned Mexicans into Americans. New Haven: Yale University Press, 2003.

Jordan, Mary, and Kevin Sullivan. *The Prison Angel: Mother Antonia's Life of Service in a Mexican Jail.* New York: Penguin, 2005.

Kamel, Rachael, and Anya Hoffman, eds. *The Maquiladora Reader: Cross-Border Organizing since NAFTA.* Philadelphia: American Friends Service Committee, 1999.

Kelly, Mary E. "Free Trade: The Politics of Toxic Waste." In *The Maquiladora Reader: Cross-Border Organizing since NAFTA,* ed. Rachael Kamel and Anya Hoffman, 47–51. Philadelphia: American Friends Service Committee, 1999.

Kopinak, Kathryn. *Desert Capitalism: Maquiladoras in North America's Western Industrial Corridor.* Tucson: University of Arizona Press, 1996.

———, ed. *The Social Costs of Industrial Growth in Northern Mexico.* La Jolla: Center for U.S.-Mexican Studies, University of California, San Diego, 2004.

Krugman, Paul. "The Uncomfortable Truth about NAFTA: It's Foreign Policy, Stupid." *Foreign Affairs* 72 (November–December 1993): 13–19.

Kunzig, Robert. "Drying of the West: The American West Was Won by Water Management. What Happens When There's No Water Left to Manage?" *National Geographic,* February 2008, 96.

Leonard, Fred. "The Logbook: Counting the Casualties of a Relentless Flood." *Los Angeles Times Magazine,* April 24, 2005, 46.

Leopold, Aldo. *A Sand County Almanac and Sketches Here and There.* New York: Oxford University Press, 1949.

Lewis, Charles, and Margaret Ebrahim. "Can Mexico and Big Business USA Buy NAFTA?" *Nation,* June 14, 1993, 826.

Martínez, Oscar J. "A Binational Region: The Borderlands." In *Regional Studies: The Interplay of Land and People,* ed. Glen E. Lich, 136–52. College Station: Texas A&M University Press, 1992.

———. *Border People: Life and Society in the U.S.-Mexico Borderlands.* Tucson: University of Arizona Press, 1994.

———, ed. *U.S.-Mexico Borderlands: Historical and Contemporary Perspectives.* Wilmington, DE: Scholarly Resources, 1996.

Martínez, Rubén. *Crossing Over: A Mexican Family on the Migrant Trail.* New York: Metropolitan Books, 2001.

Massey, Douglas S., Jorge Durand, and Nolan J. Malone. *Beyond Smoke and Mirrors: Mexican Immigration in an Era of Economic Integration.* New York: Russell Sage Foundation, 2002.

Metz, Leon C. *Border: The U.S.-Mexico Line.* El Paso, TX: Mangan Books, 1990.

Meyers, William K. "NAFTA South of the Border: High Stakes, Big Hopes, Real Fears." *Commonweal,* September 24, 1993, 5.

Miller, Tom. *On the Border: Portraits of America's Southwestern Frontier*. New York: Harper and Row, 1981.

Mongelluzzo, Bill. "Maquiladoras Rebound: Plants along Mexico's Northern Border Are Emphasizing Efficient Production and Proximity to the U.S. Market." *Journal of Commerce*, Commonwealth Business Media, February 20, 2006, 28.

Nabhan, Gary Paul. *The Desert Smells Like Rain: A Naturalist in Papago Indian Country*. San Francisco: North Point Press, 1982.

Navarro, Armando. *The Cristal Experiment: A Chicano Struggle for Community Control*. Madison: University of Wisconsin Press, 1998.

Nazario, Sonia. *Enrique's Journey: The Story of a Boy's Dangerous Odyssey to Reunite with his Mother*. New York: Random House, 2006.

Nevins, Joseph. *Operation Gatekeeper: The Rise of the "Illegal Alien" and the Making of the U.S.-Mexico Boundary*. New York: Routledge, 2002.

Ngai, Mae M. *Impossible Subjects: Illegal Aliens and the Making of Modern America*. Princeton: Princeton University Press, 2004.

Nijhuis, Michelle. "The Accidental Wetland: A Plumbing Mistake Fills a Mexican Desert with Water, Wildlife and Irony." *Orion*, March–April 2005, 25–35.

Pastor, Robert. "The Future of North America: Replacing a Bad Neighbor Policy." *Foreign Affairs* 87 (July–August 2008): 85–98, www.foreignaffairs.com.

———, ed. "The Paramount Challenge for North America: Closing the Development Gap." Final report of the North American Development Bank, March 14, 2005, www1.american.edu/ia/cnas/pdfs/NADBank.pdf.

Preston, Julia, and Samuel Dillon. *Opening Mexico: The Making of a Democracy*. New York: Farrar, Straus and Giroux, 2004.

Quinones, Sam. *Antonio's Gun and Delfino's Dream: True Tales of Mexican Migration*. Albuquerque: University of New Mexico Press, 2007.

———. *True Tales from Another Mexico: The Lynch Mob, the Popsicle Kings, Chalino, and the Bronx*. Albuquerque: University of New Mexico Press, 2001.

Quintero Ramírez, Cirila. "Unions and Social Benefits in the Maquiladoras." In *The Social Costs of Industrial Growth in Northern Mexico*, ed. Kathryn Kopinak, 285–88. La Jolla: Center for U.S.-Mexican Studies, University of California, San Diego, 2004.

Reed, Cyrus. "Hazardous Waste Management on the Border: Problems with Practices and Oversight Continue." In *The Maquiladora Reader: Cross-Border Organizing since NAFTA*, ed. Rachael Kamel and Anya Hoffman, 57–59. Philadelphia: American Friends Service Committee, 1999.

Reisner, Marc. *Cadillac Desert: The American West and Its Disappearing Water*. Rev. and updated ed. New York: Penguin, 1993.

Richardson, Chad, and Rosalva Resendiz. *On the Edge of the Law: Culture, Labor, and Deviance on the South Texas Border*. Austin: University of Texas Press, 2006.

Rotella, Sebastian. *Twilight on the Line: Underworlds and Politics at the U.S.-Mexico Border.* New York: Norton, 1998.

Rubel, Arthur J. *Across the Tracks: Mexican-Americans in a Texas City.* Austin: University of Texas Press, 1966.

Sassen, Saskia. *The Mobility of Labor and Capital: A Study in International Investment and Labor Flow.* Cambridge: Cambridge University Press, 1988.

Sayre, Nathan F. *Working Wilderness: The Malpai Borderlands Group and the Future of the Western Range.* Tucson, AZ: Rio Nuevo, 2005.

Smith, Geri, and Keith Epstein. "On the Border: The 'Virtual Fence' Isn't Working." *Business Week,* February 7, 2008, 45–48.

Smith, Geri, and Cristina Lindblad. "Mexico: Was NAFTA Worth It?" *Business Week,* December 22, 2003, 66–72.

Smith, Robert Courtney. *Mexican New York: Transnational Lives of New Immigrants.* Berkeley: University of California Press, 2006.

Spener, David, and Kathleen Staudt. *The U.S.-Mexico Border: Transcending Divisions, Contesting Identities.* Boulder, CO: Lynne Reinner, 1998.

Strathdee, Steffanie A., et al. "Characteristics of Female Sex Workers with U.S. Clients in Two Mexico-U.S. Border Cities." *Sexually Transmitted Diseases* 35 (December 2007): 263–68.

Suárez-Orozco, Marcelo M., Carola Suárez-Orozco, and Desirée Baolian Qin, eds. *The New Immigration: An Interdisciplinary Reader.* New York: Routledge, 2005.

Truett, Samuel, and Elliott Young, eds. *Continental Crossroads: Remapping U.S.-Mexico Borderlands History.* Durham: Duke University Press, 2004.

Underhill, Ruth. *The Papago Indians of Arizona and Their Relatives the Pima.* Washington, DC: U.S. Department of the Interior, Bureau of Indian Affairs, 1941.

Underhill, Ruth, Donald M. Bahr, Baptisto Lopez, Jose Pancho, and David Lopez. *Rainhouse and Ocean: Speeches for the Papago Year.* Flagstaff: Museum of Northern Arizona Press, 1979.

Urrea, Luis Alberto. *Across the Wire: Life and Hard Times on the Mexican Border.* New York: Anchor Books, 1993.

———. *By the Lake of Sleeping Children: The Secret Life of the Mexican Border.* New York: Anchor Books, 1996.

———. *The Devil's Highway: A True Story.* New York: Little, Brown, 2004.

Verini, James. "Arming the Drug Wars," *Condé Nast Portfolio,* July 2008, www.portfolio.com.

Vila, Pablo, ed. *Ethnography at the Border.* Minneapolis: University of Minnesota Press, 2003.

Webb, Walter Prescott. *The Texas Rangers: A Century of Frontier Defense.* Boston: Houghton Mifflin, 1935.

INDEX